1st 154

THE INSOLENCE OF OFFICE

THE INSOLENCE
OF OFFICE

The Story of the Seabury Investigations

BY

WILLIAM B. NORTHROP

Assistant Counsel in the Magistrates' Courts and District Attorney Investigations,
Associate Counsel in the City Investigation

AND

JOHN B. NORTHROP

Member of the New York Bar

G. P. PUTNAM'S SONS

NEW YORK   LONDON

1932

TO THOSE WHO, SEEING THE NEED FOR BETTER
MUNICIPAL GOVERNMENT, WOULD STRIVE FOR ITS
ATTAINMENT.

INTRODUCTION

THIS book is a factual narrative of the disclosures resulting from what has become known as "The New York City Investigation." For the most part the quotations are from the public records of the various public hearings. There is an occasional quotation from a brief, from argument in Court, and from judicial opinions.

In the fall of 1930, the scandals in connection with our Judiciary—especially that of our Inferior Criminal Courts—culminated in the Investigation of the Magistrates' Courts. This was initiated by the entry of an order by the Appellate Division of the Supreme Court—First Judicial Department, designating the Honorable Samuel Seabury as its Referee. He was instructed to investigate the Magistrates' Courts of the First Judicial Department (which included only the Boroughs of Manhattan and the Bronx) and the Magistrates thereof, and "report the proceedings on said investigation to this Court with his opinion thereon." By amendment to this order he was instructed to investigate and report on "any practices of attorneys practicing in said Magistrates' Courts which are obstructive or harmful to the administration of justice or unjust or corrupt, unlawful, fraudulent, or unprofessional; . . ."

Public hearings in this investigation began on September 29, 1930, and continued intermittently until May 14, 1931. At these hearings two hundred and ninety-nine witnesses were examined. The transcript of their testimony covers four thousand five hundred and ninety-six pages.

One thousand and fifty-nine persons were examined at private hearings, whose testimony covers fifteen thousand three hundred and fifty-six pages.

In addition to both these private and public hearings three

Magistrates were tried before the Appellate Division, pursuant to the statute empowering that Court to remove a Magistrate for cause.

On March 28th, 1932, Judge Seabury filed his final report on this investigation with the Appellate Division.

Before the completion of this investigation and on March 10th, 1931, His Excellency, Governor Roosevelt, appointed Judge Seabury as Commissioner to investigate and report on the charges filed against the Honorable Thomas C. T. Crain, District Attorney of New York County.

Again, many witnesses were examined at both private and public hearings between April 8th and May 29th, 1931. The public testimony covers some three thousand pages.

On August 31st, 1931, Judge Seabury reported to the Governor that the evidence presented before him was insufficient to warrant the removal of the District Attorney. Governor Roosevelt accepted and filed this report.

The Legislative Committee appointed pursuant to the Joint Resolution of the Senate and Assembly, requested him to act as their Counsel in their inquiry into the government of the City of New York.

Judge Seabury accepted this request on April 8th, 1931, although he could take no public steps therein until he finished presenting the evidence before the Appellate Division in the trial of Magistrate Silbermann which ended July 3, 1931.

The first public hearing before the Legislative Committee took place on July 21, 1931. In all, sixty-three public hearings have been held since that date down to June 1, 1932, a period of ten months and one week. The transcript of the testimony taken at public hearings numbers over nine thousand pages. More than two thousand five hundred witnesses have been examined at private hearings, whose testimony covers over sixty thousand pages.

In each of these three capacities—Referee, Commissioner and Counsel—Judge Seabury's authority was limited to eliciting the facts.

He could indict no one. He could try no one. He could convict no one. He could remove no one.

The five District Attorneys in the five counties within the city were Tammany men. The Mayor was a Tammany man. All municipal officers were Tammany men except one Alderman.

The forces arrayed against Judge Seabury were united. They were powerful. They were bitterly partisan and intensely hostile. They gained aid and comfort from Public Enemy No. 1—Public Apathy.

The city press was a tremendous power for good. Allied with the cause of good government were many estimable groups and many estimable men. From all parts of the country came, as indicative of the nation-wide interest, letters—editorials and other commendatory articles. This sentiment was diffused. These groups were disorganized and disunited and consequently—ineffective. Notwithstanding the lack of organized support and in the face of the Tammany opposition the process of disclosing the facts continued from day to day. The narrative of these disclosures is set forth in the following pages.

The authors wish to express their gratitude to all who have assisted in the preparation of this book, particularly to Mrs. Frances E. Dunn.

CONTENTS

THE INSOLENCE OF OFFICE

CHAPTER I

THE PRELUDE TO THE INVESTIGATIONS

SUNDAY, December 8, 1929. The main dining room of the "Roman Gardens," one flight up, was brilliantly lighted. The Honorary President for life was being fêted by fellow members of the Tepecano Democratic Club.

A hush fell over the diners as the Honorable Albert H. Vitale rose from the place of honor at the head of the long horseshoe table. The words of thanks froze on his lips. Masked men—guns in hand—barked out orders to line up against the wall. Vitale slid the diamond ring from his finger and tucked it in the waistband of his trousers. Former Magistrate Michael Delagi slid his in his shoe. Detective Arthur Johnson surrendered his revolver without resistance. Two more guns were taken from other guests.

Seven diners had police records—including "Jimmie the baker" and "Joe the baker"—who has since found death at the end of a gangster's ride. Chief among the figures who graced the festive board was Ciro Terranova. The latter acquired the sobriquet, the "Artichoke King," through his alleged control of the peddlers of this commodity.

This untoward incident, occurring at two o'clock in the morning, brought the evening's festivities to a close. The guests separated. Vitale hurried to the club. Within two hours he personally returned Johnson's gun—without explaining how it came into his possession. Money and jewelry surrendered at the holdup were also returned. One Bravate was tried for this crime. His alibi, that he was playing cards way down at the other end of the city, prevailed.

Fiorello LaGuardia was the Republican nominee for Mayor in the fall campaign in 1929. Among other things, he charged that Vitale while a Magistrate had borrowed $20,000 from

the late Arnold Rothstein. This apparent association of a
Judge with the underworld shocked the public conscience.
Kenneth M. Spence and George Z. Medalie, the latter now
Federal District Attorney, were appointed by the City Bar
Association to investigate his conduct while on the Bench.
Finally, a petition was made to the Appellate Division of the
Supreme Court asking his removal. The first charge grew out
of the following circumstances: one Fawcett, a Rothstein
henchman, was arraigned before Vitale for the theft of $79.43
from one Joseph Hart; he was discharged; the next day
Vitale, in writing, directed the court clerk to return to Hart
the cash taken by Fawcett, it

"being proven on oath before me to be property of Joseph Hart."

Max D. Steuer, Vitale's Counsel, succeeded in convincing the
Court that there was no proof of corruption in the evidence
adduced to support the charge, and hence it in and of itself
could not be the basis for his removal. A unanimous Court,
however, found sufficient cause for removal in the Rothstein
loan. Traffic with the underworld would not be tolerated in
a Judge. Upon his trial Vitale admitted that in four years on
the Bench he had made $165,000. During the same period
his salary aggregated $48,000.

Since the days of 1912 when Herman Rosenthal, a notorious gambler, was murdered at the instigation of Police Lieutenant Charles Becker, nothing so stirred New York as did
the murder of Arnold Rothstein. Almost four years have
passed and the murderer is still at large. Mayor Walker
shortly thereafter accepted the resignation of Police Commissioner Warren. Joab Banton, District Attorney, was denied
renomination. Thomas C. T. Crain, nominated to succeed
him, campaigned on the promise that he would solve the
murder within two weeks after taking office. When McManus,
the suspect, was finally brought to trial after election, but
while Mr. Banton was still District Attorney, Judge Charles
Nott directed a verdict of acquittal. Judge Crain took office

January 1, 1930. On January 15, he issued a wordy excuse for failing to redeem his campaign pledge.

During the period of inflation, Magistrates and Judges loaned their official position to wild promotion schemes or tottering financial enterprises. Magistrate Ewald became identified with the sale of Cotter Butte Mining stock—County Judge Vause became a director in the Columbia Finance Corporation—Judge Francis X. Mancuso became Chairman of the Board of the City Trust Company. One by one hard times overcame these concerns.

In February, 1928, the City Trust closed its doors—failed for $5,000,000. Robert Moses, the Governor's Commissioner, scathingly denounced the management of its affairs. The Bar Association undertook an investigation of Mancuso's conduct, but before their report was handed to the Governor, Mancuso resigned. Two days later, on October 12, 1929, he was indicted. Two years later, just as it seemed that he was about to go to trial, the indictment was dismissed. Mancuso was tried for perjury, and acquitted.

County Judge Bernard Vause was, at the time of his appointment, President of the Brooklyn Democratic Club. He lent the influence of "the robe" to an investment scheme which victimized thousands of small investors. While on the Bench he received a fee estimated to have been as high as $190,000 for "negotiations" which led to pier leases being awarded to the United American Lines. In May, 1930, he was indicted for the use of mails to defraud. The next month he resigned because of "poor health and limited means." In July he was convicted and sentenced to six years in Atlanta. Then the fight began. His conviction was affirmed by the Circuit Court of Appeals, and a review thereof was denied by the United States Supreme Court. Max D. Steuer then took the lists in his behalf, arguing for a new trial on the basis of affidavits charging perjury by government witnesses. By a two to one vote—Senior Judge Martin T. Manton dissenting—the application was denied. In January, 1932, he began his "stretch."

In December, 1929, ten girls lost their lives and eighteen

others were injured in the Pathé Studio fire. Long prior
thereto a violation had been placed against the building because of a fire hazard and the Company ordered to install a
sprinkler system. The Croker Fire Prevention Engineering
Company headed by Edward F. Croker, former Chief of the
Fire Department and nephew of the old Tammany boss, was
retained to file an appeal, but it was never done. The tragedy
occurred before the City officials took any steps to enforce
the order. John Flynn and Henry Lalley were indicted, convicted and fined $500 for violation of the penal law. They
were also indicted—on the theory of culpable negligence—
for manslaughter in the second degree but this indictment
has been dismissed.

The rising tide of public indignation against municipal conditions found articulation in a bill passed by both houses of
the Legislature empowering Governor Roosevelt to appoint a
Commission to investigate

> "the administration and certain local authorities in the City of
> New York."

It was charged, by Tammany of course, that the passage
of this bill was a political maneuver, designed to put the Governor in a hole. Be that as it may, corruption was rife in the
City. Governor Roosevelt vetoed the bill, refusing at that
time to lead in the fight against municipal corruption.

William E. Walsh was chairman of the City department
known as The Board of Standards and Appeals, which has
power to permit deviations from building and zoning regulations. There was no more successful practitioner before this
Board than William F. Doyle. His fees for this work aggregated some $2,000,000. Mr. Tuttle, then Federal District
Attorney, decided to check up on his income tax returns. During the course of this investigation Doyle admitted that he
split fees but refused to tell the names of the recipients. Mr.
Tuttle also developed and referred to District Attorney Crain
evidence indicating that Walsh, while a City official, had

accepted a gratuity. It was charged that he was given a $4,000 apartment for $1,500. After his indictment, he resigned. His trial resulted in an acquittal.

Doyle was brought to trial on charges of tax evasion, and also a charge of perjury. On a jurisdictional point the income tax charges were dismissed; the jury disagreed as to the tax charge, and acquitted him of perjury.

Cooley, Chief of the Probation Bureau in the Criminal Courts, resigned after being accused of falsifying the payroll by adding thereto the name of his sister who was then teaching in Buffalo.

As a climax to all that had gone before and as the overt act leading to all that has followed, came the charge that Vitale's successor, George Ewald, had bought his appointment. Evidence bearing on this charge was developed by Mr. Tuttle during an investigation which resulted in Ewald's indictment for use of the mails to defraud in connection with the sale of the Cotter Butte Mining stock.

Joseph E. Corrigan, now Judge of General Sessions (a criminal court for trial of felonies and misdemeanors), but then McAdoo's successor as Chief Magistrate, called on Ewald to resign or face charges. Mr. Justice Edward R. Finch, in the absence of Presiding Justice Victor J. Dowling, summoned the Justices of the Appellate Division to consider what action, if any, they would take in the matter.

Ewald resigned. District Attorney Crain submitted evidence in this matter to the Grand Jury, which failed to find any indictments. Governor Roosevelt designated the Republican Attorney General, the Honorable Hamilton Ward, to supersede Crain in this matter. Mr. Justice Philip J. McCook was assigned by the Governor to hold an extraordinary term of the Supreme Court. Immediately Crain expressed a willingness to resubmit the case to the Grand Jury, but Ward ordered him to desist.

Almost immediately a controversy arose as to whether or not Ward could investigate general charges of office-buying. Ward expressed the opinion that while he was limited by the terms of Governor Roosevelt's order, nevertheless the Grand Jury might investigate these charges. Justice McCook took the same view and charged the Jury that if they should discover "a system, course of conduct or understanding by force" in relation to appointment or election to public office it would be their duty to delve deeper.

The public refused to be satisfied with any such limited inquiry. Mr. Charles C. Burlingham, the able ex-President of the Association of the Bar, called on the Governor for some broader inquiry. Mr. Henry W. Taft, President of the New York County Lawyers Association, issued a statement calling for a thorough probe. Norman Thomas, the Socialist; General Harbord, the Republican; Rabbi Wise, John Haynes Holmes, and the public press criticized Governor Roosevelt for his inaction. Mayor Walker in a plea for help admitted the existence of "petty graft," but denounced those who called for an investigation as "slanderers of the fair name of the City we love." Finally Governor Roosevelt urged the Appellate Division to undertake an investigation of the "Magistrates' Court and the Magistrates thereof." In the absence of Presiding Justice Dowling, Mr. Justice Finch convened the Court, which entered an order directing that the investigation be made and appointing as their Referee, Samuel Seabury, a former Judge of the highest State Court.

Meanwhile Hiram C. Todd, Special Counsel appointed by Attorney General Ward, began presenting the Ewald case to the Grand Jury. About the middle of September, 1930, Ewald, his wife, Martin J. Healy, a District Leader, and Thomas T. Tommaney, a clerk in Sheriff Farley's office, were indicted, charged with the purchase and sale of public office. In the preceding month Healy had been suspended from his position as Deputy Commissioner of Plant and Structures, and finally resigned. Tommaney, who had been absent when wanted for questioning, finally returned and resigned to relieve Farley "of further embarrassment."

The Grand Jury continued its investigation. John F. Curry was summoned and when tendered a waiver of immunity declared himself insulted. Other district leaders were summoned, but learning from the example of their "boss" they too declined to sign waivers. All expressed the greatest willingness to testify but when they came right down to it, one by one they began to make excuses. The Mayor did nothing to facilitate the Grand Jury until the Governor, in his message, requested him to direct City Officials to sign waivers of immunity from prosecution for their "official acts." Mayor Walker issued a pronunciamento directing them to report to him by four o'clock the next afternoon whether they would sign this "trick" waiver or suffer removal. The time came and went but no official reported. The time was extended and when pressed for a reason, Walker said it was because of the Jewish holiday. Next day the papers carried a picture of Dock Commissioner Michael Cosgrove as typical of those who were prevented from reporting because of the Jewish holiday. Mayor Walker withdrew this excuse and said the delay was granted so that they might consult counsel. Since it was only too obvious that the purchase and sale of judgeships did not come within the definition of an "official act," Mr. Todd declined to permit them to testify under such a waiver.

Meanwhile ugly rumors arose to the effect that the late Judge Amadeo Bertini and the missing Judge Joseph Force Crater had bought their positions. The foreman of the Grand Jury asked the Governor to extend the terms of his order so as to permit the Attorney General and his deputies to present evidence of any violation of the elective franchise. This the Governor refused to do. Immediately the Citizen's Union offered to bear the expense, since it could not be financed out of public funds.

The gubernatorial elections came and went. Roosevelt was returned over Tuttle. The Ward inquiry began to wane. The Magistrates' investigation with its exposé of revolting corruption began to fill the public press.

Healy and Tommaney were first brought to trial in November. It was proved that at or about the time Ewald received his appointment, ten thousand dollars was passed from his wife to his sponsor, Healy, through Tommaney. The only question was whether this was a bribe or a loan. Healy explained that he borrowed it to buy a house—at that time he had some $10,000 in the bank—and the house was not bought until a year later. Mrs. Ewald did not produce the note, and it was admitted that the loan bore no interest, though not due until July, 1932. The first jury disagreed and so did the jury at the second trial in December. In January the Ewalds were brought to trial and again the jury disagreed. Following this trial all indictments were dismissed.

In 1829 John Lansing, a former Chancellor of the State of New York, left his hotel in New York City to mail a letter on the steamer for Albany. He was never seen again.

One hundred and one years later Justice Joseph Force Crater of the Supreme Court, who also functioned as a Chancellor, left a restaurant in West 45th Street, New York City. He stepped into a taxicab. He was never seen again.

Though he disappeared in August his disappearance was not announced until a month later. District Attorney Crain undertook an investigation before the Grand Jury in an effort to determine what had become of him. The Special Grand Jury looked into the rumor that at the time of his appointment in April, 1930, there had been a shift in his bank accounts of $22,500, and also to determine whether or not he had any connection with the appointment of Ewald. Both inquiries came to naught.

His wife, Mrs. Stella M. Crater, remained at their summer camp in Maine. She declined to appear before the Grand Jury.

On January 9, 1931, the Crain Grand Jury was discharged. Many witnesses had been examined and hundreds of pages of testimony had been taken, but his disappearance remained an unsolved mystery. Suddenly it was announced that on January 20, Mrs. Crater had found in the drawer of a bureau in their apartment at 40 Fifth Avenue, New York City, $6,690 in currency, a bundle of securities and a statement of alleged debts due and owing to him. After instructing her to get in touch with the people named therein who would help her to collect, the statement ended:

"Am very weary. Love.
Joe."

Since the first announcement of his disappearance the apartment had been searched by the police, not once but several times. One detective asserted most emphatically that he had searched this very drawer and found it empty, save for a fan. Confusion followed contradiction and finally the incident was forgotten.

Governor Roosevelt had appointed Crater to fill the vacancy caused by the resignation of Mr. Justice Joseph Proskauer. When Mancuso resigned he appointed Bertini. During the Special Grand Jury investigation into their appointments the Governor revealed that both had received the endorsements of many well-known lawyers.

In early October, Judge Bertini, eager to repel the rumor that he had bought his job, issued a statement expressing willingness to waive immunity and testify concerning his nomination, appointment and subsequent election. However, when called before the Grand Jury, he reversed his position and refused to sign a waiver of immunity. The city seethed with excitement. Governor Roosevelt requested Mr. Ward to send him the minutes of the Grand Jury so that he might determine whether to convene the Legislature in special session with the possibility of impeachment. Mr. Justice McCook refused to forward the minutes on the ground that it might embarrass the Grand Jury inasmuch as it had not finished its deliberations. There the matter rested until the Grand Jury announced its refusal to return an indictment and were discharged. Two months later Judge Bertini died.

CHAPTER II

SAMUEL SEABURY, REFEREE

LONDON, August 26, 1930, eleven at night. The phone rang at the Carlton Hotel. In answering it, Judge Seabury learned for the first time that the Appellate Division had appointed him Referee to investigate the Magistrates' Courts of the First Judicial Department, which comprises the counties of Manhattan and the Bronx. The reporters who then telephoned obtained no statement on the subject, as Judge Seabury had not as yet received his official notification. The next day, a cable arrived from Mr. Justice Finch officially notifying him of his appointment. Judge Seabury then announced that he was returning to America immediately to undertake his duties.

The Referee began at once to formulate his plan. How should he approach the problem?

On the fifth day, about 8:30 A.M., an airplane from out of space suddenly swooped over the ship, circled it, and disappeared into the mists again. New York was near. At Quarantine, a little later, there was great excitement. One of Judge Seabury's nephews unexpectedly came on board loaded with pictures, clippings, editorials and articles relating to the Referee and the Investigation. It seemed as if hundreds of newspaper men were there, as well as feature writers, photographers, all swarming around like bees in a hive, all asking for statements and predictions. Some innocuous extemporaneous statement was given. Pictures were taken. Thus, the first interview ended. The real work was now to begin.

Before the actual investigation and its machinery is discussed, it may be useful to paint a picture of Samuel Seabury, the Referee.

Who then is this man? No man has a broader understanding of humanity, no one is more sympathetic to the deserving, no one possesses a keener sense of humor, no one is more tolerant, no one more approachable. He is serious, he is dignified. He cannot sit and talk about nothing. He cannot sit and do nothing. He is always occupied, in reading or writing. He has powers of concentration equaled by few. His ability to change from one subject to another is due to this. His power of determination is irresistible. There is nothing mean nor small in him. He could not take advantage of any one, even his inferiors at the Bar, and their name is legion. One need have no fear, for here, without question and without cavil, but with courtesy and patience, is one who will listen and help.

Through all his public acts and opinions runs a silver skein of liberalism and progressivism. There is no reaction, no carefully worded thoughts to avoid the criticism of the mighty.

There is no one in New York more familiar with the Tammany System than Judge Seabury. Born in 1873, one year after the exposé of the Tweed ring, he watched through his youth the System in operation.

In 1894, the year of his admission to the Bar, came the Lexow Investigation. Begun by the sermons of Dr. Parkhurst, the demand grew until the investigation was ordered. It was two-fold in its conception. One part dealt with the election frauds and the other with the Police Department. The part remembered is the Police Investigation. There was no headway made until Lieutenant Schmittberger confessed. The Tammany System was then exposed and was shown to be the same foul thing that once more and in greater proportions is now being re-revealed. The same low types of graft were shown. Judge Seabury here became initiated into the Tammany System. It was revolting and repulsive. Then and there came his moment to decide. He did. He was opposed to this System and today he still is opposed. His entire political career from the time of his support of Henry George has been opposed to the Tammany Organization. His politics are Democratic, but of a school different from the school of Croker, Murphy or Curry. His elections to Judicial office, as well as his nomination for the Governorship have been forced down the throats of the Tammany Organization against its opposition.

Shortly after his election to the City Court he again saw the Tammany System befouling the Courts of Justice, by jury bribing, with the connivance of court clerks. Speedily and relentlessly he investigated the accused, proved their guilt and drove the offenders out. A few years later, in 1912, during the trial of Lieutenant Charles Becker and the trial of the four inspectors, he again saw the System at work.

Knowing, through his long years of experience, the difficulty of the task ahead, he applied to the Bar Associations of New York City, to help him in the selection of Counsel, who was to present the evidence. They responded by suggesting Isidor J. Kresel. This suggestion was eminently satisfactory to the Referee. The designation was made. By his long distinguished career at the Bar and his preëminent work in the Ambulance Chasing Investigation, Mr. Kresel had earned the honor and privilege of being Chief Counsel. His splendid work and great achievements in the Magistrates' Courts Inquiry more than proved the wisdom of the Bar Associations in suggesting him to Judge Seabury. No one could have done more, nor done it better than he. His counsel and help were invaluable to the Referee. Together they saw the necessity, if the Investigation was to be thorough, of amending the original order of the Appellate Division, by having it include the attorneys practicing in the Magistrates' Courts, as well as the Magistrates themselves. This was done on September 23, 1930.

On September 29, 1930, a day to be remembered in the history of New York City, the first public hearing was held. The presidents of the Bar Associations of Manhattan and the Bronx, together with some of the other leaders of the Bar, were present. It was here that the Referee outlined and defined the issues. It was here that he told of the necessity of preliminary or private hearings. It was here that he appealed to the young members of the profession to help him in this work, that they too might feel the exaltation of being instrumental in securing justice for the poor and helpless. A brief word is here necessary to explain the Magistrates' Courts system.

It is the court, speaking very broadly, of original criminal jurisdiction. Here an arrested person is first brought. If the accused is charged with an "offense" as distinguished from a misdemeanor or a felony, the Magistrate presiding has summary jurisdiction and may convict and impose sentence. These "offenses" are in essence mere violations of police regulations and do not amount to a crime. They embrace such acts as vagrancy in its various forms, drunkenness and various kinds of disorderly conduct and many other minor and trivial offenses, over which magistrates' tribunals have, from time immemorial, exercised summary jurisdiction. If a misdemeanor is charged, the Magistrate as such has no summary jurisdiction. He can merely hold for the Court of Special Sessions or discharge the prisoner or admit to bail, under certain circumstances. The Court of Special Sessions above mentioned is made up of three Justices who hear and determine. However, under limited circumstances the Magistrate himself may sit as a Court of Special Sessions of one, if the accused so desires, to hear and determine the matter. If a felony is charged the Magistrate can dismiss the charges and discharge the prisoner, or hold him to await the action of the Grand Jury, or further, but under limited circumstances, not necessary to enumerate here, admit the prisoner to bail.

For convenience in the administration of justice the City of New York is divided into districts, in each of which there is a Magistrates' Court. These courts transact the general criminal business of that district. Besides these regular district Courts, there are Special Magistrates' Courts. First in importance is the Homicide Court, where a person charged with having committed a homicide is brought and has his preliminary examination; then there is the Family Court, where all minor domestic disputes are adjusted; further, there is the Commercial Frauds Court, where those accused of having defrauded another in a commercial transaction are brought; also, there is the Traffic Court where cases of motor vehicle violation are handled; and finally there is the Women's Court, where all women charged with offenses or crimes of sex delinquency and shoplifting are brought. It is with this last named Court that this story opens, for there were found the greatest evils and the most sordid practices.

CHAPTER III

THE WOMEN'S COURT

HOWARD CLARK BARBER, formerly Superintendent of the Society for the Prevention of Crime (Dr. Parkhurst's Society), suggested that John C. Weston, for eight years prosecutor in this Court, could tell much about conditions therein. Finally Weston was located and Mr. Barber's prophecy proved true.

The Referee had determined to examine into the finances of all officials whose conduct fell within the scope of the inquiry. If a startling disproportion was found to exist between his total deposits and his salary while an official, the man was given an opportunity to explain this discrepancy. The examination was continued from time to time until the person under investigation had had every opportunity to check any and all records he cared to and then make his final explanation. The mere fact that the discrepancy existed was not taken as an indication of guilt, but it was made the basis for further examination. Instances have occurred where a public official has so satisfactorily explained in private the possession of hundreds of thousands of dollars in excess of his official salary, that he was never called to the public witness stand. It was only after a confession or an incredible explanation of his wealth, that an official was called to the public witness stand.

When therefore Weston was first called he was asked to furnish a list of his bank accounts from the time he first became a public official down to the date of his examination in November, 1931. Without any hesitation he listed ten banks, in each of which he then had on deposit $7,500 in cash. At that time he could not satisfactorily explain the source of this income, nor could he estimate his total expenditures. Obviously to justify these present balances he would have to show an excess

17

of income of $75,000 over his expenditures. He was asked to search his records and return the next day. Under Mr. Kresel's examination he admitted having some $93,750. According to his own explanation of income and expenditures he should only have had a cash balance of $56,100. Like a bolt from the blue came his answer to the question:

"Q. Will you tell me where you got the difference?
"A. In the Court; from the lawyers."

It remained to ascertain the details and determine whether or not this confession could be substantiated. Weston had made a practice of submitting reports on his work to the District Attorney but gave it up when he found that no one paid any attention to them. Instead, at least during the last year and a half of his tenure—January, 1928, to June, 1929, he made weekly reports to the Committee of Fourteen. It was to these that he turned for corroboration while under examination. He selected a list of cases from these reports in which he said he had been bribed. The court stenographers were then sub-pœnaed and transcribed the testimony of many of these cases. Weston testified that he had been bribed to "lay down" on the prosecution, so that the case would be dismissed. If one defendant only was involved he got $25 and if there were two or more $50. If, after the testimony at the trial had been transcribed, it was apparent that the case had been "thrown," this was accepted as some corroboration of his confession to bribe-taking. Finally after weeks of checking his story he was called to the stand. The news of his confession had been guarded with the utmost secrecy. No one suspected any such disclosure when Mr. Kresel called him to the stand. Every one rather disappointedly looked for testimony bearing upon constructive recommendations from this man who had served for seven years and more as prosecutor in this Court and whose character and ability as a vigorous prosecutor had been so glowingly extolled by the Committee of Fourteen.

In his own inimitable way Mr. Kresel, with apparent boredom to both himself and the audience, traced Weston's life history, his jewelry business and his income, his short career at the Bar and his monetary rewards, his inheritance, his appointment as a process server and his salary. In droning monotony he lulled his hearers into drowsy disinterestedness. What if Weston did inherit $25,000, made little or nothing as a jeweler or lawyer, and $3,000 as process server? Suddenly the pace quickened—people stirred. You have $90,000 and yet on your own explanation you should only have some $70,000, leaving $20,000 unaccounted for.

"Q. Where did you get that?
"A. ...I got it from the lawyers around the Court, around the Women's Court.
"Q. To put it rather succinctly and boldly, Mr. Weston, this $20,000 is a total of bribes that you took and received as representative of the District Attorney's office in that Court?
"A. I am sorry to say that is so, Counsellor."

The spectators sat bolt upright—shocked from their stupor by this breath-taking disclosure. The gentlemen of the press could hardly contain themselves. Through them Weston's story of corruption in the Women's Court was broadcast to a skeptical and apathetic public.

Jefferson Market is one of the landmarks of "old New York." It is a dingy castellated pile of red brick situated on the upper fringe of Greenwich Village. In the southern wing—until recently—grocers, butchers and others sold their wares in lawful trade. In the northern wing, in a room on an upper floor past the windows of which thundered the Sixth Avenue elevated trains, a coterie of lawyers, bondsmen and Vice Squad police who had robbed women of their liberty sold it back again for cash.

The Magistrates presiding over this Court exercise summary jurisdiction over the so-called vagrancy cases. Every woman arrested on such a charge in Manhattan must be tried in that Court. Statistics show that most of the women so arrested are tried on the charge of offering to commit prostitution. The evidence before the Referee showed that this was the easist type of case to "frame."

The stool-pigeon used by the Police selected some defenseless woman, one who appeared to have some money and to whom the publicity of arrest on such a charge would be unbearable, and then in company with the Vice Squad officers he went to her apartment. Admission was gained on some pretext or other by the stool-pigeon. Once inside the "pigeon" planted a bill in some conspicuous spot and peeled off his coat and vest. Suddenly there was a great rapping on the door, the officers demanded and gained entrance "in the name of the law." Thereafter the program was stereotyped; The Officer: Are you married? No.—Did you come here for a "good time"? Yes.—To the stool-pigeon: Did she offer to commit prostitution? Yes.—Did you pay her any money? Yes, pointing to the bill he had "planted." While one officer picked up the bill and marked it with his shield number, the other pretended to eject the "pigeon" by force.

Once outside the "pigeon" telephoned the bondsman, who proceeded to the station house where the prisoner was to be "booked." The Desk Lieutenant freed the defendant on a $500 station-house bond. Bewildered, shocked and frightened, the victim executed an assignment of the bank passbook, then the bondsman taxied to the prisoner's home and got physical possession of the book.

Next morning, after visiting the savings bank, he introduced her to a lawyer who demanded his fee. The formal appearance was then made and the lawyer entered a plea of "not guilty." Back again to the bank went victim and bondsman where the amount of the fee was actually withdrawn. The "fee" was then divided, if it was to be a divided fee, between the bondsman, the police, and the lawyer.

The case was then called for trial. Mr. Lawyer whispered to the prosecutor "This one is O.K." The stool-pigeon, of course, was not brought to trial. The arresting officer took the stand and although he had sworn to a complaint setting forth all essential elements of the offense, he now testified in such a way that one essential element was not made out. Mr. Prosecutor made no attempt to strengthen the case. As soon as the prosecution rested, counsel for the defense was on his feet and moved for a dismissal. In the interests of justice the prosecutor joined in the motion. His Honor, the Magistrate, discharged the defendant. Within the course of a day he would, in similar cases, discharge just such other defendants. Oh— it was a grand comedy. Broken in spirit, outraged and tormented in mind, the victim went home in dazed bewilderment to start life anew; gone were her savings, her faith and her hope. The stool-pigeon spotted another victim—in company with the Vice Squad officers, he went to her apartment. . . . Incredible—unbelievable!—but it happened day after day, week after week, and year after year, in the Women's Court of Manhattan.

That is what happened when the victims were willing to pay; when they would not, the officer adhered to his sworn complaint, the Magistrates accepted the officer's testimony— even over the denial of the defendant, whose credibility was supported by the testimony of character witnesses. A speedy conviction followed.

The facility with which a conviction could be obtained seems to have been too highly regarded by the Committee of Fourteen as indicating a satisfactory administration of justice. It is obvious that the ease with which a conviction could be obtained was one of the chief reasons why a "ring" could operate so successfully.

The defendant could, of course, take the stand. She might also call witnesses to testify to facts at issue and also to her good character. Often she did, but in most cases it was all to no avail. Magistrate Norris, who frequently presided in the Women's Court from 1920 to the date of her removal, gave the following testimony:

"Q. So that we may infer that during your entire experience in that Court, you never observed a police officer before you who, you thought, was testifying falsely?

"A. No, I did not."

Magistrate Renaud attached great weight to the police officer's testimony. He also developed the practice of dismissing a charge if the arresting officer did not appear the second time the case was called. This last practice was taken advantage of by certain attorneys who saw to it that the police officer should not appear, thus facilitating the defendant's discharge.

In the seven months of 1930 before the Inquiry opened two thousand one hundred and eighty-one women were arraigned there on charges of vagrancy. After the Inquiry opened arraignments began to fall off. In August two hundred and twenty-four were so arraigned; in September, two hundred and ten; October, one hundred and twelve; November, fifty-two; and December, nineteen. Thus it is shown that after the Investigation got under way and up to December 31, 1930, only six hundred and seventeen were arraigned. It then became evident that these practices could no longer continue. This precipitate decline in arraignments indicates that prior to the disclosures made in the Investigation a large number of arrests were illegal and made for revenue only. The Mayor displayed his eagerness to discredit the Inquiry by publicly stating that vice was on the increase because the officers had become afraid to perform their duty.

Weston named twenty-one lawyers, who, he swore, had bribed him during his tenure of office. The Referee in his report to the Appellate Division submitted that testimony for such action as might be proper.

The Court appointed former Judge Clarence J. Shearn as Referee to take the testimony and report. Messrs. Einar Chrystie and George B. Adams presented the evidence on behalf of the Association of the Bar, assisted, in the preparation, by Mr. Haberman of the Referee's staff. Judge Shearn concluded that Weston was an accomplice and, in the absence of what he deemed sufficient corroborative testimony, recommended the dismissal of the charges against all the accused lawyers save two. The Appellate Division has not yet acted on that report.

The very physical surroundings of the Women's Court indicate a deplorable condition. The members of what might be called the West Tenth Street Bar are housed in a row of two story buildings directly across the street. The plate glass window running across their "stores" is a veritable billboard. Tremendous letters and a big red seal indicate that within one may secure not only legal talent, but also bail bonds and the services of a notary public. Prior to this Inquiry it was quite generally the practice of these men to rent out desk space in their outer offices to one or more bondsmen. The exchange of business worked to their mutual advantage.

Their suite of offices generally consists of two rooms. In the outer one sit the bondsmen and in the practitioners' office a stenographer. Behind a door marked private sits a member of the West Tenth Street Bar. A book of forms, a Criminal Code and Bender's Diary constitute his library. A court calendar giving the assignments of the Magistrates is the only mural decoration. A desk that has seen better days and a couple of chairs complete his office furniture. Books of account would take up entirely too much room so they are dispensed with. The stubs of current checkbooks give his financial history, at least for the last few months.

Business falls like manna from the Heavens. It just follows in the wake of success. They don't advertise. They don't pay "runners." They pay neither court clerk, prison attendant nor bondsmen for bringing in cases. The well-spring of their practice is so remote as to be almost undiscoverable. As one of their number explained, he would sometimes get a case from "a friend of a friend who was arrested by a friend or a common-law husband."

No discussion of this Court and the influences operative therein would be complete without calling attention to the self-styled private welfare agencies, which have made this Court their special study. Chief among these is the Committee of Fourteen. This Committee was formed in 1905 by a group of citizens who probably believed that they could be instrumental in accomplishing good results. Their annual reports indicate that they had little conception of what was going on about them. The reports and especially that of 1930 when compared with the facts disclosed in the Appellate Division's Investigation reveal a sad spectacle.

Their 1930 report asserts that the Committee's own record has been one of long continued constructive criticism. It claims credit for the good the Inquiry has accomplished, but berates it for lessening the number of convictions on charges of prostitution. It endeavors to shift the blame for its own failure to discover Weston's bribe-taking proclivities and guardedly apologizes for its continued endorsement of him as a just and able prosecutor. It refers to the Weston bribes as "petty cash gratuities." Mr. George Worthington, the Committee's Secretary, in his book entitled "Specialized Courts Dealing with Sex Delinquency," applauds as "progressive, sympathetic, and at the same time scientific" the Magistrates who sat in that Court. Two of the Magistrates who sat in that Court have since been removed from office by the Appellate Division. The book also commends as excellent the Probation System attached to that Court which the Referee has so severely criticized in his report to the Appellate Division.

After thus eulogizing the work of the Court, and those officially connected with it, the author concludes:

> "The trials were conducted very carefully and there were so many checks on the police that the writer believes that there is practically no possibility of an innocent woman being convicted of prostitution in this Court."

CHAPTER IV

THE VICE SQUAD

THE specialty of some of the members of the Vice Squad of the New York Police Department, at the inception of the Magistrates' Courts Investigation, was in many instances the framing and bleeding of innocent women and prostitutes. It is undoubtedly true that there were honest men in this Squad who refused to pursue the practices indulged in by some of the others.

Three different groups made up this Squad. First, there was the group operating from Headquarters, or the 19th Division; these men worked on a roving commission throughout the Greater City. Second, there were the Borough Squads, under a Deputy Chief Inspector, who was in charge of each Borough; these groups could operate only within the territorial limits of the Borough. Thirdly, there were the Divisional Squads, the activities of which were confined strictly to the Division limits.

The function of the men making up the Vice Squad was the suppression of gambling, liquor violations, and prostitution. Some few performed none of these duties but on the other hand secretly fostered and nurtured all three offenses for in so doing they kept alive the business which gave them their victims and their profits. They did this by means of threats, false arrests, and stool-pigeons or *agents provocateur*. In a statement on October 27, 1930, Commissioner Mulrooney said, disarmingly, that the Department as such had never employed stool-pigeons.

These remarks of Commissioner Mulrooney had their speedy answer on December 3, 1930, when Chile Mapocha Acuna, a confessed stool-pigeon, walked around the courtroom and picked out and identified certain members of this Squad for whom he had worked in various parts of the city. This extraordinary person was so sure of himself and was so familiar with each that he boasted he could be blindfolded and then identify these men merely by their voices. These men were ordinary uniformed patrolmen assigned to duty in plain clothes. They worked on complaints written or otherwise sent in to Headquarters and the various station houses throughout the city, as well as on information they themselves obtained by observation and other means throughout their districts.

There were two types of arrests these men made, the "direct case" and the "indirect case." In the direct case, the officer himself was the inducing factor, who led the victim on by falsely making her believe that he was approaching her on a purely business basis. As soon as she believed that, and accepted the proposition and endeavored to carry out her bargain, the officer would reveal himself and arrest her. In the indirect case the inducing factor was the stool-pigeon, who, working with the police, would falsely lead the girl on, take her to some room and then, when she attempted to carry out her bargain, at a given time the police, who knew about it all, would break in, pretend to slap and cuff the stool-pigeon or "unknown man" around, throw him out, and would then arrest the victim. These two methods were used almost exclusively, the latter more than the former.

One form the indirect case took came to be known as the "Doctor's Racket." Here these officers, in conjunction with their "stool-pigeons," would send him to a doctor's office, where they knew nurses were employed, while the doctor was out. The nurses subjected to these practices worked in the offices of chiropractors, osteopaths, and masseurs. Here the stool-pigeon, or in one or two cases the officer himself, would pose as a patient and request a treatment. He might be told by the nurse that she could not give it while the doctor was out; that, however, made no difference, for this pseudo-patient would commence to undress, not before, however, he had placed five or ten dollars in a conspicuous place, money supposed to be in payment of the treatment, but in reality only to supply one of the elements of the offense of offering to commit prostitution, namely the demand and payment of money. If a stool-pigeon were being used in this racket, the officers would, after a given time, break in and arrest the girl for offering to commit prostitution. If it were the officer himself, he would reveal his official capacity and arrest the girl for the same offense.

Another type of indirect case was one that came to be known as the "Landlady Racket." Here, in the cases found, only the stool-pigeon was used, the officer himself never. It was worked as follows: in the morning of a given day, the stool-pigeon would go to an agreed address, which was known to be a rooming house, and apply to the unsuspecting landlady for a room. After being shown a room, he would tell the landlady that his wife was coming into town from somewhere about noon and that he would bring her up shortly thereafter. Before leaving, he would pay the landlady five or ten dollars on account of rent, merely to get the money, usually marked, in her hands. In the afternoon he would return with some girl, pretend she was his wife, and go to the room assigned. Almost immediately thereafter the officers would break in, arrest the girl for offering to commit prostitution, and the landlady for maintaining a house of prostitution. The women preyed upon were generally middle-aged women or widows trying quietly and unobtrusively to earn a living. It was a good racket. It gave the officers a double chance for a shakedown—the landlady and the girl, although the latter may sometimes have been in on the job.

It is not necessary here to go into every form of framing these men devised; but there was no restraint if they thought they were safe. They never attacked the powerful.

Of the companions and tools of the Vice Squad—the stool-pigeons—the most important was Chile Mapocha Acuna. He was a man of about thirty-one, of slight build, beady brown eyes, curly brown hair, about five feet and weighing about one hundred and twenty-five pounds. He came to America in 1919, from his native country, Chile, speaking no English, with

about $2,500. His only reason for coming was, he said,
". . . just fancy and illusions. I had in my mind of becoming
something; that was only an idea. There was no definite purpose in my coming here, because I had a better opportunity
in my own country. Every one of my family had it, but I had
it in myself perhaps some kind of an adventurous spirit." He
had his adventures. His story is perhaps one of the strangest
ever told, as he himself was one of the most remarkable of
witnesses. Coming here, as he said, in 1919, he shortly found
that he had spent all his money and, speaking very little English, he wandered to New York and found a job in the C. & L.
Restaurant on Broadway and 80th Street, as a dishwasher.
This former student of the Institute of Pedagogy in Santiago,
Chile, rose quickly from a dishwasher to counterman in various restaurants where he worked, until in 1927 he became a
waiter at Reubens on Broadway near 81st Street.

Some time after he went there, he became acquainted with
two detectives. They, learning after a while that he spoke
Spanish and other foreign languages, thought that in his wan-
derings in that district he might hear of things going on of
interest to them and, if so, they asked him to tip them off
and they would pay him for his information. It so happened
that about that time he had learned the name of the perpetrator of a murder recently committed. He told them. They
acted upon his information. Out of this case he made from
fifty to one hundred dollars. As he was naturally shrewd, he
saw the pecuniary advantage of this relation and agreed to
help them further, particularly among Spaniards and Ital-
ians. His function in those districts was to mix among sus-
pects and their companions, after some crime had been reported, and endeavor to turn up the perpetrator and then
report him to the detectives. He continued to do work for
detectives on crimes of a more serious nature until January
of 1929, when he first became associated with the Vice Squad.

According to his testimony, one day, while he was at the
68th Street Station House talking, a sergeant was introduced
to him. This officer was then working for the 19th or Head-

quarters Division under Inspector Boland. Acuna was pointed out to this officer as one possessing information which might be useful. Acuna produced a list from his pocket of about four gambling joints and one house of prostitution, which he says he turned over to the sergeant. The following day, the raids evidently having taken place that night, Acuna appeared at the station house to collect his share. He received, he said, only fifty dollars, on the ground that the places turned up were cheap places. Shortly thereafter Acuna was sent from this district to the station house at 123rd Street and told to report to Inspector "Ryan." He reported there to some man, whom he believed to be Inspector "Ryan," but the person thus referred to was not Inspector Ryan. His availability for working uptown was that this district embraced the Latin or Spanish section of Harlem, and he spoke the language fluently. Here, from "Ryan," he got his instructions about giving a false name and address, about the "comedy" or slapping around that would take place when he was caught in the raid, and also about never going to court, and always denying that he knew the arresting officers. After these preliminary instructions from "Ryan" he was introduced, as having a great deal of good information, by "Ryan" to two of the Squad working the district, one of whom was Officer Tait. Tait is now in Sing Sing for perjury for having testified falsely against a negress named Icie Sands. Acuna, according to his testimony, had worked out in minute detail with these men the method to be used in getting into the place, his conduct inside and what was to be done when the raid occurred.

Some time later Acuna came to the Investigation. He had been double-crossed, and sent to jail for a year. The city was in an uproar over stool-pigeons. Some wanted them for information, others wanted to get rid of them for the information they had. Besides, he was not sure that the Inquiry was sincere or that it would give him what he wanted—protection. However, he finally came on October 28, 1930. He insisted on seeing Judge Seabury and Mr. Kresel, and would tell his story to no one else. He did tell them briefly. They sent him to talk to

Mr. Cooper, whereupon he unfolded his story in greatest detail, without a record of any kind in front of him. To check his story, every record referred to was subpœnaed from the Courts. These corroborated his story in the minutest detail. At last the key to the system was found. There was no detail that he did not know. He knew the Vice Squad, the lawyers and the bondsmen who made up this trinity. He knew the other stool-pigeons that worked for the Squad,—"the Dove," Pinto, Harry the Greek, Meyer Slutsky, Chico and Harry Levey. Their stories, with the exception of Levey's, were the same. Levey's story was different in that it showed a different phase of this almost perfect graft-extracting system.

Levey is apparently a native New Yorker. He had served for a while in the army in some capacity. After he was discharged he became acquainted with Louis Taube or "the Dove," who is now in the Penitentiary on Welfare Island for fleeing the jurisdiction. On one occasion the Dove asked Levey if he knew where he (the Dove) could have a "good time," as the expression runs. Unsuspectedly and in apparent good faith, Levey told him. This favor the Dove reciprocated in stool-pigeon fashion, by raiding the place and having the girl arrested. Levey first testified under the name of Joseph Lesser. He had been down to the headquarters once or twice when he disappeared, and then of a sudden it was learned that he had been arrested in New Orleans. Immediately he was indicted for conspiracy to defeat justice by fleeing the jurisdiction when wanted as a witness. He was shortly thereafter returned to New York and lodged in the Tombs. It was then the story of his disappearance was learned in full, and also another aspect of the system used by some of the Vice Squad, i.e., the practice of spiriting away those who knew.

His story is this: one day, after leaving the headquarters, he was accosted by three unknown men and told to meet William M. O'Connor, one of the Vice Squad, the following Friday, in the waiting room of the Grand Central Station. Levey pretended he didn't know why he should meet

O'Connor; nevertheless, after some discussion of the subject, he agreed to do it. He did. He met O'Connor, who escorted him from the waiting room to a secluded spot on the gallery surrounding the main room of the station. There he was given $50, according to his testimony, and told to leave town immediately. O'Connor, so he testified, told him he didn't care where he went, but to get out, and that the necessary money would be forthcoming. A day or so later, he decided to go. He told his wife he was going to New Orleans to get a job and then he left. He went first to Baltimore to the Emerson Hotel, where he received his first payment for expenses. Thence he went to Washington, and finally to New Orleans, stopping at the Marberc Hotel, where he was later arrested. In each of these places he received money. This money was sent by way of telegraphic money order, ostensibly sent by a "Harry Lewis" of New York. In reality, according to Levey, it was from O'Connor and Quinlivan. All of Levey's requests were signed Leo or Leo Baker. As O'Connor had had experience in the telegraphic branch of the Police Department, he was not unfamiliar with the ways to disguise and send money by wire. While in New Orleans, Levey telephoned O'Connor's house at Navarre 4343, Brooklyn, and talked to both O'Connor and Quinlivan, trying to agree on terms,—when the money would be sent. All of these telegraphic money orders were produced before the Referee. All receipts for telegrams signed by some one in O'Connor's or Quinlivan's families and finally the hotel bill from New Orleans, showing the record of the call to Navarre 4343, which was admittedly O'Connor's home number, were put in evidence. Despite this flood of documentary proof, these two men took the stand and blandly and simply denied the whole scheme. In all, in the space of a month, to keep him away and his mouth shut, they had paid Levey around $700 or $750.

After this story had been proved at a public hearing, Levey went on to explain his part in the collection of graft in speakeasies. This collection, according to his testimony, was done on a regular basis, each speakeasy having a fixed monthly fee to pay. The fee depended on the size of the place and the business done. Between the first and the fifth of each month, Levey, so his story runs, in company with two members of the Vice Squad, would drive around the circuit and collect the tribute. Approximately $5,000 a month was collected and split between the officers. Occasionally a dispute would arise with a speakeasy proprietor who claimed that he was already paying tribute and ought not to be further taxed. The method of collection was fairly simple. Levey would drive the officers to some point near the place, then he would get out, go in and see if the "boss" was in. If so, he would either pick up an envelope with some fictitious name on it, such as Cohn and Ginsberg or the "X" Construction Company, take it out with him and deliver it to the men waiting in the car. If the boss was in but didn't have the money ready, Levey would report to the officers and they would go in and see him. Seldom, if ever, according to his testimony, did they come empty away. If the boss was not in they would simply return later for payment.

The methods and practices of the last of the triumvirate, the bondsmen, will now be discussed.

One of the bondsmen encountered was a person by the name of John Steiner, who operated across the street from the 100th Street Station House in New York.

Up to April, 1930, he and another person by the name of Abraham Treibitz were partners. In that month, the State Insurance Department revoked Steiner's license. Since then he has operated, as he testified, merely as a clerk in Treibitz's office, just doing errands and answering the 'phone. He had no connection with the police. He knew them only to say "Hello." He emphatically denied knowing the stool-pigeons, but despite this, every now and then in his testimony, another fact would slip in, which showed that he knew some of the Vice Squad officers who operated in that district, and all of the stool-pigeons. All this crowd used to congregate in his office to play cards and wait for the victims to be brought in. In the Sigrid Johnson case, later described, Steiner denied overcharging, in fact, denied everything that connected him with the case; nevertheless he was convicted of this crime by the Court of Special Sessions and sent to the penitentiary.

According to the testimony of the victims and the stool-pigeons who made a clean breast of the whole matter, the bondsmen were the pay-off men. It was the bondsmen who would collect from the victims and it was they who would divide the proceeds among the interested parties. Many witnesses testified the bondsmen invariably charged in excess of the legal rate. These witnesses produced their bank books showing the withdrawals of large sums. These amounts were shown to have been withdrawn within a day or two of the arrests. There is, therefore, on one side: the testimony of the victims, substantiated by their bank books, as to the overcharges, and on the other side only the unsubstantiated and recordless denials of the bondsmen themselves. All the bondsmen testified exactly alike. None ever solicited any business, none ever took cases to lawyers or others, none ever split fees, and none ever went into the station houses. It was just coincidence that their "stores," as they called them, were next to or across the street from the station houses. They were unanimous in calling every single person who testified against them and their practices, a liar. There is, however, no difficulty in determining where the truth lies.

In order to trace and find out about this money which Acuna and Levey had testified they knew was collected, the accounts of certain officers were subpœnaed and analyzed. In the instances which are enumerated below, the analyses were startling, but no more so than the stories as to how this money was accumulated.

Officer James Quinlivan, who has since been convicted by the United States Government for filing false income tax returns, had been, up to the time of his public examination, on the Police Force for eighteen years. His and his wife's accounts were examined for only the past five years. In that time, he himself had banked about $31,000 in cash and his wife, the sum of $57,744.67, of which $30,016.20 was in cash. They had a joint safe deposit box, but it was used, he testified, merely for the safe-keeping of insurance papers and jewelry. When asked to explain his accounts he told a tale startling in its naïveté and remarkable in its conception.

Ten thousand dollars of his money came from gambling but it was won, he asserted, before he went on the Force. This money, in cash, was kept by this gentleman's mother at home, in a trunk, for about ten years. At her death, his father assumed the burden of caring for this. He, too, kept it in the trunk. His death occurred in about two years and then Quinlivan himself took care of it in the good old trunk. He kept it in this fashion until he married and gave it to his wife, as he says, "as soon as I got married." It had grown, however, from $10,000 to $20,000. The good father who died, left James, although there was another son, $10,000 in cash. When pressed as to why the other brother didn't get any of the money he told the Referee that the brother could have had all he wanted, but he died, thereby relieving himself from the need of money. This $20,000 grew too, very speedily, for we find that on his honeymoon, Quinlivan picked up $3,000 more at the Havre-de-Grace, Maryland, race track, where betting is legal.

Of the first $10,000 which his mother kept, $9,000 was won on a wonderful horse named Flora Belle. The year of the race and the race itself in which this horse was supposed to have run were never discovered.

He first heard about this horse in return for doing a drunken jockey a generous favor. Quinlivan took this jockey home one night in his drunken stupor, and on the very next day this thoughtful jockey reciprocated the favor by telling Quinlivan to bet on Flora Belle.

It is all a very charming picture, because it shows that beneath the gruff exterior of this brass be-buttoned policeman, there beats a heart of gold. Besides this $23,000—$8,000 more was discovered. He told of this amount, but refused to tell how he acquired it, on the ground that to do so would tend to incriminate or degrade him.

He played cards as well as the horses, but this apparently was a sore subject, for when he was asked about his winnings, at cards, he gave this explicit answer, "Well, I can answer that question one way, I can refuse to answer the question on the ground when I was in the Department I refuse to answer where on the same ground, that it may tend to incriminate or degrade me, but while I was out of the Department, I played cards at different places in Yonkers." There his story ended— it was interesting, it was explicit and convincing to all, probably, except the Referee, who said at the close, "This covers the incident. I think this whole record that we have listened to, this evidence of corruption and perjury, ought to go to the District Attorney of the County for action, and I hope the minutes will be sent to him. . . ." The Referee was never fortunate enough to hear Mrs. Quinlivan's story. On the day scheduled for her visit, Quinlivan learned that, four weeks before that day, she had gone to some unknown destination in Pennsylvania with both children, to visit some unknown friends. She had never told her own husband of this. In those circumstances resort to the colorless story of an accountant to explain her bank accounts became necessary. She was indeed, from the analysis given, a very saving woman.

Another of the interesting stories was that of Lieutenant Pfeiffer. This story, as ludicrous and ridiculous as it is, has two very important aspects: one, it brings into the Investigation the first "tin box"; two, it indicates the amount of money spent by the taxpayers each year in only two of the five Counties of New York City, i.e., Manhattan and the Bronx, for the information bought from stool-pigeons.

Pfeiffer's story in accounting for the money in his bank accounts is incoherent, rambling and contradictory.

In essence, it is this: he had about $1,000 when he joined the Department thirty-four years ago, earned in truck driving and working in some marble business. Since then he and his wife have accumulated their wealth by savings from his salary, and rents. The rents were derived from houses, which one minute he had and the next minute didn't have because his wife had inherited the houses from her mother. First he would tell how he owned a mortgage on a house and in the next breath would say his wife inherited $12,000 or a house, he wasn't sure which, and therefore he didn't own that house or mortgage but it was another house and mortgage. This story went on for about fifty pages of testimony, contradicting itself, changing all around—getting more and more complicated, telling nothing and ending in utter confusion, so that no one knew which mortgage fitted each house, nor could any one know what his wife had inherited or saved, nor how much.

The second aspect of his story dealt with his "tin box." The facts about this are very simple, his explanations ridiculous and incomprehensible. All that he said about this box was that he kept in it his insurance papers, his wife's jewelry and "different papers." No one ever discovered what these "different papers" were. He said that he never put cash in the box and that the only thing he ever went to the box for was to look at the insurance papers and take out or put in his wife's earrings, though on one occasion he admitted he put his own ring in the box. To check this fanciful tale, an official record of his visits to his safe deposit box was obtained. This showed that in a little over one month, Pfeiffer visited his box no less than five times. On one occasion he stayed for just one minute. He was asked if on this occasion he just opened the top of the box and dropped cash in, but as usual he said no. His inspection of the insurance papers that day must have been a bit cursory. Finally, to sum up his "tin box" story, he was asked this question:

"Q. So that you kept putting in the life insurance and fire insurance policies and taking them out, is that it?
"A. Yes, sir, different papers, yes, sir."

The last and most important feature of his story concerned the amount of money spent by the taxpayers for information bought from stool-pigeons. On the stand Pfeiffer figured that the average monthly bill submitted by the twenty officers of his squad was $35 per man, or, in all, about $700. This would amount to $8,400 per year for his squad alone. On this basis for the two Counties of Manhattan and the Bronx, there being about 120 men on this squad, Pfeiffer computed that the taxpayers paid out approximately $50,000 annually. Using the same method of calculation the City as a whole pays nearly $100,000 a year to these stool-pigeons. The money was paid without any checkup or investigation whatsoever. What the officers said they spent was approved by Pfeiffer without any question. He testified about that as follows:

"A. Well, we believe the men, what money they spend they put in an honest bill for it.

"Q. In other words, you take it for granted that they are not lying to you?

"A. Yes, sir....

"Q. Is that all you do?

"A. Yes, sir....

"Q. You don't make any investigation whatsoever, do you? You take their word for it?

"A. We take their word for it....

"Q. And whatever they tell you you believe?

"A. I take it for granted, yes, sir."

The story of Robert E. Morris, another member of the Vice Squad, is surely as pathetic as any that was heard. The facts were very difficult to elicit because of the complete collapse of Morris's memory. All things past had faded completely from his mind. He couldn't even recall whether or not he had any bank accounts at all or whether or not there were six or seven. Two were found. On the stand he volunteered the fact that he had inherited or saved some $50,000. The method was interesting, but unusual. Forty thousand of it came from an uncle. Ten thousand from gambling.

As to the $40,000: about twenty-one years ago, he (Morris) was down at Coney Island one day, when he bumped into his Uncle George Waring. It seems that Uncle George was

in a generous mood that day, for immediately on meeting
Morris, he took from his pocket forty brand new one thousand
dollar bills and handed them over to his nephew. It was never
learned what he was doing in Coney Island on that day; it
must have been coincidence, for Uncle George lived in Lake-
view, New Jersey, at the time. Answering another question
as to what business Uncle George was in, Morris said:

"A. Well, I know his business, but I don't think it is fair to
ask that question if a man was not in a legitimate business, I don't
say ... but he is dead, a man should stand here and run down
my relative with the lowest."

Thus the true source of Uncle George's wealth was never
ascertained. Uncle George had at the time a wife and three
children. Morris had two brothers and two sisters. When
questioned as to why Uncle George had singled him out as
the recipient of this present when there were so many others
who might expect some token of generosity, Morris replied:

"A. No, he just gave it to me. I was always his favorite
nephew, he always thought a lot of me, and gave me the money."

It was thought by Counsel that Uncle George could cor-
roborate this story, but when he endeavored to learn his
whereabouts Morris informed him that Uncle George had
died, as had all of Uncle George's family, and that they were
all buried somewhere in California, perhaps near Los An-
geles. Thus Morris's tale of forty of his fifty thousand dollars
ended.

The remaining ten thousand he said was won in gambling,
playing the races and shooting craps at Patty Shay's on the
Bowery. He refused to tell whether or not any of this money
was won in gambling while he was on the Force, on the ground
that:

"A. If I testify where I was gambling, and if it was a gambling house, I am not supposed to be in there, I am supposed to
report the gambling house, and by not doing so, I am subject to
a complaint, and that will subject me to dismissal."

All the other questions as to his gambling activities were answered by "I don't recall" or by some meaningless statement intended, in substance, to be the claiming of his constitutional rights.

All of this $50,000 was kept at home in a tin box, the second tin box of a long procession. As to where it now was he said that his wife had gotten all of it. He was then asked where his wife was and in response he told the Referee that they were now separated and had been since June, 1927, but that he had since the separation given her money and made her a monthly allowance. Counsel next showed him his signature card from the Fulton Savings Bank opening his account with a cash deposit of $2,025. The account was dated July 8, 1927. When asked where the money came from he said first, that it was his wife's (even though they were then separated), and second, that she had given it to him because she was building a house. In reply to the question why his separated wife banked this cash in his name he said:

"A. Because my wife was building a house, and my wife thought that being I had children, I would look after them, and it was better for me to have the money in my name, that I could attend to paying off, as the house was being built, being a man, than it would be if she was a woman, so I done it for her, for the sake of the children. That is the reason I made those deposits in the bank, and put that in my name, and that is the reason it shows in my name, but otherwise it is no more my money than it is yours."

There were two more items of cash deposited, one of $1,000 in August, 1927, and one of $1,150 in October. Both of these amounts were later withdrawn by check, he said, to pay for the house. These withdrawals were said to have closed the account. Under date of February 28, 1928, the sum of $1,700 in cash was withdrawn. This completely confused him. His answers trying to reconcile this fact with his statement that all was withdrawn by check were unintelligible. As to that he said:

"That might have been in cash and I got a check from a man, and on the back of the check it showed what the money was for, it was for this house."

He was asked the name of this check giver. It turned out to be Benny, who works in the Surrogates Court in Brooklyn. To prove that it was Benny, he said:

"I believe it was still ... I believe it was his checks that I gave him the cash, or I had it in check form from the bank itself, I don't recall years ago, this check, because I don't recall. That is what the money was for."

After this explanation, the question was not pressed further. He closed the account on May 16, 1928, eleven months after he opened it and paid the balance of $2,573.09, which was withdrawn in cash, towards the house. He was shown another account in the Dime Savings Bank that was opened on March 3, 1924, with a cash deposit of $4,000. This, too, turned out to be his wife's money, but as to why she gave it to him, all he could say was: "I can't explain the reason for that." He closed this account eight months later, returning the money to his wife.

The courtroom regretted the close of Morris's tale for it had, by its consummate imagination, reawakened in them the long dormant thrill they once had over a good story or fairy tale.

There were many other accounts and many other stories of similar purport and tenor, even though not so imaginative, not necessary to detail.

CHAPTER V

THE TECHNIQUE OF FRAMING

THE alliance between the Vice Squad, bondsmen and lawyers which had so long existed was dissolved as a result of disclosures made in the course of the Investigation. The Mayor remarked concerning the part played by the police in the matter: "a few had faltered." His concern apparently was not with the victims, but with the defense of his administration. He attempted to discredit the Inquiry by broadcasting statements declaring that the disclosures made were attempts to libel the entire Force. The patent absurdity of both excuses and statements was made even more manifest when Mulrooney, the Police Commissioner, abolished the Squad and returned its members to ordinary police duty.

The stories of victims of the "ring" drove home to the public the extent of its atrocities.

"It is," the Referee said, "only by humanizing this Inquiry that we can translate our findings into a language the great mass of the people can understand. The public will not be aroused to an awareness of conditions as they actually are in the Magistrates' Courts through graphs, charts and reports. We must divorce it as far as possible from legalistic machinery. There is more eloquence in the testimony of an illiterate witness telling of oppression suffered through abuse of legal process, than in the greatest sermon or editorial or address ever written."

Their victims ranged from women of high to low estate. Reluctant to live again those hideous scenes, but willing to help eradicate this caricature of justice, these women haltingly told their stories. Wives snatched from their husbands, sweethearts torn from their lovers, and women from the streets, followed one another to the stand. With trembling lips they told how they had been hunted, jailed and bailed. Sordid stories of brutal assault, inhuman bestiality and stealthy deception were spread upon the public record.

One young woman requested that she be allowed to testify under the fictitious name of "Betty Smith" so that her job might not be put in jeopardy. Although separated, she and her husband remained on friendly terms—in fact, he paid the rent for her apartment in the city.

On the 18th day of November, 1929, her husband asked her if she would dine with him and a mutual friend. This, she testified, was a frequent occurrence. She accepted his invitation, telling him to meet her at her apartment in New York about five in the afternoon. While she and the friend, who had arrived a few minutes before, were waiting for her husband, the doorbell rang. She opened the door and to her amazement a total stranger burst into the room and slammed the door behind him. This stranger turned out to be Officer Robert E. Morris of the Vice Squad. He immediately pushed her into the bedroom and slammed that door too. When her friend protested at this unwarranted outrage, the officer summoned his partner. They then told him he was in a house of prostitution. He remonstrated and assured them that that was not so. He gave them his card, explaining why he had come there, but, nevertheless, they put him out.

After he was gone she too did her best to convince them they had made a mistake. She showed them her marriage certificate and business cards, but all to no avail. They insisted she was a prostitute, arrested her, put her in a cab and took her to the police station. Before they left, however, they took the precaution to cut the telephone wire.

Her friend, who had been waiting in a drugstore downstairs, saw them take their victim away. He telephoned his attorney and together they went to the police station, where his attorney bailed her out and took her home.

There she found her husband, who on arriving at his wife's apartment had been informed by some one of her arrest, but had not known where to find her. By this time she was so distraught they took her to a hotel, and called a doctor to attend her.

The next morning, for the first time, she learned that she was charged with offering to commit prostitution with one Joseph Clark "and then and there demanded and received the sum of $20 therefor, and did thereupon expose her person to the said Joseph Clark for said purpose, the truth whereof defendant did thereupon admit." This, the usual and uniform complaint, was then sworn to by the partner of Officer Morris even though he had not made the actual arrest.

Her attorney demanded and received, as was his right, an adjournment. Her bail nevertheless was increased from $500 to $1,000 and although she had already put up jewelry worth $1,200, as security, she was forced to put up $500 more in cash.

Her trial took place before Magistrate H. Stanley Renaud, another of the regular Women's Court Magistrates, on the day before Christmas.

Incredible as it is, this Magistrate found her guilty on the uncorroborated word of the officer, who had not even come into the room until he had been called by his partner Morris. She and the other persons who were present took the stand and in no uncertain terms denied the charge. In addition to that, an elevator boy swore that he had not taken both of the police officers up to the apartment at the same time. Her husband, the manager of the house and two other friends swore to her good character. The defendant was convicted nevertheless. This outrageous injustice was "righted" by the Court of Special Sessions, but not until Mrs. "Smith" had been forced to serve over five and a half months of her sentence on probation. In the meantime she was forced to endure almost unbelievable humiliation.

No sooner had the Magistrate pronounced her guilty than she was locked up in a cell in the Jefferson Market Prison. They then proceeded to subject her to the usual tests prescribed by law as to her condition of health. Be it said to their credit, the prison matron and a doctor, one from the Police Department, treated her with a kindly helpfulness.

A few days later when she was again brought into court, she pleaded with the Magistrate, that if he would only send her to a hospital where she could get proper medical treatment, she might soon be well enough to undergo the required examination. The Magistrate promised her medical care and treatment, but nothing was ever done, so she remained locked in a cell from Christmas Eve until January 2nd, when she was able to take the tests, and these having been taken, she was admitted to probation.

Unfortunately, however, "Betty Smith" declined to appear before the Grand Jury to testify against these two officers. After a departmental trial Morris was discharged from the Force because of some other matters brought out in the Investigation. Because of an indictment then pending against the other officer he was not tried by the Police Department. When his case came on for trial, the jury disagreed, and his bail was discharged.

"Catherine" Nolan breakfasted with her fiancé on November 22, 1924. They discussed plans for their wedding, which was to take place during Christmas week. After breakfast he went to his work and she, feeling unwell, went home to bed. She had left an accounting job that she had held for six years in the hope of bettering her position. Momentarily she hoped for the telegram telling her to report for this new job. In the afternoon she was aroused by the incessant ringing of her doorbell. Finally she got up, slid the chain bolt into the slot and cautiously opened the door. "Telegram," said the caller. Expectantly she reached through the opening. Instead of a telegram her hand was seized in a vise-like grip—pressed down across the chain until her fingers bled—all the while she was ordered to open the door. Dazed, she became hysterical and the colored janitress rushed to her aid, only to be ordered away by the officer. While the janitress fled down the stairs to find a uniformed patrolman—with the cry—"Here goes the door" the cop burst into the room.

Enter, Patrolman Abe Dicker.

The impact sent Miss Nolan spinning. In falling she hit her head against a chair. Dicker pulled her into a chair, struck her twice, and called her all manner of vile names. Just then the janitress returned with a uniformed officer, who quickly left when Dicker told him that he and his partner were making a prostitution arrest.

She was booked at the 68th Street Station House, where Dicker, feigning helpfulness, told her to call some one and tell them to take $50 and go to Jefferson Market and get Bondsman Lange to write the $500 bond (the legal rate for which was $15). He also urged her to hire Lawyer Lange, the bondsman's brother.

At her trial Dicker, the only witness for the prosecution, testified that he had observed her apartment for some time after he had taken his post. One man came out—in fifteen minutes another man entered—he left and a third entered. Fifteen minutes later this officer gained entrance. He testified at the trial that upon entering he found one Jack Steinberg of 490 E. 56th Street (which would be about the middle of the East River) in bed, who admitted that he had paid her $5 for a "good time," and that she admitted it and had returned the money. On cross-examination he maintained that there was no chain lock on the door. To show the falsity of this, the broken lock taken from the door itself was put in evidence. Miss Nolan, though subjected to a brutal cross-examination by both the Magistrate and the prosecutor, denied the charge and gave the lie to Dicker. In spite of the testimony of the janitress as to what happened, and in spite of the testimony of her character witnesses, among them her former employer, she was found guilty.

They packed her off to jail, where she was subjected to brutality and insults by the woman doctor who made the physical tests. In due course she was sentenced to six months' probation. Though she was condemned by law, her fiancé's faith never wavered, they were married and have been living together happily ever since. Their wedding trip was, however, necessarily shortened by reason of the fact that she had to report to the probation officer once every week.

After her conviction, Mr. Samuel Marcus, Counsel to Dr. Parkhurst's Society, prosecuted her appeal to the Court of Special Sessions. By a two to one vote the judgment was affirmed. With dogged tenacity Mr. Marcus stuck to his guns. In the latter part of May, 1926—after she had served her complete sentence—the Appellate Division reversed the conviction on the ground that it was against the weight of evidence, and ordered a new trial. Miss Nolan's troubles were not over yet. She appeared first before Judge Silbermann— Weston joined in Mr. Marcus' motion to dismiss, saying that the People had no additional evidence and in view of the determination of the Appellate Division it was useless to re-try the case on the same evidence. Due to some procedural technicality the case could not be disposed of that day. Before the case came up again Mr. Marcus had an interview with District Attorney Banton, who directed his Assistant to inform the Court that the People had no further evidence and to join in a motion to dismiss. Magistrate Jean Norris, before whom it came the second time, declined to dismiss, saying: "In this Court, when cases are sent back here for trial, there is always a new trial." The matter came on again before Magistrate Silbermann. Not only did he refuse to dismiss but in addition directed that a warrant issue for her arrest. In vain Mr. Marcus told him that he could reach her by telephone—that the only reason she did not appear was the fear of losing her job. Mr. Marcus wrote Judge Norris complaining of this treatment to Miss Nolan. Upon receipt of this letter Judge Norris got in touch with Mr. Marcus and on July 21, 1926—almost one year and eight months from the day of arrest—she honorably discharged Miss Nolan.

Subsequently, in 1927, Abe Dicker was dismissed from the

Force, but for an offense other than the illegal arrest of Miss Nolan.

Josephine Olen was a middle-aged woman of quiet respectability who made her livelihood by taking in boarders. One Saturday afternoon she answered the doorbell. The caller asked for a Mrs. Lewis; she was not there any more, but, said Mrs. Olen, a friend of hers, Miss Janice, lived downstairs. At his request she took him down to see if he could find where Mrs. Lewis went. Mrs. Olen left to answer the telephone and then she was again called to the door. This time, two policemen, exhibiting their badges, demanded to be taken to the room where she had taken the other man. She obeyed, and when they reached Miss Janice's room, they found Meyer Slutsky, the stool-pigeon. The officers arrested the girl for prostitution and Mrs. Olen for keeping a disorderly house.

An officer at the 100th Street Station House told them that they better get busy and get bail or they would have to stay in jail all night. With usual helpfulness he suggested that they get John Steiner. Mrs. Olen agreed and before long Steiner appeared and put up bail, taking the customary assignment of her bank book which showed a balance of $1,095. When they went home to get the book Steiner cheerfully remarked, "You are already cooked," but he said he knew the detectives and might be able to do something for $1,000. Innocent as she was Mrs. Olen refused to be gouged in any such manner as that.

Mrs. Olen could not get in touch with her own attorney, so she acquiesced in the suggestion of Miss Janice that they employ another attorney. He at first suggested a fee of $800, but finally reduced it to $500, according to Mrs. Olen's testimony. At his office Mrs. Olen signed a paper without knowing what it was and without the benefit of any explanation. Afterwards she discovered that it was an order on her bank to pay out $1,080 to one Abraham Treibitz, whom Steiner helped in his bail business. The attorney, according to Mrs. Olen, said he had to charge a big fee to "take care of detectives and people in the Court."

In due time the two women were tried and acquitted. Weston, who had prosecuted the case, testified that the attorney met him before the trial and told him he had a case there he wanted "to go out," and after the acquittal paid him $50.

After it was all over Mrs. Olen began to wonder what had happened to her bank book which she hadn't seen since giving it to Steiner. She enlisted the aid of her own attorney, Daniel Polansky. Finally after correspondence and telephone calls to Steiner he retrieved $368.

This illegal arrest cost Mrs. Olen $712 in addition to the mental torture and unwarranted interruption of her daily affairs.

Quinlivan, one of the arresting officers, is in Atlanta doing time for failure to have due regard for the income tax laws. Both of the arresting officers were dismissed from the Force and both were indicted for perjury and conspiracy to obstruct justice.

Steiner in another case was sent to the penitentiary under an indeterminate sentence for the overcharging on bail bonds.

A woman was arrested and arraigned in the Women's Court on a charge of prostitution. She was then taken to the office of a "fixer" who told her that he was "a big man in the Grand Street boys" and that for $600 he could fix everything in such a way that it would make no difference if she were guilty or innocent, this sum to include in addition to his charge, the attorney's fee and bribe to the officer.

Mr. "Fixer" retained an attorney, but it subsequently developed that he had received no part of the $600, so the victim had to pay him another $200, but even this did not include his services at the trial.

Her case came on for trial. Mr. "Fixer" brought the president of the District club bearing the name of the Tammany leader responsible for the appointment of the Magistrate holding Court. This service cost the victim another $150. They all met, not in the Court, but in a drug store opposite. From there they pretended to telephone the Magistrate. The victim was then informed that the Magistrate told them he couldn't dismiss her case unless she had "witnesses." She said she had no witnesses, so they told her the case would have to be adjourned until a different Magistrate was presiding. Before that date Mr. "Fixer" told her he had fixed the new Magistrate. This cost her an additional $50. Again the case was called. This time they had the victim wait in a nearby restaurant. Her bail was forfeited for nonappearance. Later upon the suggestion of Mr. "Fixer" she surrendered and the forfeiture was revoked, and a further adjournment granted. Again it was represented that the new Magistrate had to be fixed and she paid an additional $200. Up to this point they had "bled" the victim of $1,200

No further funds being obtainable, Mr. "Fixer" allowed her to go to trial. She was convicted. For seven weeks she was confined to the Kingston Avenue Hospital for medical treatment. Thereafter she was returned for sentence, and placed on probation for six months.

Upon completion of her sentence, she enlisted the aid of the probation officer. Together they went to Mr. "Fixer's" office, to try to recover the money. In the presence of the officer the defendant said:

"You are a nice one. You certainly fixed it all right for me. Instead of getting me out, as you said you would for that fee, you certainly got me in there."

To which he replied:

"I couldn't help it. I have been double-crossed."

Mr. "Fixer" finally returned $100 of the amount which he had collected in exchange for a general release.

When called Mr. "Fixer" said he was a "tax expert," though he was neither lawyer nor accountant. He could not satisfactorily describe just what he did in his capacity as a "tax expert." He admitted he participated in this case, but was unable to give any justification for his interference.

Still another girl was permitted to testify under the name of Betty Smith. Orphaned at an early age she was brought up in a Greek orphanage in Philadelphia. After some vicissitudes she arrived in New York on December 28, 1928. The preliminaries leading up to her arrest were substantially as follows, according to the testimony of Acuna.

In June 1929, according to the testimony, "the Dove" and Acuna met Officer John J. Glenn and two other officers. The Dove put in a telephone call to Betty Smith and over her protestations said he was coming right up. For some reason Acuna was substituted. One of the officers gave him a ten and a five-dollar bill and they all drove (in the officer's car) to 73rd Street and Amsterdam Avenue. Acuna gained admittance and found the intended victim "in bed half asleep, covered." Acuna sat between the twin beds and introduced himself as "the fellow from the drug store."

After a brief interval the four detectives broke into the room and after the usual comedy arrested her. On the way to the police station they found out that she had no money. Some one had blundered. In an effort to get out of this predicament they bluffed her into pleading guilty. They said, as she testified, "You might just as well plead guilty because if you don't we will make you guilty." So, without benefit of counsel, that is what she did and upon that plea the Magistrate sentenced her to The House of the Good Shepherd. After being confined there for ten months she was put on parole for a further period.

At the time of this hearing before the Referee she was still serving her sentence. This was also the case with a few other girls. To relieve them of further punishment, the Referee laid the facts before the Governor, who granted them pardons.

Shortly after giving this testimony, in early December, 1930, Betty disappeared. Subsequently—a year later—a pri-

vate detective was convicted of conspiracy for his part in bribing her to leave the state.

Even more recently Glenn was convicted of perjury and
sentenced to Sing Sing for four and a half to seven years.

After her husband was sent away to an institution, Mrs.
Potocki carried on alone. From 8:00 P.M. to 4 A.M. she
worked as a charwoman. When she got home she could only
sleep an hour or so before she had to get up and give her two
little girls breakfast and get them off to school. Another
"forty winks" and she went downstairs to work for a Mr.
Meyers in his restaurant, until 3:30 P.M. Thursday after-
noons she reserved for the meeting of St. Monica's Guild,
held in the parish house of Old Trinity at the corner of Broadway and Wall Street. It was hard work but she kept at it until
the day of her arrest—September 23, 1930.

On that afternoon—about 5:30, her children had just returned from school—she was entertaining her friends Marie
Barry and Jack Keeve. Before long she answered a knock at
the door. Two men in plain clothes said that Henry Lewis
had sent them up there to get a drink. She protested that she
could not let them in because she sold only to her friends.
Finally they persuaded her that they were "all right" and she
let them in. They turned out later to be William B. Lewis and
Edgar McFarland of the Vice Squad.

They put a five and a ten-dollar bill on the table. She then
poured drinks for all. This drinking continued until Mrs.
Barry and Keeve left about 7:00—in the meantime she had
given her two children their dinner and they had gone out to
play. She told the officers she couldn't give them any more
and started to take away the bottle.

She never did get the bottle, for just as she reached for it
Lewis grabbed her and when she protested he struck her first
on one side of the jaw, then the other. At the second blow
she fell. Amid her screams and his violent outbursts of pro-
fanity he hit her again, and began clawing at her clothes. Just

as he finished tearing off every stitch of her clothing there
was a knock at the door.

McFarland, who had been sitting there all the time, got up
and opened the door. Mrs. Barry had returned to get a pack-
age she had left behind. She had scarcely put her foot in the
door when McFarland hit her in the jaw with such terrific
force as to make the blood fairly spurt from her mouth.

All this time Lewis had been wrestling on the floor with
Mrs. Potocki. When he found that he couldn't overcome her
resistance with his hands and feet he began to bite her—not
once, but several times. Finally he grabbed her and dragged
her over to the bureau and called for the patrol. During the
interval before the wagon arrived five policemen were crowded
into that tiny little apartment, all of whom testified that they
were there to arrest these two beaten and exhausted women.

About 9:00 she and Mrs. Barry were locked up in adjoining
cells in the Old Slip Station. There Mrs. Potocki, who is corroborated by Mrs. Barry, testified that she cried for a doctor
who would do something to relieve her suffering. No one
came. They were forced to spend that night in the station
house, bruised and beaten, without medical attention to relieve their suffering.

The next morning before they were arraigned in Jefferson
Market Court, a lawyer came to them and told them that he
had been sent to defend them by Mr. Meyers. He entered
pleas of "not guilty" and bailed them out. He went home
with Mrs. Potocki and took her bank book, which he had
already taken the precaution to have her assign to him. Later
it developed that he took $1,000 from her on the representa-
tion that it was for security. It was only after Colonel Bur-
leigh, whose sympathies had been enlisted by the Rev. Dr.
Kinkaid of Old Trinity, got after him, that he returned $590.
The rest he took for his services and bondsmen's fees.

The trial finally came on before Magistrate Earl Smith,
who was so shocked at this evidence of police brutality that
he not only discharged both Mrs. Potocki and Mrs. Barry,
but sent the minutes to Chief Magistrate Corrigan.

Dr. Louis Goldblatt of the Beekman Street Hospital testified before the Referee that he examined Mrs. Potocki on September 26th, at which time he made the following findings:—contusions below the left eye—on the right and left arms and upper sternum—"marks above her right breast, which resembled teeth marks," contusions on both breasts, the abdomen and upper thighs on both inside and outside surfaces—and tenderness over the ribs in front so that it hurt her to breathe.

These two officers emerged from the hearing before the Referee and a news photographer snapped them executing a little jig on the courthouse steps. This picture, typifying their callous disregard of human suffering and their insolent arrogance, was given wide publicity and earned them the sobriquet of the "Smirking Cops."

Both were convicted on the charge of second degree assault and sentenced to Sing Sing—Lewis for two and a half to five years and McFarland for two to four years.

There were many other stories of a similar nature not necessary to detail here.

CHAPTER VI

THE BOOKMAKING AND POLICY RACKETS

THE stories of this chapter show, as did the story of the Women's Court, other aspects of the slovenly and slipshod procedure which prevailed at the time of the Investigation in all the Magistrates' Courts. The first is that of a pseudo lawyer by the name of Joseph Wolfman.

Wolfman was born in Austria about twenty-six years ago. Shortly thereafter he was brought to this country by his parents. He attended public school up to the sixth grade when he was forced to leave and spend about two years in the hospital on account of a tubercular hip. He is a small man, about five feet, five inches in height. Two characteristics mark him, his unusually wide head and his limp. On leaving the hospital he got a job as office boy with the Automobile Chamber of Commerce. He apparently held this for only a short time. His next job was with the Marcus Embossed Sign Company, where he did general office work at $22 per week. While employed here he, in his off hours, took an extension course in law at LaSalle University. One of the requirements of the course was the attendance at different courts to learn the procedure. This he did.

He attended the Supreme Court and later the Magistrates' Court, selecting the one in West 54th Street. He attended this Court for about a week. During that time he noticed an Italian woman sitting next to him. Her son was about to be arraigned when she leaned over to Wolfman and told him that she could not speak English but that she wanted to speak to the Judge. Wolfman volunteered to do it for her. While he was proceeding to the Bench, the Magistrate called the case, put the complaining officer on the stand and examined him. Meanwhile Wolfman had been standing at the rail

54

before the Judge. After the Judge finished examining he turned to Wolfman, who he thought was the defendant's lawyer and asked him if he wanted to cross-examine. Wolfman said "no." Thereupon the boy was held in $2,500 bail. As he was leaving the woman, after telling her what had happened, a bondsman approached Wolfman and asked him if he wanted to bail the boy out. Wolfman sent him to the mother, who accepted the bondsman's invitation to let him bail her son. The following morning in Court this bondsman gave Wolfman $10 as his split or fee and told him that any business brought by Wolfman to him would be compensated. That was his first case. He returned the following day and for many days until he himself got into trouble and was discovered as a pseudo lawyer. He described in great detail his activities and methods from that day on.

A typical day was as follows: each morning he would arrive at Court about eight o'clock. Leaving his hat and coat on a bench, for he had no office, he would wait for the detectives or patrolmen to come in. As they came in (by this time he knew them all by their first names) he would ask them what they had on that day. The officer would tell him that he had a Mr. "Smith" who had about $60 or $70 in his pocket. There was a client. Wolfman would rush to the clerk's office, file a notice of appearance for the defendant, even though he had not even seen him, give a copy to the Pen-Keeper and go in to see the prisoner. Wolfman would tell the prisoner that he was an attorney and that as he had noticed the prisoner's case on the daily calendar, he thought he could help him. If the prisoner was suspicious that Wolfman was not a lawyer, the officer, who told Wolfman of the case, would be called over by Wolfman to identify him as a lawyer. This the officer would do. The prisoner would be impressed by the fact that the officer knew him. The retainer would then be obtained and the balance of the fee to be paid would be fixed. After this was done, Wolfman would then, according to his testimony, seek out the complainant and endeavor to have him withdraw his complaint or else, that failing, would arrange to have the officer change his testimony or as a last resort he would have the assistant clerk prepare a form known as "014."

This form was a printed one addressed to the Magistrate advising him that he (the clerk) had heard the facts and in his opinion they did not warrant the drawing of a full complaint. This would be presented to the Judge, who never once, according to Wolfman, ordered a full complaint drawn after receiving this form from the clerk. The usual price for this form was five dollars, although at times it would cost ten dollars. The case would then be dismissed and the split made. It would always be in cash. In the three years that Wolfman practiced in the 54th Street Court, he was the attorney of record in six hundred and seven cases of which, he says, seventy per cent or four hundred and twenty-four were dismissed, mostly by the methods above described.

Besides obtaining cases from the officers, he got them from the bondsmen, clerks, keepers, attendants and every one else in and around the Court. There was always a fifty per cent split of the fee. In his best weeks Wolfman made about $500 a week. He lost it in gambling and other ways so that when trouble inevitably and finally overtook him he was practically penniless. The lowest fee he ever took was $15, and the highest he ever received was $2,000. The great majority of his cases were those of gamblers who had been arrested on a charge of bookmaking.

Here the case was generally dismissed on an "014," sometimes after there had been a hearing. The testimony on the hearing was often meaningless. It is true, theoretically at least, that the true facts and circumstances of the arrest had been stated to the clerk and that there was in fact no cause of complaint. It would seem, however, that the Magistrates could have discovered, from the extraordinary number of daily dismissal of complaints, that in many cases these "014" forms had been improperly procured. They seemed never to discover and from the testimony on the hearing of these "014's" seemed not even to have tried to find out the actual state of facts of the arrest. In the testimony of the cases given below it is perfectly clear that no true effort was made except to get rid of the case quickly. In the case of Weltman & Rappe, where an "014" had been obtained, the complete testimony is:

"Mr. Wolfman: In view of the fact that there is insufficient evidence, I move to dismiss.

"The Officer: It is one of these cases where I went into the room and found them at the psychological moment.

"The Court: Motion granted."

That was the end. That was the complete trial. Surely there was no effort made here to learn anything at all about the case.

The William Lawrence case was similar. Here the complete record reads:

"The Court (after reading 014 form): Any other evidence beside what you have here, officer?

"The Officer: No, sir.

"The Court: No complaint, discharged."

The same thing, though the case was much worse, happened in the case of William Duffin. This man had been arrested five times for bookmaking within two and one-half months. He was discharged every time. When he appeared again in this case, Wolfman represented him. Here follows the entire proceeding before Magistrate Rosenbluth.

"The Court: Where was this arrest made?

"The Officer: In front of 128 West 49th Street, 2:00 o'clock yesterday afternoon.

"The Court: Defendant discharged."

There were many other similar cases. The testimony differed little. The only effect of these hearings was that they gave the court reporter something to do.

One sure way to secure a dismissal in these bookmaking cases was to have the officer say he heard no conversation; that insured an "out." The reason for this was never stated

nor made clear. It was, as Wolfman says as to all these practices, just a "custom" of the West 54th Street Court.

There was another "custom" of the Court in regard to
gambling arrests where sixty or seventy prisoners would be
brought in. All the prisoners would be arraigned and admitted
to bail. On the hearing, the following morning, perhaps fifty
or more would fail to show up. When the case was called an
equal number of spectators or hangers-on sitting in the room
would be substituted, and all would be discharged. The substituted defendants took no chance, the whole proceeding had
been previously "fixed up." Besides, they received one dollar
apiece for their labors. Here ended Wolfman's extraordinary
story of the customs in the West 54th Street Magistrates'
Court of New York City.

The Harlem or 5th District Court presented another
aspect of this almost unbelievable System.

As in the Women's and West 54th Street Courts, a horde
of lawyers and bondsmen were found, ready to prey on the
unfortunate victims who were arrested, so here in Harlem
the same System prevailed. One whole day at the public
hearing, witness after witness took the stand to tell his or
her story or how he or she came to be bailed or how he or she
happened to have a lawyer to represent them at the trial.
From their own lips it was learned how the clerks and attendants pointed out and supplied bondsmen and lawyers, how
bondsmen recommended and obtained lawyers and vice versa.
All that one had to do was to be arrested and suddenly, as if
by magic, a bondsman and a lawyer would appear.

Mary Toth had this experience. She was arrested some
time in 1930. On arriving at Court some one appeared and
offered to be her lawyer. She didn't know him. Her testimony
to this fact is:

"Q. Did you have a lawyer, Mrs. Toth?

"A. There was a lawyer there, he came in, he wanted to take
my case, but I told him I don't need any lawyer, so of course,
when they called my name, he stepped up for me.

"Q. Was this lawyer a stranger to you, Mrs. Toth?

"A. Yes, he was.

"Q. What did this stranger, who said he was a lawyer, say to you?

"A. He said I better take a lawyer for my case."

This person, her lawyer, pursued her even to her home to collect the fee from her husband. The husband also testified that the lawyer was a total stranger to him and that he never saw this man except once when he came to the house to collect his fee. The bondsmen were the same. One Harford testified to that situation as follows:

"Q. Did you have a bondsman?

"A. Yes, sir.

"Q. Did you call for the bondsman?

"A. No, he came to me.

"Q. Was he a stranger to you?

"A. A total stranger.

"Q. You were behind the bars there at Harlem Court?

"A. Yes.

"Q. And he spoke to you?

"A. Yes, sir."

Thus it was in many hundreds of cases. The victim had no chance. He was fair prey for the first lawyer and bondsman who could get their hands on him. Generally when they were through the victim might be free, might be in jail, but one thing was sure: he was penniless. This unseemly race of lawyers and bondsmen took place not only in general arrests but also in the "policy" arrests of which there are literally, yearly, hundreds.

The game of "policy" or "numbers" in New York City, is apparently indigenous to the colored section in Harlem. It is a simple and elementary form of gambling. The yearly intake of money is astounding. There is no way of estimating the amount except by drawing inferences from the accounts of the "policy" bankers, whose name is legion. It is a tremendous industry employing thousands of people. A brief and general description of the game may help the reader to appreciate its ramifications.

The game is this. Each morning the banker determines what numbers are to win. He selects from the statement of bank clearing or any other large set of figures, certain numbers. For instance, he may select the first, fifth and sixth figures of the bank clearing statement. Then all the players will, without knowing what figures have been selected, try to guess it. They write their guess, which is generally based on a hunch, down on a slip of paper and place their bet, which ranges from one cent to $1.00, no more. The odds against winning are figured at 600 to 1. It is extremely profitable for the player to win and very expensive for the banker. If the player wins it is called a "hit." If there has been a big "hit" or a lot of winners the banker sometimes stages a fake raid to get out of paying his losses. After placing the bet, the slip and money are turned over to a "pick up" girl or boy. They take the money to a "collector" and turn over the money and slips to him. The collector takes the money to a "controller." This person takes the slips, adds up the money received and reports to his banker. The banker then waits for the publication of the statement and pays off the winners. Some bankers testified that they took in as much as $2,500 or $3,000 daily. For one banker alone this amounts to over a million dollars a year.

As there are hundreds of bankers and innumerable players it is easily seen that the business is gigantic. It was testified to by the bankers subpœnaed that they obtained bondsmen and lawyers for their employees if arrested and if convicted and sentenced they would take care of the families while the person convicted was serving his sentence. Certain bankers armed their employees with buttons bearing certain initials. The object of these buttons was to let the officer know, if he intended arresting some one, that that person was employed by Banker So-and-so, the theory being that Banker So-and-so was paying protection and therefore he and his employees were to be given immunity. The buttons were changed at intervals so that no outsider would be able to get protection by wearing one. All the bankers denied using these buttons, but buttons taken from players were produced in Court. One of the employees by the name of Lucas testified, "He invested me with a button."

There are one or two of the "bankers" whose stories describe the System. Banker Roberts testified that he had been a collector for about three years and a banker for two. Due to the danger of detection and arrest he was constantly on the move. There were about one hundred people in his employ. His daily intake was between $2,500 or $3,000. He had in his employ a mysterious girl named Peggy. She apparently was a "fixer" for the cases of Roberts' employees in the Courts. As he says: "her duties were to see if she could not make the cases lighter against those men that were arrested."

"Q. Then the field of her operations was the Court?
"A. Yes."

As to her seeing the right people to fix the case, he testified, "Officers or anybody that had to be seen, it wouldn't make any difference, an officer or Judge or attorney, or what it was." This lady subsequently died and his operations ceased.

Following Roberts, a Porto Rican by the name of Jose Enrique Miro was examined. Miro came to this country from Porto Rico in 1916. Locating himself in New York he found a job as a common laborer at which profession he worked until 1924. He quit work about then, took up gambling, got married and lived on the proceeds of his gambling activities. Some time in 1926, he testified, he started in the policy game. His testimony disclosed the fact that he began as a "banker" employing about six collectors whose names he didn't know. His sister and brother-in-law worked for him in the business, adding slips and performing other clerical duties. All were paid thirty dollars a week including the six collectors, whose names he didn't know. Miro denied using buttons to identify his men, but admitted supplying bondsmen and lawyers. On that subject he testified:

"Q. And what assurances or guarantees did you give them?

"A. I promised them to give them a lawyer, and a bondsman, and if any of them were caught, and make time I will see that their families were protected."

While the victim was serving the sentence Miro paid $20 or $25 to the family at home. This occurred three or four times during his career as a policy banker, which lasted, according to him, for two years, from 1926 to 1928. Since 1928, his testimony was, whatever money he made or had was from gambling other than playing the policy game.

This story is almost impossible to believe because since 1928 he deposited his greatest amounts and bailed more people for playing policy than before.

Miro's accounts are very interesting, as they are those of a poor ignorant Porto Rican, who up to 1924 was merely a common laborer. They show also the tremendous income derived from the ignorant of Harlem. In all, he had six admitted accounts in which, between July 7, 1927, and December 12, 1930, he deposited $1,111,730.08. Of this amount, in these admitted accounts, he deposited $876,885.21 up to the time he claimed he had severed his connection with the policy game. There were three other accounts which he denied were his. These were under the assumed names of Jose Casanova, Jose Jimenez and Victor Martin. These accounts were all opened on the same day, March 28, 1929, and all closed on the same day, January 13, 1930. The balances on January 13, 1930, were transferred to one of Miro's accounts, which was under the name of Enrique Martin. He didn't deny the transfers, nor did he imply that the bank was wrong in so doing, nor did he refuse to accept the money, all he did was to deny that the accounts were his. Into these three accounts in about a year he deposited $139,826.21. This was, of course, after he said he had quit. The grand total of all his accounts was $1,251,556.29. The testimony that he gave at the public hearing was so contradictory and different from his previous story that on leaving the witness stand he was arrested and subsequently indicted for perjury. His case is now one of the untried cases reposing in the District Attorney's Office. He has since been convicted in the Federal Courts on some income tax dereliction, and is now serving his sentence.

There was another of these policy bankers by the name of Wilfred Brunder. He was better known than Miro and had been longer in the game. He testified at the private hearings on one or two occasions, but by the time he was to take the stand in public, he had disappeared. He was not seen again until some time late in November or early in December, 1931, when he returned to America from Bermuda. During his absence he had been indicted for filing false income tax returns by the Federal Government. On his return he appeared at the Office of the Federal District Attorney, pleaded guilty to the charge, was fined and sentenced to serve a term in prison. Even though he was not publicly examined his accounts were put into evidence. They showed that between January 1, 1925, and December 31, 1930, in the Dunbar National and Chelsea Bank, Brunder deposited the amazing total of $1,753,342.33. This amount was deposited actually in four and one-half years. His indictment in the Federal Court resulted from the testimony presented before the Referee in this Investigation.

CHAPTER VII

OBSTRUCTION AND DELAY

SHORTLY after the appointment of Judge Seabury as Referee to investigate the Magistrates' Courts, Mayor Walker stated that he would give the Investigation his fullest coöperation and further that he would also instruct every agency of his administration to do the same. He hailed it as "fair and impartial." A few months later when the disclosures made before the Referee had rocked the very dome of City Hall the Mayor took a different attitude.

To carry on the Inquiry successfully it was essential to have a staff of lawyers, in addition to accountants, stenographers and process servers. Witnesses had to be examined, the relevancy and admissibility of their testimony had to be determined, legal documents and briefs had to be prepared. The statute pursuant to which the Inquiry was ordered provided that the "reasonable expenses of the Investigation" should be paid by the City. The Administration, going far afield, raised the question as to whether or not the salaries of legal assistants came within the statute.

At the suggestion of Presiding Justice Dowling, the Referee discussed this question with the Mayor, at the Hardware Club, and received his positive assurance that the bills would be paid immediately. He realized the public importance of the Investigation and thought the objections of his Corporation Counsel—Arthur W. Hilly—to be without any substantial basis. The Referee, after this positive assurance, felt satisfied that he had overcome what threatened to be serious opposition.

However, the next day, the Referee received an opinion from Corporation Counsel Hilly that only the disbursements and not the assistants' salaries would be paid. Surprised at this position taken by the Mayor, in view of his promise of the day before, the Referee wrote the Mayor and again asked him to direct their prompt payment. To this letter the Mayor never replied.

The Referee thereupon immediately instituted a mandamus proceeding against the Mayor and the Comptroller to compel their payment. In answer, the Mayor set out that he knew nothing of the case, and that it was just one of the thousand that are brought against the City. Both he and his Comptroller not only insisted that there was no warrant under the statute for paying these salaries but also that the whole statute was unconstitutional, null and void. The bad faith of the second contention as charged by the Referee was demonstrated by the fact that under and pursuant to this very statute the City had paid out some $10,000 for disbursements incurred by the Referee in this Investigation.

The Court riddled the Mayor's contentions, upholding the constitutionality of the statute and directing payment of the legal assistants. After the Comptroller's refusal to participate in any appeal, it was abandoned by Mr. Hilly.

This incident showed what the Mayor's idea of help and coöperation amounted to.

One of the most shameful disclosures of the entire Investigation was the fact that there were fifty-one girls then confined in Bedford Reformatory under illegal commitments. When this evidence was presented Dr. Palmer, Superintendent of this institution, announced that he understood it to be his duty to hold these girls until some court upon application for a writ of habeas corpus directed their release.

The situation in a nutshell was simply this: in 1923 a statute was passed empowering the Magistrates to adjudge girls between sixteen and twenty-one to be *"wayward minors,"* upon a proper complaint, but only *"where the charge is established upon competent evidence upon a hearing."* Obviously this provision was made to safeguard girls from being "railroaded" to the Reformatory on their "confession" alone. In spite of this unambiguous language certain Magistrates had incarcerated some seventy-seven of these girls without any real trial whatsoever. In fact, each commitment on its face read "and whereas such charge having been duly established *by the confession of the defendant on her plea of guilty,*" and that part of the form containing the wording of the statute "upon competent evidence upon a hearing" was stricken out.

The Mayor immediately went into a conference with Chief Magistrate Corrigan, Corporation Counsel Hilly, Police Commissioner Mulrooney and Mr. Worthington of the Committee of Fourteen. This matter obviously did concern the Mayor. Such, however, was not the purpose of this official meeting, as appears from a reading of the lengthy statement issued by the Mayor. This statement not only criticized the presentation of this evidence but weakly sought to justify these commitments.

The Referee at the first public hearing thereafter took cognizance of this second attack by the Mayor. He read the Mayor's statement into the record, and then pointed out the inapplicability of the Pagoda case relied on by these lawyers and Mr. Mulrooney. In addition he read into the record letters to Dr. Palmer from the former Attorney General, Hamilton Ward, and the then Attorney General, John J. Bennett. Mr. Ward advised Dr. Palmer that he might now expect many writs which would be granted,

"for the Magistrates have shown utter disregard of human rights or an absolute ignorance with regard to the law, which amounts to the same thing."

Mr. Bennett also pointed out the illegality of these commitments and the inapplicability of the Pagoda case. However, he fell into the error of advising that the whole thing could be cleared up by bringing these girls before the Court to be re-sentenced. The Referee pointed out that one cannot, by a re-sentence, legalize a commitment made in the first instance without jurisdiction.

Shortly thereafter all of these girls were loaded into buses and brought to the city. Before nightfall, however, they were all returned. Nobody has yet determined the reason for this excursion, but it is certain that only a few begrudged them this holiday.

At the designation of the Bar Associations, John McKim Minton secured a writ of habeas corpus for one of these girls, Anna Pelz, in order to test the question said to be involved. The case went to the Supreme Court, the Appellate Division and finally to the Court of Appeals which upheld the contentions of Judge Seabury and discharged the girl from custody. Subsequently the other girls were also discharged.

Thus ended the second attempt to discredit the Investigation.

In the examination of police officers assigned to plain clothes duty startling differences were discovered between their aggregate salaries and their bank deposits. Some attempted to explain this difference in various incredible stories. One officer had a friend, McDonald, who assisted him. Morris had his Uncle George; both benefactors, however, were dead. Quinlivan took care of a drunken jockey, who in turn took care of him. Such beautiful relationships as these three had would scarcely be suspected in the Police Department. There was another policeman who endeavored to tie up and hamper the Inquiry. He was Charles A. Wund.

This man descended the social scale from a milkman to a Vice Cop. This descent was accompanied by a corresponding rise from poverty to riches. However, "the embarrassment of riches" was his lot. His first three years as an ordinary patrolman were uneventful, and he viewed with some dismay on January 1, 1925, his total accumulated wealth of $244.20. In the next three years, though his total salary was less than $3,000 a year, he deposited $13,000. This was better, but it paled into insignificance compared with his deposits of $70,000 during his tenure as a Vice Cop from January, 1928, to February, 1931. His total salary during this period was only $8,000. He testified that the difference was due to his profits in the market. An accountant from the Inquiry staff took the stand and proved that far from making a profit Wund had suffered a net loss of $20,000. During this same period he had made three hundred and sixteen arrests of which number two hundred and thirty-eight were discharged. He was asked if, for money, he had changed his testimony at the time of trial so that those whom he had arrested might be discharged. He denied, however, he had done so.

When he was asked to identify his various bank and brokerage accounts his lawyer, sitting in Court, gave him the high-sign as to his answer, whereupon Wund drew from his pocket a typewritten statement, which he read to the effect that he refused to answer upon the ground "that this inquisitorial body or court has no such right to inquire into the same, because it exceeds the authority vested in it by the Appellate Division."

The futility of these obstructive tactics was made plain immediately. He was asked to step down. Then followed a procession of men from banks and brokerage houses who identified various transcripts of his accounts with their respective banks, whereupon the accounts were then received in evidence. His attorney procured an Order to show Cause why the Referee should not be prohibited from pressing these questions. The Referee appeared in person at the Special Term and Appellate Division of the Supreme Court where the Writ of Prohibition was denied.

Harry Singer, another cop, changed from "the waist and dress line" at $40 per week to patrolman at $1,000 a year. That was in 1917. Around January 1, 1925, he, too, became attached to the Vice Squad. Between that date and January 1, 1930, he made five hundred and eighty-seven arrests of which only eighty resulted in conviction. There were but few questions he would answer when he took the stand, because of a fear that the Inquiry was illegal and an invasion of his right of privacy, etc., etc. He was most emphatic, and also thoroughly naïve, in saying that he had never heard of a policeman making an arrest simply to extort money. Although his salary, too, during this period, was never in excess of $3,000 a year, he and his wife nevertheless banked some $40,000, over half of which was in cash, between January 1, 1925, and September, 1930.

Singer was even more embarrassed about his bank accounts than was Charles A. Wund. He even refused to look at his canceled checks and deposit slips, all, of course, on the ground that the inquiry was illegal. Just at this point in his examination the minutes read:

> "(At this point an interruption in the proceedings by an attorney named Sylvester.)"

Sylvester stood before the Referee and offered the ridiculous suggestion that the Referee suspend his examination of Singer until he (Sylvester) could get a court order restraining the examination. The Referee looked at Sylvester, and then at the papers handed him, and, determining that there was no stay in the papers given him, proceeded with the hearing. Just as Wund had refused to testify when his bank accounts were in question, so Singer likewise refused. On Singer's refusal to testify as to his bank accounts, the Referee had him step down, and put in all his accounts through witnesses from the banks. Another interesting feature as to Officer Harry Singer appeared in relation to his bank accounts.

It so happened that the papers of New York City, on the morning of December 22, 1930, published a list of names of various police officers whose bank accounts had been subpœnaed. Singer's name was on the list. A little later, while he was under examination, he was asked whether or not the fact that his name was on this list had anything at all to do with the withdrawal on the same day of all the balances in all of his accounts. This he declined to answer. If, in fact, the two were unrelated, it was indeed a most startling coincidence.

In the motion which Wund had previously brought to restrain the Referee from inquiring into his bank accounts, Harry Singer now joined. He, too, seemed interested that his modest savings be not made public. On the argument before the Appellate Division, the attorneys for these two Vice Cops raised the cry that their savings and their moneys were private business, to which the Referee replied: "I say it is not private business; I say it is public plunder."

CHAPTER VIII

THE RESIGNATIONS AND THE BRODSKY CASE

MAGISTRATE FRANCIS X. McQUADE resigned on the morning of his examination in public—to devote time to the protection of his business interests. Thus was cut short a judicial career, the beginning of which had been sponsored some time ago by such citizens as "Big" Tim Sullivan, Charles F. Murphy and Mayor Hylan.

While a Magistrate he was active in sponsoring the stock of the Ajax-Texas Corporation. This "speculative venture of questionable merit . . . is no longer in existence, and apparently those who invested in its securities have suffered a complete loss."

While he was a Magistrate, Judge McQuade had a financial interest in the gambling room of the Havana Casino. The negotiations leading up to the purchase were initiated by a conference between McQuade and others at the Pennsylvania Hotel in 1920. Thereafter representatives of the Magistrate and his associates personally inspected the properties in Havana. The Third Securities Corporation purchased a seventy per cent interest. For the 1923-1924 season the profit on this investment was $162,960, yielding McQuade $8,148.

Also during the period he was a Magistrate, Francis X. McQuade was active in the Polo Grounds Athletic Club, Inc., an organization which promoted fights. His stock was held in the name of Jack Flanagan, a dummy. Payments of his distributive share were made in a very circuitous manner. In one instance a check for $2,000 was drawn payable to Flanagan, who endorsed it over to one Hoffman, and a day or two later this very check was deposited in McQuade's account. In other instances checks were made payable to others

71

who reduced them to cash before they turned the proceeds over to McQuade.

Besides these extra-judicial duties he was connected with the corporate owner of the New York Giants baseball team. Litigation between it and the Magistrate over some internal dispute has been pending in the courts for some years. There was no evidence whether or not this matter was a distraction from his judicial duties.

The Referee certified to the Appellate Division that he found no evidence of corruption in connection with Magistrate McQuade's judicial activities, but stated that the Magistrate was in some respects temperamentally unsuited to the discharge of his duties.

On January 17, 1931, shortly before his appearance for examination in public was scheduled, George Washington Simpson resigned as City Magistrate. Ostensibly, the reason was arthritis in one finger of the right hand. Chief Magistrate Corrigan denied his request for a sixty-day leave of absence, and offered him a leave of absence for thirty days, but this Magistrate Simpson refused, saying he needed sixty days in which to recover, whereupon he resigned.

For many years Magistrate Simpson had presided over the Commercial Frauds Division of the Magistrates' Courts. From time to time during the progress of the Investigation, persons who had been litigants in that Court complained to the Referee. In one case, involving the sale of an obscene book, irregularities were disclosed which, had they been known to Magistrate Simpson, would have necessitated the filing of charges against him.

Henry M. R. Goodman, a friend of the ocean flyer Charles Levine, abruptly resigned on January 6th, 1931, while his affairs were still under examination. He, too, ascribed ill health as the reason for his retirement.

Louis B. Brodsky obtained his appointment from his district leader, James J. Hagan. The following are excerpts from his (Brodsky's) own testimony:

"I spoke to Mr. (James J.) Hagan and I mentioned the fact that I had rendered services to the organization and that I felt that I ought to get some recognition.... Later on I understood there was to be a vacancy, a temporary vacancy, and Mr. Hagan said to me, 'Louis, there is to be a temporary vacancy; how would you like to take it?'... And he said he would urge my appointment to the party ... and eventually I was appointed a temporary magistrate.... He told me he had presented my name to the leader of Tammany Hall (George W. Olvany)."

The district leader gave him the "job"—the reward or as Brodsky terms it the "recognition" for years of party service. In 1929, Mayor Walker reappointed him for a full ten year term after Brodsky, according to his own admission, had again seen the district leader.

After Judge Brodsky's public examination was completed, the Referee requested the Appellate Division to exercise its authority under the Constitution and laws of the State and remove him from office as unfit. The Referee charged that Brodsky speculated on margin in the market and engaged in many real estate transactions for profit after his appointment as Magistrate.

Under the Constitution a Magistrate may be removed for "cause." What constitutes cause, as the Referee said, "depends upon the standards of conduct which guide the judicial judgment of those in whom the power of removal is granted."

There was, however, nothing so indefinite about Section 102 of the Inferior Criminal Courts Act, which reads:

"... No city magistrate shall engage in any other business or profession or act as referee, or receiver, but each of said justices and magistrates shall devote his whole time and capacity so far as the public interest demands to the duties of his office."

This Statute was nothing more than an enactment into law of the Canon of Judicial Ethics:

"He should therefore not enter into such private business ... nor should he enter into any business relation which, in the normal course of events reasonably to be expected, might bring his personal interest into conflict with the impartial performance of his official duties."

In addition to this specific prohibition the canons further forbid speculation on margin:

"... It detracts from the public confidence in his integrity and the soundness of his judicial judgment for him at any time to become a speculative investor upon the hazard of a margin."

In addition to the admitted facts that Brodsky's marginal operations involving $7,000,000 which resulted in a loss of $170,000 and his realty transactions resulting in a loss running into "hundreds of thousands of dollars," left him financially embarrassed, the Referee further charged that Brodsky's unfitness was demonstrated by the following facts: (1) He gave to the son-in-law of the district leader to whom he owed his "job" a power of attorney to operate a margin account opened in the name of Brodsky's secretary, Kitty Carr; (2) That Brodsky's speculations necessitated his borrowing hundreds of thousands of dollars in which transactions he "kited" checks; (3) That shortly after discharging Robert H. Loeb on a charge of disorderly conduct, he opened a margin account which was guaranteed by Loeb who paid the $30,000 loss suffered in this account. This account was closed out in the 1929 crash and yet Brodsky had not repaid Loeb up to the time of the filing of charges against him in 1931; (4) That he wrongfully discharged gamblers who were operating within the confines of his district—the leader of which at that time was James J. Hagan.

In his report to the Appellate Division, the Referee summarized the charges by saying that some related to his conduct on the Bench and others to his extra-judicial activities, but he said:

"Whatever the sphere in which these acts were done, it seems to me that the nature and quality of the acts themselves are such as to demonstrate that his conduct has fallen far short of adherence to the minimum standards to which it is essential that a judge shall conform."

There was, the Referee said, but one question to be decided whether under the Constitution, the Statute or the Code of Ethics, it did not matter which, to-wit:

"Is it consistent with the standards to which a judge must conform for him to be actively and constantly involved in heavy speculation in the stock market upon the hazard of a flimsy margin? Is the administration of justice weakened and the judge brought into disrepute to such an extent as to impair his usefulness if while in office he becomes continually and deeply involved in extra-judicial activities for personal gain, necessitating the constant borrowing of money from numerous sources and the frequent kiting of checks resulting in a state of uninterrupted serious financial difficulties? ... these activities disclose a willingness on the part of the Magistrate to cheapen the judicial office and to pursue a course of conduct for personal gain which forfeits public confidence in him as a judicial officer."

The trial of Magistrate Brodsky took place in the courtroom of the Appellate Division. Presiding Justice Dowling and Justices Finch (now Presiding Justice), Merrell, McAvoy and Sherman sat in judgment. Brodsky presented his defense under the guidance of Terence J. McManus. Mr. Kresel presented the evidence in support of the charges.

The Court by a majority of four to one held that Brodsky was not "doing business" within the terms of the Statute, and that there was no "cause" for his removal. Mr. Presiding Justice Dowling dissented and voted for his removal on the ground that his real estate and stock market activities constituted "doing business" in violation of the Statute.

Following this decision the Association of the Bar of the City of New York adopted the following preamble and resolution of its Executive Committee:

"*Whereas,* the Appellate Division of the First Department has held in the Matter of Brodsky that extensive operations of the City Magistrates in the City of New York in real estate and speculation in stock upon margin do not constitute doing business within the meaning of Section 102 of the Inferior Criminal Courts Act;

"*Therefore, be it Resolved,* that, in the opinion of the Executive Committee of the Association of the Bar of the City of New York, such extra-judicial activities on the part of any judicial officer are unbecoming and unseemly, involve a lowering of the standards to which judicial officers should conform, and are calculated to bring the judicial office into disrepute, and be it

"*Further Resolved,* that this Committee recommend that proper legislation should be enacted to make such activities on the part of any judicial officer of this State unlawful and ground for removal of such judicial officer. . . ."

A copy of this was sent to each legislative leader of both parties and the Governor who urged, but failed to rally sufficient support to secure, passage of such a bill.

When Brodsky became a Magistrate he was the sole owner of seven pieces of real property and owned a two-thirds interest in another. Obviously he was not obliged to do anything more than to dispose of these properties within a reasonable time, but it is also obvious that their management demanded some of his time and thought.

Criticism, however, was made of his ventures into new realty speculations after he became Judge Brodsky. He, in connection with others, purchased income producing properties in Flushing and Belle Harbor, Long Island. The former represented an investment of some five or six thousand dollars, and just the month before his trial, he and his associates, faced with foreclosure proceedings, deeded the premises over to the mortgagee. Brodsky testified that he collected the rent from the Belle Harbor piece, deposited it in his bank, and drew checks to the others for their interest.

He made a deposit of $5,000 on a $50,000 contract to purchase what he conceived to be a "key piece" of property just off Park Avenue. For some reason or other he did not go through with this speculation, but instead forfeited his deposit.

After a great deal of quibbling and refreshing of Brodsky's

recollection it was developed that he had organized a corporation which took over an apartment building for $450,000.
Later Brodsky negotiated the sale of this property to the
Hyman Corporation. Sam Augenblick, with whom Brodsky
had been actively associated before, originally took a lease to
this property. He couldn't swing it so Brodsky took it over;
bought the property under the option in the lease and then
resold it.

Before Brodsky went on the Bench he owned a leasehold
on No. 571 Park Avenue. When asked if he had negotiated for
the purchase of this parcel after going on the Bench, he first
answered "Personally, never," then said he didn't remember. Mr. Kresel then produced a letter offering to purchase
the property for $575,000. It was on the stationery of the
A Park Avenue Corporation which was wholly owned by
Brodsky. Mr. Kresel directed Brodsky's attention to the initial
"L.B.B." and asked if that didn't show it was dictated by him,
to which he evasively replied that it simply "showed that the
typewriter wrote L.B.B." This smart "Mr. Attorney" tactics
benefited him not at all for Mr. Kresel quickly showed that
since Brodsky was the sole owner of the corporation, the offer
could not have been made without his consent. In the end the
letter went in evidence without objection from Brodsky or
Mr. McManus, which removed any doubt as to its authorship.
Still later, on his official stationery he wrote the owner's representative requesting him to "grant me an interview at your
office," to discuss terms of a longer lease to a corporation which
planned to erect a fifteen story apartment.

Thus after he went on the Bench he entered into negotiations for the purchase and sale of real estate involving over
a million dollars—executed deeds and leases—collected rents
—discussed building loans—attended closings and supervised
the management of his real estate holdings. Sometimes in his
Chambers at the Court—sometimes at home and sometimes
at the office of his real estate corporations, he would direct
Miss Carr or Miss Solomon in regard to these matters. He

was president of six corporations, an officer of three others, and director in all nine.

His widespread realty interests resulted, as he himself testified, in losses "running into hundreds of thousands of dollars."

In 1926 Brodsky began to play the stock market. He had, as his testimony shows, some doubt about the propriety of this step, and so he opened an account in the name of his secretary Miss Carr.

"Q. ... So we have it now that you opened this account in the name of your secretary because you felt you were a judge and you ought not to be too active in the market; is that it?
"A. That was right."

Blindly Miss Carr signed papers in relation to the account at the request of Brodsky. Chief among these was a power-of-attorney to Edward J. Byrne, son-in-law of District Leader Hagan to whom Brodsky owed his appointment. This document by its terms gave Byrne "the same authority over my account which I myself might exercise." In other words Byrne could buy and sell as he chose, and deposit and withdraw funds at any time. The account was, as were his other ten accounts, carried "upon the hazard of a margin." It was closed in 1928 with a loss of some $9,000.

The circumstances leading up to the opening of Judge Brodsky's account with Weisl & Company are as here detailed. Mr. Robert H. Loeb and a companion were leaving the Hotel Sherry-Netherland. A dispute arose between Mrs. Winifred M. Stoner (whom Loeb had previously known) and himself, as a result of which Loeb was brought before Magistrate Brodsky on a charge of disorderly conduct. Further, Mrs. Stoner claimed that the lady who was accompanying Loeb was wearing her bracelet and it was stipulated that, if the evidence warranted, a complaint might be drawn for grand larceny. Brodsky dismissed the charge of disorderly conduct and held there was no basis for a larceny charge. Subsequently he sat as sort of a mediator between these two people at his house. This involved, to quote Brodsky, "the ownership of the bracelet, in the first place, and in the second place, it involved the question of an assault." One would have supposed that both of these questions had been determined by Brodsky's dismissal of the charges in the Magistrates' Court. As a result of this informal hearing Loeb paid Mrs. Stoner $12,500, which Brodsky said "represented the value of the bracelet." The whole thing is quite confusing. Loeb freed on the larceny charge and yet, according to Brodsky, paying the complainant $12,500, "the value of the bracelet."

Brodsky didn't see Loeb after that until the fortuitous meeting two months later which he described as follows:

"... I was walking on Seventh Avenue and a man came out of the subway—'How-do-you-do, Judge'—'How-do-you-do.' It was Mr. Loeb. We shook hands. We had a pleasant little chat. He appeared to be grateful."

And then after a short discussion about the market, Loeb said:

"Judge, why don't you open an account with my house. I am sure I could make some money for you."

Thereafter Loeb and Brodsky met several times, and in March, 1929, Brodsky opened a margin account with Weisl & Company. Brodsky's account was covered by Loeb's general guarantee to Weisl, and later by a specific guarantee.

In September, 1929, Loeb called on Brodsky for some collateral, whereupon Brodsky gave him $25,000 of class "D" bonds of one of his real estate corporations, saying, "I think very highly of those bonds." He, Brodsky, was then permitted to continue trading but then the "big crash" came and the account was wiped out with a $30,000 loss.

Brodsky couldn't pay but he gave Loeb his demand note for $30,000 secured by $32,000 face amount of these bonds. While Brodsky thought very highly of these, the Referee termed it a payment in "stage money." At that time the bonds were in default and so they were at the time of Brodsky's trial. There was no market for them. They were junior to class "A" first mortgage, "B" second mortgage, and "C" third mortgage bonds—over two million dollars of obligations ahead of them. At about that same time $17,000 "C" bonds were sold at public auction for $1,000.

Brodsky's total speculations, on both sides of the ledger, reached a total value of approximately $7,000,000—through eleven different margin accounts in a little over four years.

"Presiding Justice Dowling: Could you tell, Judge, about what your gross losses were in the stock exchange operations?
"A. Approximately about $170,000."

To carry on these realty and stock market operations Brodsky borrowed vast sums of money, "on numerous occasions kiting checks. . . . He was at the time of his trial indebted to persons who loaned him mnoey to an aggregate of upwards of $115,000 and was at that time without any means from which to repay the same."

Tammany was jubilant over Brodsky's acquittal. Another Magistrate termed it "The happiest day of my life." The Referee made no comment upon the decision, but continued from day to day presenting evidence of conditions in these courts.

CHAPTER IX

THE TRIAL OF MAGISTRATE NORRIS

ON October 27, 1919, a woman lawyer by the name of Jean H. Norris was appointed by Mayor Hylan to become New York City's first woman judge. She was appointed a temporary Magistrate. Throughout the length and breadth of the land women's clubs rejoiced, for in New York, at last, a woman held public office as a Judge. Prior to her appointment Jean Norris had been co-leader with George W. Olvany (later leader of Tammany Hall) of the Tenth Assembly district in New York City. This and the fact that she was a woman were her qualifications for judgeship. The story of her fall and subsequent dismissal from office is a sad one. It was brought about solely by her own shortcomings. Here was an opportunity unparalleled for a woman to render an outstanding public service, by treating those arraigned before her with firmness, yet with understanding, humane sympathy and not with the "fist of steel." Unfortunately, she failed.

From almost the very beginning of the Investigation there were rumors and stories of Judge Norris's harsh and over-bearing attitude towards those who came before her. From an examination of the records which were subpœnaed from the Women's Court it appeared that a greater proportion of defendants were convicted by her than by other Magistrates who presided in the Women's Court; that she convicted more often on the uncorroborated testimony of a police officer and imposed harsher sentences than the other Women's Court Magistrates. She told the Referee as to these "sworn officers of the law," that she invariably believed them "because I have supposed the men who came before me naturally were telling the truth." She never suspected "frame-ups," although at the very outset of her career in the Fannie Greenspan case such an instance was called to her attention. Nor did she, according to her testimony, suspect that the police officers used stool-pigeons.

An examination of appeals from judgments rendered by her revealed the Bodmer and Landry cases discussed later. Information as to the deSena case was called to the attention of the Referee, as was also a stockholders' list of the Equitable Casualty and Surety Company, which disclosed the information of her stock ownership in a company whose bonds she was approving and if need be forfeiting and canceling the forfeiture. An attorney in good standing disclosed to the Investigation the facts concerning her endorsement of a commercial product,—yeast.

On Lincoln's Birthday, 1931, the Referee and two of his assistants went to the Investigation headquarters to sift the evidence in the deSena case and determine what there was to it, if anything. The attorney who tried the case was consulted as to the facts. He told of changed records. The stenographer who took the minutes at the trial was sent for and examined as to these changes. He produced from his files in the Women's Court his original notebooks and also the original changed minutes, which for some reason he had always kept. All the changes which had been made were in the Magistrate's own handwriting. The Magistrate was summoned by the Referee to appear at a public hearing. She appeared, took the stand and told her story. Her explanations were long drawn out and evasive but failed to overcome the facts which she was obliged, reluctantly, to admit. Following the close of her public examination her official conduct became the subject of the Referee's second report to the Appellate Division.

After the necessary formalities she was called for trial on June 22, 1931. It was a sweltering day. The courtroom was crowded and tense. Proud she came in, proud she remained during the trial, but defeated she left after the judgment of the Court had been pronounced.

The case was called. "Proceed, gentlemen," announced Mr. Justice Finch. Judge Seabury, the Referee, who was to present the case to the Court called Mr. Peter F. L. Sabbatino, the attorney who had tried the deSena case, to the stand and said to him: "Mr. Sabbatino, will you tell the Court whether or not you have any recollection of any incidents that occurred on that day and the day following in the course of the trial of that case?" In reply Mr. Sabbatino said, " . . . the Judge asked me several times whether I was going to put the defendant on the stand or not. I evaded answering the question. And some time during the process, when I was putting in my defense, the Judge ordered the defendant to take the stand. A court attendant physically grabbed the defendant, and forced the defendant from the chair where she was then seated on to the chair occupied by witnesses." Presiding Justice Finch interrupted and asked:

"Q. In the presence of the Magistrate?'
"A. In the presence of the Magistrate."

"Any other incident?" Mr. Sabbatino was then asked by Judge Seabury. To which he replied: "The Magistrate asked me to plead the defendant guilty. . . ."

Again he was asked as to other incidents and in answer Mr. Sabbatino said, "I think the Magistrate sought to limit the defense in the amount of time the defendant could have in putting in her defense and also in the number of witnesses she could use in proving her defense."

The other outstanding event of the trial which he remembered was the interruption in the deSena case by the Magistrate to try another case involving some twenty-two girls accused of being wayward minors, who had been herded into the courtroom. This interruption lasted, even according to Judge Norris, at least an hour. Finally, however, the case was finished. Mary deSena was convicted.

Mr. Sabbatino decided to take an appeal from the Court's judgment and accordingly ordered the minutes of the trial. When he first received them from the stenographer he noticed that page forty-three was missing entirely and that pages six and seven appeared to have been changed. These changes resulted in a long contest with the stenographer about furnishing him (Sabbatino) with a true copy of the minutes. Finally he succeeded and the stenographer thereupon sent him true copies of what had taken place. Mr. Sabbatino then very carefully compared the new pages with the old ones, and found therein many serious differences on the copies first furnished him from those, the true copies, he had later received. The first and incorrect copy given him completely misrepresented the Magistrate's remarks and attitude during the trial and were so changed by her for that very purpose as the Appellate Court found. Below are parallel columns showing these changes. In the left hand column is what truly was said, in the right hand column is what the Magistrate hoped the Appellate Court would think had been said.

The True Record	*The False Record*
The Court: "Too late."	This was stricken out.
The Court: "... You know what to do, plead her guilty and throw herself on the mercy of the Court."	"What is it, counsel, do you wish to plead her guilty and throw herself on the mercy of the Court?"
The Court: "How long will it take you to try this case? You are going to be limited. This case has been pending since the 26th of April."	"How long will it take you to try this case? It has been pending since the 26th of April."
The Court: "I won't try this long case, ..."	"try" is changed to "hear."
The Court: "Never mind 'about.'"	Stricken out.
Mr. Weston: "Less than ten minutes."	Stricken out.
The Court: "I won't hear any more witnesses. Next case. Step aside."	Stricken out.
The Court: "No argument. Will you put the defendant on or not?"	Stricken out.

The True Record	*The False Record*
Mr. Sabbatino: "I cannot rest without putting in the full case."	Stricken out.
The Court: "Step aside."	Stricken out.
The Court: (To Defendant) "Get up."	Stricken out.
Mr. Sabbatino: "I will have to call the janitress."	Stricken out.
The Court: "Take the stand."	Stricken out.
The Deft.: "He is my counsel, I beg your pardon."	Stricken out.
The Court: "Will you stop arguing?"	Stricken out.
Court Attendant: "Do as the Judge tells you."	Stricken out.

From a reading of the two columns it is plainly apparent that all the prejudicial remarks made by the Magistrate were stricken out. No Appellate Court would have been able to know what had actually occurred in the trial Court had not the defendant's attorney insisted on having the true record. On the appeal the conviction was affirmed, but, however, with one Judge dissenting, who said: " . . . I am constrained to hold that the record in this case clearly indicates prejudice on the part of the Magistrate [presiding], which affected, in my opinion, the substantial rights of the defendant so that she was not accorded a fair and impartial trial."

The Appellate Division, which tried her, in sustaining the Referee's finding, said: "That in the deSena case Magistrate Norris changed or attempted to change official records in material respects, to the prejudice of the defendant, in an effort to eliminate from the record on appeal remarks and rulings by her as Magistrate which presented evidence of unjudicial and unfair conduct at the trial and thus to prevent the substantiation in the Appellate Court as to what had in truth occurred." Further on in its opinion the Court said: "During the course of the hearing an issue was tendered, met and tried as to whether Magistrate Norris forced the defendant deSena to take the witness stand in violation of her constitutional rights. We find that the evidence preponderates in proving this charge." Her only excuse for her actions in this case was that she merely wished to correct inaccuracies in the record. Her own expert stenographer at her trial testified that the original stenographic notes were, with one or two trivial exceptions, correctly transcribed and if the notes had been taken down correctly in the first place, then the typewritten transcript was correct. Her wrongful act in this case was the changing of the record which imports, to an Appellate Court, absolute verity, in an endeavor to hide her own prejudice at the original trial.

The second case in which the Referee found her actions wrongful was that of one Mina Landry. This woman was charged with maintaining a house for disorderly purposes. She was tried and convicted. She was then remanded to jail for forty-eight hours to undergo certain physical examinations, and have her past history checked up by one of the Probation Officers of the Court, before she was sentenced. On the day of her sentence a Mrs. deLima, the probation officer in this case, was ill and therefore could not be at Court to present her report. However, she had prepared it but had not had the time to have it typewritten and knowing she would not be at Court, had given it, in longhand, to Miss Smith, the senior officer, to present it at the time of sentence to Magistrate Norris. This Miss Smith did. She testified, "I stepped up on the Bench and placed the report, . . . either gave it to the Magistrate or placed it just before her, and explained that Mrs. deLima was absent. . . ." This report, as all probation reports are, was, theoretically at least, to have an important effect in determining the nature of the sentence imposed. If the report were favorable a light sentence generally followed, if unfavorable a more severe sentence was imposed. The report read: "Mina Landry: Defendant appears to be thoroughly repentant. She is clean and orderly and gentle in speech and action. Defendant is well thought of by her roomers. Defendant's rooming house is well cared for. The rent is $1,300 for thirty rooms, and the net profit is so small that it barely covers her food expenses. Would recommend the hospital if diseased; if not diseased, probation." Magistrate Norris despite this favorable report imposed a sentence of one hundred days in the workhouse.

Just after the defendant had been sentenced Miss Smith turned to Magistrate Norris and said, "The place has a bad reputation, I know it from years back; it also has a speakeasy connected with it. I know the proprietor."

Magistrate Norris, according to Miss Smith, then said, "Tell Mrs. deLima to make a more thorough investigation as I understand there is going to be an appeal."

Miss Smith following the Judge's directions dictated those remarks to her stenographer in a letter addressed to Mrs. deLima. The letter read as follows: "Mrs. deLima: Judge Norris wants a very thorough investigation of the premises 161 East 23rd Street, due to the fact that there have been many more arrests from there and the lawyer intends starting an appeal immediately."

In accordance with this direction Mrs. deLima made another investigation, but the information which she obtained was not of her own finding, but was obtained over the telephone from some one at the office of the Committee of Fourteen. She didn't know whether or not it was true, but nevertheless she took it and typewrote it into a report. This information was very damaging to the defendant and better calculated to support the Magistrate's sentence when it was read by the Appellate Court. The minutes were ordered, and submitted to the Magistrate. Once again she changed them in her own handwriting, keeping out the first report made, in longhand, by Mrs. deLima and directing the incorporation of the second and damaging report. The Appellate Court never saw the first report.

Once more she had changed the record, which, as said above, "imports absolute verity."

The Appellate Division in sustaining this finding of the

Referee relating to this charge said: "That in the Landry case the acts of Magistrate Norris in reference to the record on appeal were calculated to prejudice the rights of the defendant on that appeal to a proper review of her sentence." Had the lawyer not appealed from this judgment of Magistrate Norris the true facts would never have come out.

The Bodmer case presented to the Appellate Division another aspect of Magistrate Norris's actions and attitude toward those brought before her. This girl of twenty was living with a man, not her husband. One day a deaconess, who had learned of this situation, went, together with a policeman, without a warrant or any other authority, to this girl's room, got in in some way, captured her and brought her into Court, charging her with the offense of being a wayward minor. It would be obvious, even to a layman, if he but read the statute governing such cases, that there was no case against this girl under that statute. Here, nevertheless, the deaconess and policewoman brought her and within two hours of her arrest, without any advice as to her constitutional rights and without a lawyer, she was put on the stand by the Magistrate, tried and convicted. No evidence except hearsay evidence was introduced, no one asked her any questions except the Magistrate. No admissions made by her were introduced, only those made by some one else which, of course, were not binding on the defendant on trial. The conviction was reversed on appeal, the Appellate Court in its opinion saying in part: ". . . For errors committed on the trial we must reverse the judgment in this case. The defendant was not warned of her rights before trial, and the People's case consists almost entirely of hearsay evidence, which was, of course, inadmissible against the defendant. . . ."

On her cross-examination Magistrate Norris swore absolutely that the defendant was advised at the trial as to her constitutional rights, whereas in her answer to the charges, also sworn to, she said "Respondent believes that this direction was given. . . ." She was asked by Judge Seabury if she wished to change one of these two irreconcilable statements. She replied: "My response is the same." This remark meant little except that she couldn't reconcile the two statements. In sustaining this charge, the Appellate Division said, "That in the Bodmer case the respondent (Jean Norris) placed a twenty-year-old girl on trial summarily upon her arrest, without a warrant and without counsel or the opportunity to obtain counsel, and convicted her without advising her of her rights and on testimony which was obviously insufficient in law and almost exclusively hearsay. The constitutional rights of defendant were thus violated in an inexcusable manner." On cross-examination Magistrate Norris was asked to point out any advice given as to the defendant's constitutional rights. Her only answer was, in substance, that it must have been given for it always was. She was asked also to point out any common law evidence. There was none to be found, so she fenced and evaded answering until in desperation she blamed the trial stenographer, saying, "I might say I thought a great deal of the testimony was missing, that I do not consider that this is a true or a complete transcript." Judge Seabury then proved that the minutes were correct and once more asked her the question:

"Q. And you find no common law evidence adduced against her, do you?"

To which she replied: "Now, Judge, am I being tried on the way in which I conducted the Court?"

This question of hers, to which the answer was obviously yes, ended the discussion of the Bodmer case.

Another charge against her was that she owned stock in a bonding company whose bonds she was called upon to approve, forfeit or revoke the forfeiture. Magistrate Norris admitted she owned the stock but said in her answer that that fact in no way influenced her judgment. Also, she denied that the acts of approving, forfeiting or canceling the forfeiture were judicial acts. She could not or did not see the impropriety of such ownership although she admitted it would have been wrong for her to have owned all of the stock in the company.

Apparently the impropriety incident to the ownership of the bonds never occurred to her. In fairness to Magistrate Norris it must be said that nothing suggestive of corruption appeared in any of her acts. To this charge, the Court in sustaining it said: "That Magistrate Norris purchased and held stock in a bonding company with whose representative in the Magistrate's Court she was in close contact and as to whose bonds she was frequently called upon and did act in her judicial capacity."

The other action of hers which was complained of and which contributed to her removal was her endorsement, for money, of the advertisement of a commercial product, namely, yeast. Here, Magistrate Norris allowed her picture as a Judge to be used with an accompanying letter, signed by her, attesting the excellence of yeast. This letter read in part. "Recently one of my friends suggested that I try eating Fleischmann's Yeast, which I did—skeptically enough in the beginning but thankfully enough at the expiration of only two weeks, as the improvement in my digestion resulted in more restful sleep than I had had for years." The "friend" referred to in the letter was the business agent of the company who had already paid her the $1,000 before Judge Norris signed the letter. It seems too, that the "friend" had told her that the company required two weeks' trial before they would accept her endorsement. The "friend" had first offered Magistrate Norris $500 for the endorsement but when she refused to accept this amount, raised the figure to $1,000 which was the amount paid. Magistrate Norris testified that it was the intention of the company to feature, in their advertisement, the fact that she was New York's only woman Judge and that she had been a Magistrate for seven years. She also admitted the Referee's Finding No. 74, which read as follows: "The said testimonial letter, by its reference to Magistrate Norris's official position and judicial duties, directly connected her judicial position and career with the advertisement of Fleischmann's Yeast." The Court trying her said, in regard to this action of hers: "That for money Magistrate Norris underwent a course of treatment and sanctioned the exploiting of her judicial position in the advertising of a commercial product contrary to the essential dignity of judicial office."

Viewing each of the acts above related as a part of a whole, the Referee at the end of his opinion to the Appellate Division said, "These acts on the part of Magistrate Norris are not simply departures from the technical rules of correct procedure. On the contrary, they evince a course of conduct resulting in injustice to defendants, which, in individual cases, must have been followed by tragic consequences. I see no good reason why, in the future, the rights of defendants should be jeopardized by subjecting them to her determination. The public interest certainly requires that they should not."

With these remarks the Appellate Division found itself in accord, saying at the end of its own opinion, "The Court, therefore, unanimously finds the respondent guilty and, acting under the provisions of law, directs her removal from office. An order will be entered accordingly." Such an order was entered.

CHAPTER X

THE TRIAL OF MAGISTRATE SILBERMANN

JESSE SILBERMANN had been a Magistrate for ten years. According to his own testimony it was not his educational equipment or legal ability that got him the "job." Political considerations, his race, and partisan political activities were the determinative factors. He testified that these were the reasons:

"I learned that the Mayor decided to appoint a Hebrew from the Bronx.... I was active in the party; I was chairman of the Law Committee of the Democratic party up there prior to my appointment; I was active in politics."

It was to his District Leader, James W. Brown, Public Administrator of Bronx County, that Silbermann went with his petition for "recognition." It was but the irony of fate that Brown's influence on Silbermann's decision in the Grabsky case brought about his removal as a Magistrate. No case other than this better supports the following statement of the Referee in his report to the Appellate Division:

"The selection of Magistrates upon the recommendation of District Leaders results in the creation of a debt from the Magistrate to the Political Party responsible for his appointment, which he spends the rest of his term of office in repaying."

From the date of his appointment in 1921, until his removal in 1931, after a trial before the Appellate Division, in which he was defended by Mr. Herbert C. Smythe, Judge Silbermann sat in the Women's Court approximately one-fourth of his time. Indeed, according to Judge Corrigan, who succeeded Chief Magistrate McAdoo, Judge Silbermann came to him and asked to be assigned to that Court. Through the years

Silbermann came to know certain members of the Vice Squad who often appeared in the Women's Court as complainants. He knew Harry Katz, the bondsman who shared the office of Emanuel Busch—a prominent practitioner in that branch of the Court. He knew, quite intimately, another member of Lawyer's Row—Mark Alter. Alter used to visit him in Chambers; Silbermann occasionally dropped into Alter's office on his way home with Weston.

These relationships with members of the "ring" charged with responsibility for this condition in the Women's Court were pertinent in bringing home the charge that Silbermann knew or should have known of the conspiracy to defeat justice then operative in that Court.

> "Here," as Judge Seabury said in his summation, "you had a Trinity of three dominating powers in that Women's Court in Manhattan. Representative of the Bar stood Mark Alter. Representative of the Prosecutor's office stood the confessed bribe taker, Weston; and on the Bench, to referee and determine between these contestants, sat Judge Silbermann, who had observed the fact that, for years, officers had been giving perjurious evidence."

To support this charge that Silbermann knew or should have known of this conspiracy Weston was placed upon the stand at Silbermann's trial. There he told his story reciting the details from the receipt of his first bribe down to the voluntary relinquishment of his office in 1929. He told of his own relations with Silbermann and praised him unstintingly as an honest and upright Judge. This eulogy of Silbermann by Weston is important in showing that Weston's testimony as to the practices that were pursued in that Court was not motivated by hatred of or vindictiveness toward Silbermann.

Silbermann himself took credit for initiating the so-called "green-sheet." This reform was brought about because of Silbermann's observation that many police officers gave false testimony. In his own words, he instituted this reform, "so that the officer could not change his testimony, or change the facts, or testify to different facts from those which really occurred."

Of course, it is at once apparent that the "green-sheet" would be valuable on cross-examination. Indeed, he admitted that he used it for that purpose, until 1927, when Weston and Magistrate Renaud convinced him that by using the "green-sheet" he was obtaining evidence outside the record and hence its use was not only unethical but illegal. Although he claimed that he took drastic action in cases where the officers testified falsely he could not show a single instance where, on his complaint, an officer was dismissed from the force. Silbermann also swore that he never used the officer's sworn complaint to check the truthfulness of the latter's testimony on the stand. He characterized Weston as a vigorous prosecutor, sometimes "vicious" or "brutal." While on the stand he was shown ten or twelve cases, in which Weston admitted that he was paid money by defendant's attorney, and yet he insisted Weston did his duty and produced all the evidence.

The Appellate Division in passing on this charge said: "We conclude that the proof offered to sustain charge No. 1 is insufficient to establish that the respondent knew or should have known of the conspiracy set forth in the charge, or that his failure to discover such conspiracy was due to wilful neglect."

The third charge was that Silbermann decided cases improperly and from considerations outside the record.

A young typist was arrested for stealing a dress from Klein's Coat & Dress Store on Union Square. Klein's business is conducted on a self-service basis. The losses from shoplifting necessitated employment of private detectives. One of these detectives noticed this young girl walking out of the store with a dress on for which she had not paid. Whenever she took a step a big blue tag appeared from under a panel on the back of the dress. The detective noticing this, beckoned to her co-worker. They followed her out in the street, and after it became evident that she had no intention of returning they apprehended her and brought her back. She and the two detectives went up to Mr. Klein's office, and she there admitted that she took the dress, saying that she had lost her purse in the store and in fear of her mother, had taken the dress to make up for her loss. She was taken to the station house where she again admitted her guilt and typewrote a note to her mother saying she was sorry for what she had done.

At the hearing before Silbermann on September 8th, she was represented by Mark Alter. Although the Magistrate's sole function in this case was to determine whether or not the testimony showed that a crime had been committed and that there was probable cause to believe the defendant guilty, he discharged the defendant.

Klein, unable to understand why the girl had been discharged, unsuccessfully sought an interview with Silbermann. He finally complained to the District Attorney, who sent him to Chief Magistrate McAdoo, who arranged with Silbermann to reopen the case.

The case finally came on for a rehearing before Judge Silbermann. Weston informed the Court that Klein was opposed to having Silbermann preside because he had already expressed his opinion that the girl was innocent. Alter then took the position that Silbermann was the only proper Magistrate to hear the case. Silbermann then said, "No reason appearing why this Court should not hear the matter, the Court will proceed with the hearing."

In view of the fact that Silbermann had discharged the accused on the first hearing on the ground of "insufficient evidence," Klein himself took the stand and in addition produced both store detectives, an officer from the police station to whom she had admitted her guilt, also Officer Gallagher, who swore that he looked at the note she had typed while in the station. Opposed to all of that testimony, he had the girl's testimony, and even she admitted that she put on the dress and that she didn't pay for it. Although she denied walking out of the store, Silbermann himself testified that he believed she did walk out. Finally, Silbermann in the effort to justify his position was driven to the position that he did not believe that the girl had formed any intent to steal, and then he lost himself in a maze of contradictory assertions as to why he did not believe the State had made out a prima facie case sufficient for him to hold the accused for trial in Special Sessions.

It is impossible to reproduce the atmosphere of bias, prejudice and unjudicial conduct that prevailed in this second hearing.

Shortly thereafter Klein had another girl, one Minnie Hanasty, arrested for shoplifting. She also was arraigned and had her hearing before Silbermann and again he dismissed the accused. This time Klein had one of his employees order the minutes. The stenographer transcribed them and left a copy thereof on Silbermann's desk; he kept them a few days, but in the meanwhile Klein had become so insistent that the stenographer sent him a copy. Shortly thereafter Silbermann, not knowing the minutes had already been delivered, called the stenographer in and dictated a long outline of the facts together with arguments supporting his action in the case. The stenographer swore that Silbermann told him to insert this in the place of the three or four line opinion that he had delivered at the end of the trial in Court. Of course, the whole phraseology of this "memorandum," as Silbermann called it, indicated an intent to use it as an opinion and put it in the copy of the minutes to be furnished to Klein. Silbermann stoutly denied that this "memorandum" was intended to be used as an opinion in the case.

The Appellate Division, in its opinion relating to this subdivision of the charges, said:

> "There was probable cause to believe that the defendant was guilty of the crime and that the respondents, in wilful disregard of this prima facie proof, arbitrarily and with apparent bias refused to hold the defendant for trial. The hearings as conducted by the respondent disclosed an unfair attitude towards the complainant and his witnesses and unjudicial conduct on respondent's part and indicate that he was actuated by improper motives.
>
> "The Hanasty case, likewise, comprised in Charge No. 3, presents another instance of unfair and unjudicial conduct."

Charge No. 2, related to the Grabsky case and was that

Magistrate Silbermann "was improperly influenced by political considerations" in his disposition of that case.

Hyman Grabsky and his nephew Philip were fur manufacturers. The Rhoda Coat Company gave them a pattern and ordered forty-seven fur sets to be made in accord therewith; but after completion, the coat company tried to return them on the ground that they did not conform to the pattern. It was, of course, true that so long as the Grabskys had the pattern they could disprove this claim. In selecting the person who was to secure the return of the pattern the Rhoda Company chose a man over six feet and weighing two hundred and twenty-five. Hyman was partially paralyzed and weighed one hundred and fifteen pounds. Nevertheless, when the Rhoda agent started to walk off with the pattern Hyman resisted and shouted to Philip for help. Thereafter a free-for-all fight took place during which Philip Fetbrandt, the Rhoda agent's helper, was hit in the face, the blow breaking his glasses and cutting his eye. He preferred charges of assault against both Grabskys.

After a hearing upon these charges, Magistrate Jesse Silbermann found the Grabskys guilty and remanded them without bail.

On August 29th, Philip's brother Paul, who had changed his name to Gray, immediately got into touch with a friend, who suggested that he enlist the aid of District Leader Brown, who "put Silbermann on the Bench."

Gray called at Brown's house in the late afternoon of the 30th. Brown agreed to intercede, and then and there tried to get the Judge on the telephone, but failed.

The next day—the day they were to be sentenced—Gray called at Brown's house and picked up Brown and his lieutenant, Danny Byrne, Clerk of the Bronx County Court. They then proceeded to the Magistrates' Court, arriving there before the Grabskys were sentenced. They all entered the courtroom. The Grabskys testified that Brown had an interview with Silbermann and returned telling them that Philip would be let off with a small fine but that he could do nothing for Hyman, who did not reside in his district. Silbermann sentenced Hyman, the paralytic, to ten days in the workhouse, but Philip, whose record showed arrests for disorderly conduct and larceny, was let off with a fifty dollar fine.

Brown admitted that he went to Court to intercede for Philip, but denied that he had done so. Both Silbermann and Brown admitted that the latter had interceded in behalf of other prisoners at the Bar. It was admitted that the man with the worst record, Philip, was let off with a fine, while the paralytic, Hyman, went to the workhouse. Documentary evidence was adduced to prove that the price of Brown's aid was that Philip and Paul join the Organization and that they fulfilled their agreement. Indeed, if anything more were needed, Brown himself made the proud declaration: "That's how we make Democrats."

As Judge Seabury said in his summation:

"I say to your Honors, will you consider this Grabsky charge in the light of the probabilities, in the light of facts that are known to every lawyer in New York City.... The great curse of those Courts today, in my judgment, and I think it is proven by the evidence, is the influence of politics in them, and there can be no better condition in those Courts until you drive it out.... Of course, I have to prove it by circumstantial evidence. They don't make contracts for that sort of thing. Your Honors... can say that in a case, where it is proven, a judge who allows his judicial action to be influenced by it must cease longer to be a Magistrate. ... If you take that ground, much will have been done to make even a City Magistrate's Court what it ought to be, a Temple of Justice and the Bench itself the altar in the Temple, not the bargain counter that it has become, the bargain counter over which justice is bought and sold by the bribery of witnesses and District Attorneys, and by the political brokers that undertake to deliver decisions because of the influence they have."

In its opinion, the Court said:

"... Respondent was improperly influenced by political considerations in imposing sentence upon Philip Grabsky, in that the respondent did permit the imposition of such penalty to be affected by a person interceding who had been selected solely because of

his supposed political influence with respondent, and who was
unconnected with the case, uninformed of the facts and had no
knowledge of the character, career or surrounding circumstances
of the offender."

In the Silbermann case, while personal unfitness was proven,
even a larger issue was involved. The Court met this issue
squarely and by its decision, in effect, served notice that: all
District Leaders and politicians must keep "hands off" the
Magistrates' Courts; prostitution of these Courts to mere en-
rolling places for Tammany would not be permitted: Democrats must be made somewhere else; it is no part of a District
Leader's "civic duty" to influence judicial decisions.

CHAPTER XI

THE MAGISTRATES' COURTS REPORT

UNFORTUNATELY space does not permit of the republication of the Magistrates' Courts Report. On the other hand, it is difficult to condense it, for it is already condensed. It is our hope, however, that the following excerpts will indicate its nature and recommendations. It sums up the facts which present the need for change and proposes a true remedy.

As the Referee proceeds from fact to fact, the central evil of these Courts—political influence—is thrown into bold relief. In closing, he sounds the knell of the district leader's influence in these Courts.

"I cannot believe that the facts which have been shown in regard to the City Magistrates' Court can fail to arouse a public demand that these conditions be changed.

"The abuses that have been disclosed do not strike at people of wealth and power. They oppress those who are poor and helpless, under circumstances where the oppressor enjoys practical immunity. A court in which these practices could have obtained, or in which they may obtain again, is not a Court of Justice. True, we are assured that the Vice Squad has been abolished, that the employment of stool-pigeons has been discontinued, and that other changes of like character have been made; but what assurance is there that these evils will not be revived? Even more important is it to recognize the fact that the chief abuses now resident in the court lie much deeper and are not obviated by changes of the character which have been made.

"There can be no remedy for these conditions unless the court can be entirely freed of political control. That will not be a task easy of accomplishment, necessary and vital though it is to the proper administration of justice. There is too much patronage and rich opportunity for spoils to allow the necessary changes to be made, if the political forces that now dominate can prevent it; but change there must be if these evils are to be severed from the administration of justice.

"I believe that the initiative to bring about the necessary changes in this Court should come from the Bench and the Bar in the First and Second Judicial Departments. If, however, the Bench and the Bar do not act, or if they assume to act and limit their action to technical and procedural changes which consist in the adoption of noncurative palliatives, it is my belief that other agencies within our city life should come forward and exert themselves to cause the necessary changes to be made.

"The basic recommendation which should be given effect is simple. The power of appointment of magistrates and justices should be taken from the political district leaders, where in truth it at present resides, and vested in the Justices of the Appellate Division. Selfish and partisan reasons can be urged why this should not be done, for it will diminish the spoils that can be distributed as political rewards; but no honest minded man will doubt that this change will restore integrity to these Courts, and will rescue them from the disgraceful depths into which they have been plunged."

He compares with regret his findings with those of the Page Commission of 1910, which also made a study of these courts, and finds a tragic similarity.

"The reason why we are no better off today ... is that the Inferior Criminal Courts Act (passed as a result of the findings of the Page Commission) left unimpaired and free to flourish the basic vice in the Magistrates' Courts, i.e., *their administration as part of the political spoils system.*"

No official from the Magistrate down to the attendant at the gate is immune from its withering touch. Some Magistrates by the quality of their work have shown that they are deserving of their place both by character and ability. As to others:

"... the evidence shows the applicant for judicial office standing abjectly and, figuratively, with his hat in his hand, before the political district leader, begging his recommendation to Tammany Hall, which was recognized to be the *sine qua non* ... a situation which is a scandal and a disgrace, as well as a menace, to the City of New York."

In support of this most serious charge, quotations from the testimony of eight of the twenty-five Magistrates of the Boroughs of Manhattan and the Bronx are set forth. The testimony of Magistrates Brodsky and Silbermann in regard to their appointment has already been given.

Magistrate Dreyer went to his district leader and said:

"Here is my position, my practice absolutely gone, . . . what am I going to do? I think I am entitled to get a judgeship for all I have done for eighteen years. . . ."

Magistrate Gottlieb was quite frank, saying:

"I took care of things politically. I helped get the house that our clubhouse is in. I have done things to help build up our organization in our district. . . . A call came to fill his place, as temporary Magistrate. There seemed to be no logical man for the position. . . . The job, as we call it, really belonged to our district. That is a rule, sometimes broken, but I spoke to Briarly, and I spoke to Judge Mahoney."

Former Magistrate Goodman testified:

". . . I spoke to Judge Friedlander about it and whether he spoke to Mr. Murphy . . . I don't know, but I do know he spoke to Mister Hylan because I had an interview with Mayor Hylan. I assume it took the usual routine . . . submitted to the County Leader by the District Organization and then submitted to the Mayor."

The Referee concludes that this manner of selection creates a debt

"from the Magistrate to the Political Party responsible for his appointment, which he spends the rest of his term of office in repaying."

This appointment of Magistrates by the Mayor—a political agency—is the central evil resident in these Courts. No progress can be made unless and until this appointive power is transferred to some non-political agency which will look for character, ability, and judicial qualifications rather than party subserviency, race, nationality or creed. Palliatives have been tried and failed. The real and lasting cure can only be attained by the appointment of qualified men free from political obligations.

There is a clerk in charge of each court. His position is appointive—for a four year term. It is not dependent upon civil service examination. These jobs also are farmed out to the district leaders. Sixteen of these clerks admitted upon examination that they were active politically, and that the job was the reward for party service.

The following is a typical instance:

"Q. Are you a member of a Democratic club?
"A. Yes.
"Q. What is the name of the club?
"A. The John F. Curry Association.
"Q. John F. Curry, and Curry, of course, is the leader of the club?
"A. Yes, the district I was born in and still live on the same avenue where I was born. . . .
"Q. Now, when you were appointed corporation inspector, who sponsored your appointment?
"A. Mr. Curry.
"Q. Mr. Curry did?
"A. Yes.
"Q. And when you were appointed a clerk of the First District Court, he also sponsored your appointment?
"A. Mr. Curry, yes.
"Q. Were you active in the club?
"A. For 25 years, but never held no political jobs.
"Q. Were you ever a captain?
"A. I was more than a captain. I was very active. . . ."

Another instance is:

"Q. What political club are you affiliated with?
"A. Chickopee Democratic Club, 21st Assembly District. . . .
"Q. Who is the leader of that club?

"A. At the present time Thomas F. Murray, the last year.

"Q. Who was the leader prior to that?

"A. Edmund P. Hallihan...."

The Clerk has general supervision over all other clerks and attendants in his particular court. He supervises the records and routine. He controls all moneys deposited in his court. The proper functioning of each court depends in a great measure upon the integrity, fitness and intelligence of these clerks and their staff. The fact that the clerk is a political appointee makes him a useful aid to political leaders in favoring those of their henchmen who are haled into court. Several clerks testified to the intervention of the district leader, but qualified their admission by saying they never intervened in felony or misdemeanor cases. This qualification must, as the Referee points out, "be taken with a large grain of salt." The following quotation from the testimony of one of the clerks shows how the District Leader exerts his influence in these courts.

"Q. Help the man that was served with the summons out?

"A. Yes. That was it. Sometimes I might go in to the judge in his chambers and ask if he would consider it, and sometimes he would say 'No' and sometimes 'Yes,' and I give it to him....

"Q. What do you tell the judge when you come into them with a case in which you want to help the defendant?

"A. Why, I just have a memorandum marked 'John Smith' or 'John Doe' and say, 'Corporation ordinance, officer so and so. Judge, this man is a poor man and says he is broke and has not any money and if you can see your way clear to help him out, O.K.'

"Q. Does he?

"A. Sometimes.

"Q. Does the judge know from whom the request for a favor has come?

"A. Sometimes. I won't say 'sometimes.' All the time.

"Q. That is, he knows that it is that particular leader who is asking the favor?

"A. Yes; yes....

"Q. How often do you say you have been asked to speak to the judge about a defendant in a pending case, such as that pushcart case? Do you get many of those requests from district leaders or other people?

"A. Occasionally we do. We get a few.

"Q. How many would you say you would get during a year, roughly?

"A. Oh, we might get fifty. . . ."

The next ranking officer in the court is the Assistant Clerk. Of the forty-eight Assistant Clerks examined, thirty-nine stated that they had been, or were, members of political district clubs. Ostensibly their appointment depends on competitive civil service examination. But this in turn may be made the subject of political influence. The following is an illustration:

"Q. The Assistant Clerks, nevertheless, have to pass a Civil Service examination?

"A. No, they don't—

"Q. The Assistant Clerks?

"A. Oh, yes.

"Q. But you do not think that the examination at present is adequate?

"A. I do not think the requirements are adequate. It ought to be open to the public and should not be closed.

"Q. There are two grades of Assistant Clerks, are there not, a second, a third grade?

"A. Yes.

"Q. What is the difference between them?

"A. I could not answer it, except what they make them at headquarters, I guess. There is another thing, look at Mr. McAdoo,—carrying his pets, like he took—I took a competitive examination, as I did the last, and you would have to sign a waiver so that one or two of his men could get in over there. He wanted a man appointed by the name of Broderick, and we all took the examination, I was sixth on the list of assistants in all the boroughs, and Broderick was twelfth. Everybody before twelve had to sign a waiver so that Broderick could get in, and he got it, and headquarters have been working with that kind of stuff for years.

"Q. What was Broderick made as a result of this?

"A. Some kind of a job McAdoo picked out for him, some

kind of a Deputy Recording Clerk, you know how you can mess up a thing, make a lot of soft jobs, that is what he did. He wanted to get him in at an increased salary, and he got him. Everybody laid down, I signed a waiver myself, though I was bitter, and I told Broderick: 'You come and ask a man to sign a waiver?' He said: 'What do you care?' He said: 'I am going to get it anyway.' I said: 'Go ahead and get it.' That situation should not exist, should it? . . ."

The Assistant Clerk's most important function is to draw the complaint. There was in common use, up until this investigation, a form known as the "O-14." This form prepared by the Assistant Clerk indicates to the Magistrate that he is in doubt as to whether or not the facts justify a complaint. The Magistrate's duty then is to conduct an examination and determine whether or not a complaint should be drawn. In most cases, especially those of book-making, it was the Magistrate's practice to dismiss the case, when presented with such a form. The abuses springing from the use of this form have already been described in an earlier chapter.

The court attendants—also ostensibly civil service appointees—vied with the clerks and assistants in acting as "steerers" to favored court practitioners. This corrupt practice, revealed by the bogus lawyer Wolfman, who frequently split fees with them, has also been told.

The only other court official is the People's representative—the Assistant District Attorney. In the last analysis these men also are appointees of the district leader. They are not the most able men on the District Attorney's staff. Assignment to these courts is given to the novices in the office. As is evidenced by Weston's tragic story they work without effective supervision. The Referee reported that for the most part, "He stands in court, apparently merely as a casual and indifferent observer," and concludes that he "might just as well have been non-existent."

Thus it will be seen that every official of this Court is at some time touched with the blight of local organization politics. The Magistrate or the attendant in charge of the prisoners' pen is subject to it, either in his appointment, his advancement or in keeping his job.

The Referee next turned his attention from the official inhabitants of these Courts to the police, the bondsmen, the "fixers" and the lawyers. Concerning the latter he said:

"Those members of the Bar who are sensitive to the honor and dignity of their profession have long suffered embarrassment as a result of the fact that so many members of their profession have been engaged in unworthy practices in the Magistrates' Courts....

"The lawyers who are most conspicuous there, operated under circumstances inconsistent with proper professional standards. They have found entrée to the defendants through traffic in favors with court officials, or, in some instances, by definite corruption. The proof shows that many practitioners in these courts frequently exact unwarranted fees....

"The fact that these lawyers did not render any appreciable amount of legal service is shown by the testimony of Joseph Wolfman, who had functioned as a lawyer in the Magistrates' Court for three years without any legal training at all. He said that on one occasion he had spent a week studying procedure in one of the courts, but that beyond this he had little preparation. It is most interesting to note that no one suspected for three years that he was not a lawyer."

The ways of the police officers and bondsmen are thus described:

"Nearly all the cases which come into the Magistrates' Courts emanate from arrests by members of the Police Department. The outcome of these proceedings is largely in the control of the arresting officers, upon whose testimony the case must stand or fall. Experience shows that many police officers have not been blind to the opportunity for extortion which this power puts into their hands. In some cases they would make arrests and immediately offer to sell immunity without requiring the prisoner even to go to the Police Station. If the money was paid, the matter was ended then and there. If the money was not paid, the person arrested was arraigned in the Police Station. Here a bondsman, whose virtue is extolled by the policeman, is quickly provided, the prisoner having previously been refused permission to communicate by telephone or otherwise with any one else. The prisoner, unfamiliar with legal processes, wonders at the magic which unlocks the door of the cell, but unlocked it is. The prisoner is taken by the bondsman, as his pawn, to the bondsman's office, usually near by, where further inquiry as to the prisoner's financial status is made. Here the bondsman learns that the prisoner has a savings bank account. The prisoner is put into the bondsman's automobile and taken home, where the bank book is delivered and assigned to the bondsman. The next morning the bondsman, having the bank book and its assignment in his pocket, takes the prisoner to the bank, where sufficient money is drawn out to pay what is supposed to pave the way to freedom, and this is given to the bondsman. This amount includes an exorbitant charge for the bail bond, rarely less than twice the legal fee, and an additional sum, which the bondsman advises is to be used to pay for a lawyer, whom he will provide to represent the prisoner, and to 'fix' the case, by bribing the officers to testify so as to make the proof insufficient to hold the defendant, and the representative of the District Attorney, to 'go easy.' Where the bondsman has discovered that the person arrested has additional funds, the victim is held up for additional amounts, on the ground that alleged complications have intervened, requiring the payment of larger amounts than were originally contemplated. When the defendant has been mulcted of all the money possible, the play proceeds: the case comes to trial, the officers testify to a state of facts insufficient to make out a case, the representative of the District Attorney stands mute, and the defendant is discharged.

"If the money demanded by the bondsman is not paid, the officers testify to a complete case. Being officers of the law, as one Magistrate put it, their testimony is presumed to be true, and the defendant is convicted, no matter what the defendant may say, the theory being, as another Magistrate put it, that the person arrested would naturally give evidence consistent only with innocence."

The formidable front that these characters, acting in concert, presented to the due administration of justice in these Courts is thus lucidly described by the Referee:

"The ring operating mainly in the Women's Court was a

shocking example of the lengths to which distortion of law to illegal ends was carried in the Magistrates' Courts. It was made
up of interlocking halves, the lawyers, the bondsmen and the fixers,
on the one hand, and members of the so-called Vice Squad of the
Police Department and their stool-pigeons, on the other.

"The system which I have described, by which cases were dismissed in large numbers, because of the insufficiency of the testimony of the police officers, were continuous over a long period.
During that period the same Magistrates presided time and again
—so often, indeed, that they came to know well the various
members of the Vice Squad. It would, in my opinion, be impossible to reconcile the prevalence and the continuance of this
system with competency and uprightness on the part of the presiding Magistrates. Among those who sat there most frequently
were Magistrates Jesse Silbermann, Jean H. Norris, H. Stanley
Renaud and Earl A. Smith.

"Magistrate Silbermann, for instance, says that in case after
case he rebuked the police officers for their perjurious testimony.
In case after case he told the officers that they could not do that
kind of thing to him, but he could not name a single case where
he had taken any effective action in order to correct these conditions, much less to have the officer removed from the police force.
Whatever the motives of the Magistrates may have been in sitting
back and permitting this outrageous spectacle to be enacted before them day in and day out, the effect of it is not in doubt: it
permitted the lawyers, the fixers, and the bondsmen who operated
in these courts to reap a rich harvest. There was absolutely no
excuse for these Magistrates in permitting the police officers to
testify as they did, without intervening, because at the very time
the officers were testifying there was in the court, as the Magistrates well knew, the so-called 'Green Sheet,' which consisted
of a written report made by the police officer promptly after the
arrest, attested by the Desk Lieutenant, setting forth all the circumstances attending the arrest. A mere reference to the 'Green
Sheet' would have demonstrated to any Magistrate who was suf-
ficiently interested to find out, that the officer's version, given
on the stand at the trial, was different from the facts to which
he had subscribed in the 'Green Sheet.' Indeed, the 'Green Sheet,'
for which Magistrate Silbermann took credit, was initiated because of the recognized prevalence of perjury by police officers

and for the very purpose of preventing it. The theory of the 'Green Sheet' was that by making the police officer write out the circumstances attending the arrest immediately after making the arrest, he would be prevented from changing his story when called upon to testify at the trial, as the result of considerations passing to him between the time of the arrest and the time of the trial. Notwithstanding this, the 'Green Sheet' was ignored and the police officers were permitted, day after day and in case after case, to give testimony contrary to the 'Green Sheet' signed by them, with the result that the defendants were discharged. I am not now criticizing the fact that they were discharged; in a great many cases they had been framed in the first place and they were entitled to be discharged. What I am criticizing is the supineness of the Magistrates in the face of palpably perjurious testimony by police officers."

Never before in the history of the minor criminal courts in New York City has any one presented such a comprehensive plan for their reorganization along lines best calculated to eradicate the abuses therein, as did the Referee in his final report.

There are in the city today three inferior criminal courts which cost the taxpayers over three million dollars annually. The Referee recommended the abolition of the existing Magistrates' Courts, Children's Court and Court of Special Sessions, as by law constituted and the creation of a new court of Special Sessions of the City of New York, in which shall be vested the jurisdiction now possessed by said three courts, and such other powers as may, by law, be conferred upon it; the judges of said court to be appointed by the Appellate Division. Another recommendation was that all "terms" or "parts" of this court be held in a central courthouse—one in each borough.

"The true reason for consolidation, however, is found not in the mere financial benefits to be derived therefrom—although these would be great and no good reason exists for ignoring them; an even more important reason is that upon such a consolidation the present haphazard and illogical distribution of the work could be eliminated, a new and better distribution could be substituted, considerable duplication of work avoided and a much

smoother and better coördinated system put into operation. This
would not only be of benefit to the courts, but of great advantage to the members of the public having to do with them."

Much has been said as to the advisability of keeping the
Children's Court separate and distinct from the other courts.
The Referee, too, would keep it distinct. Under his plan of
reorganization it would be a separate part of the new court
and housed in a separate building. Furthermore it would have
the advantage of better qualified judges—free of political influence—and it would be under the supervision of a centralized
authority in the person of the new President Justice. Thus it
would have all the advantages that it now has together with
the advantages that come from centralized control and non-
political and better qualified judges.

The Referee's most important suggestion and the one that
is vitally necessary to the improvement of the administration
of justice in these courts, is the transfer of the appointive
power from the Mayor to the Appellate Division.

Unless this change is made there is no hope for improvement.

As the "system" now operates, Magistrates are appointed
first and foremost as a reward for party subserviency. Tammany appoints Magistrates for the purpose of strengthening
the party and not for the furtherance of justice. After months
of patient, thorough and intelligent investigation, the Referee
said:

> "I am convinced that without a radical change in the method
> of the selection of Magistrates—a change which will result in
> eliminating political control of the appointments—*any other in-
> novation will prove futile.*"

There are now ten or more separate district Magistrates'
Courts in Manhattan, each with its retinue of clerks—assistant
clerks and court attendants. It is all the product of the spoils
system. Since a centralized court would throw some of these
parasites out of their sinecures, we may expect their unlimited
opposition to this proposal. Only an aroused public sentiment,
and an organized Bar determined to discharge its public duty,

can bring about this and the other changes suggested by the Referee.

In furtherance of the spoils system these courts even as presently constituted are overmanned. The clerks are not subject to Civil Service—thus the most important post in each of these courts is politically controlled. By virtue of the iniquitous system of "waivers" the person who should be appointed to a responsible position is forced to give way to a politically active but inferior assistant clerk. Thus even where Civil Service ostensibly controls, in reality, promotions come only through political channels. Again, examinations for these jobs are restricted. Unless a person has been an attendant, interpreter or fourth-class clerk in these courts he cannot even take the examination.

By virtue of what has come to be known as "form O-14" these clerks can insure the discharge of a defendant with political influence. In this form as previously described the assistant clerk charged with drawing complaints informs the Magistrate that he is in doubt as to whether or not the facts warrant the drawing of a complaint. Wolfman testified that he bribed clerks to use this form and that, where this form was used, the Magistrate invariably dismissed the case.

The remedy for all this lies in doing everything humanly possible to wrest these courts from political control.

The Referee early concluded that the only possible way to cleanse the courts of extortion, bribery and corruption was to make it economically unprofitable for any thieving bondsman and unscrupulous lawyer to operate therein. Basing his recommendations on instances where it was proven that bondsmen had charged in excess of the legal premium for bail-bonds and lawyers had overreached their unfortunate clients, he suggested, first a system of cash bail not to exceed twenty-five dollars except in cases of felonies; the designation by the Appellate Division of a group of lawyers to attend these courts and upon designation by the Magistrate to defend the accused, in return for a reasonable compensation to be paid out of the public treasury.

This procedure would at once insure the presence of the accused in court with competent counsel, and would obviate overcharging. It is superior to the idea of an elective or appointive city official in that there would be an absolute freedom from political control. Again it is an advance over the theory that these persons should be represented by the Legal Aid Society, because that Society is dependent on voluntary public subscription and charity. "The public obligation of manning these courts with honest and competent lawyers is an official obligation which should not be dependent upon the ability of a charitable organization to raise funds."

The evils to which helpless women have been subjected by being brought first to the police precinct station house have been described. Recently, too, our Court of Appeals has had reason to reverse a murder conviction because of the "third degree" practiced on the defendant in the station house. To obviate these abuses the Referee suggests that all persons arrested be arraigned immediately before a Magistrate. Such a reform would insure to the accused the immediate protection of counsel, prevent robbing by bondsmen, eliminate the "third degree" and centralize the detention of prisoners.

All of the foregoing changes seem at the present time more or less assured of consummation, with the exception of unification into one court and the transfer of the appointive power from the Mayor to the Appellate Division. And yet strangely enough all other changes pale into insignificance beside the two last mentioned. The reason why those last two are not more vigorously pressed is to be found in the public idea that since this latter change would necessitate a constitutional amendment it would be too much trouble, and further because they are opposed by Tammany,—the entity which represents the beneficiaries of the present system. In closing his report the Referee said:

"There can be no remedy for these conditions unless the Court can be entirely freed of political control. . . .

"I believe that the initiative to bring about these necessary changes in this Court should come from the Bench and the Bar in the First and Second Judicial Departments."

And if, said the Referee, the Bench and Bar do not act or in acting adopt only non-curative palliatives,

"...it is my belief that other agencies within our city life should come forward and exert themselves to cause the necessary changes to be made."

CHAPTER XII

THE INVESTIGATION OF DISTRICT ATTORNEY CRAIN

IN New York City the instrumentalities for the discovery and prosecution of crimes are under the political control of the dominant machine. Every District Attorney in the city is a Tammany man and so is the Police Commissioner. The administrations of Theodore Roosevelt as Police Commissioner, and William Travers Jerome and Charles S. Whitman as District Attorney, show that Tammany Hall does not fare well with such diligent and effective men in these offices. It is no wonder then that they viewed with alarm the appointment of Judge Seabury, as the Governor's Commissioner, to hear and report his recommendation in regard to the City Club's charges of incompetency, in which it petitioned the Governor to remove Judge Crain.

Mr. Samuel Untermyer undertook the defense of Judge Crain. In contrast to the high regard of judicial fairness on the part of the Commissioner, there was, some thought, a complete disregard of these proprieties on the part of Mr. Untermyer, as was exhibited by his newspaper campaign of attacks on the Commissioner. Through the press he assailed the Commissioner as unfair, biased and prejudiced, although in private assuring him of his confidence in his (the Commissioner's) sense of fairness and impartiality. His attempts to provoke the Commissioner to an open quarrel through the medium of the newspapers was unsuccessful. Besides his newspaper attack, he addressed letters to the Governor objecting to the Commissioner. Governor Roosevelt uttered no word of protest about these attacks until after the case was finished, when he said through a spokesman:

"The Governor resents and has long resented the attitude of Counsel for Mr. Crain in this case."

Various city newspapers had from time to time reviewed the District Attorney's administration. The citizenry were therefore not altogether surprised when in their charges the City Club said:

"His conduct of the office of District Attorney...has been incompetent, inefficient and futile...."

Every one remembered his unredeemed promise to point out Rothstein's murderer within fifteen days after taking office; his failure to prove anything conclusive in regard to Doctor Doyle; his ineffectiveness in the Ewald-Healy matter, which resulted in the Governor's taking the case out of his hands; his admitted inability effectively to curb "racketeering"; his failure to follow through his inquiry into the Magistrates' Courts; his failure to bring promptly to justice stock dealers against whom charges had been made; his failure to bring Judge Mancuso and others promptly to trial in the City Trust crash; and his shifting the burden of the trials in the Bank of United States failure to Mr. Steuer.

Although loaded down with work in his investigation into the Magistrates' Courts, Judge Seabury accepted the Governor's designation and set to work with a staff headed by Mr. John Kirkland Clark.

The charges of incompetency against the District Attorney grouped themselves under four heads: "racketeering"; the situation in the Magistrates' Courts; the stock fraud cases; and, lastly, particular cases, such as Doctor Doyle, Magistrate Ewald and Abraham Pols.

"Racketeering," at least for the purpose of this case, may be defined as the unlawful levying of tribute upon legitimate business.

Complaints in regard to conditions in the Fulton Fish Market in New York City, which serves "approximately one-fifth of the population of the United States," reached the District Attorney in November, 1930. He immediately undertook to make war on the racketeers then operating and on racketeers in general. He testified before the Commissioner, however, that even though he received full coöperation from the police, he was powerless. The Commissioner in his report to the Governor concluded that he was ineffective, saying:

"The evidence before me compels the conclusion that the much heralded warfare upon racketeers ended in a complete and abject surrender by the law-enforcing authorities in New York County."

District Attorney Crain in his defense said that in this war he had made radio speeches on the subject and had formed a "Committee of Public Safety." He testified that he had given out statements to the press and sent out questionnaires to the industries affected. He described how he had put a sign over an office door "Complaint Room," and how he introduced his assistants to the gentlemen of the Committee, and for their education had paraded before them as a typical racketeer "Tough Jake." His conclusion was that nothing more could be done, inasmuch as he himself had presented the case to the Grand Jury and they had not acted.

Obviously, to determine the effectivenes of his presentation it was necessary to read the Grand Jury minutes. To the Commissioner's surprise, District Attorney Crain refused to consent to the Commissioner's application for a copy of these minutes and also sought, affirmatively, to hinder the inquiry by opposing it. These obstructive tactics were condemned in the Commissioner's report where he said such lack of coöperation on the part of a public officer whose conduct is under investigation,

"constitute defiance of the lawful authority of the Governor of the State and may of itself present a situation where the Governor would be justified in removing such public official,"

but since this was a case of the first impression he would not urge its consideration in connection with the pending charges.

The Court, after argument, granted the Commissioner's motion and an inspection of the Grand Jury minutes revealed

"not only ineffectiveness but, in my judgment, incompetency... in dealing with this serious question."

They disclosed a failure to ask the chief witness the one important question as to whether or not he had paid "Socks" Lanza, an alleged "racketeer," any money and they further disclosed the District Attorney's failure to prove a payment by any other evidence. The Commissioner, with more limited power to obtain evidence, showed not only one, but a regular series of payments to racketeers; and the further fact that although these racketeers rendered no legitimate services, they were on the payrolls of the various companies. In one instance he showed that the payment to a racketeer on condition that the labor contract be renewed at the rate then in existence rather than at a higher rate, was $12,000; and in another, that although the racketeer demanded $7,500, he settled for $5,000; and that this unlawful charge had the effect of increasing the cost to the consumer.

It was alleged that racketeers also preyed on the millinery trade. The leading racketeer in that trade was one who had succeeded "Little Augie" when the latter met a violent death at the hands of his fellow gangsters. The Commissioner found that the District Attorney's conduct in failing to bring these millinery racketeers to justice was excusable on the ground of the reluctance of witnesses to testify. In spite of this difficulty the Commissioner secured witnesses who testified that they paid as high as $100 a month to the leader of this group for "protection" and that these payments were so designated in their books.

One Mezzacapo was alleged king of the racketeers in the cloth shrinking trade, victimizing chiefly not the employers but the worker. The District Attorney, in his investigation into racketeering in this industry, never examined into the extent of Mezzacapo's activities; in fact, he did not know that Mezzacapo was under indictment in his own office at the time complaints were made to him. The evidence before the Commissioner showed that in his accounts in the period from 1925-1930, Mezzacapo deposited $332,000.

The District Attorney set out to examine racketeering in thirty industries. He presented five matters to the Grand Jury who returned indictment against two persons who were still awaiting trial eleven months later—August, 1931. Two other matters were presented to the Magistrates' Courts, one defendant pleaded guilty to petty larceny—the other, though held for the Grand Jury, had not been indicted at the time the Commissioner handed in his report.

As to the second charge, the District Attorney's ineffectiveness in dealing with the situation in the Magistrates' Courts, the Commissioner concluded:

> "A dispassionate review of the minutes of this Grand Jury, and of the action that was taken by the District Attorney, compels the conclusion that the effort on the part of the District Attorney to eradicate these abuses which existed in the Magistrates' Courts was almost wholly ineffective. Little good came of it, and no aggressive steps were taken to eradicate the chief evils inherent in the system which prevailed there."

In undertaking this Inquiry on January 27, 1930, District Attorney Crain said he wished to get all the information he could in order

> "to take steps to punish all conduct that is in violation of any criminal statute."

Upon the hearing he asserted that his sole object was to make a presentment as to conditions, and yet in the next breath he claimed credit for the entire results of the investigation then being conducted by Judge Seabury, as Referee under the Order of the Appellate Division. The fact remains, however, that the sum total of District Attorney Crain's activities was institution of criminal proceedings against seven bondsmen. In three of these cases there was no prosecution, in two, one was acquitted or the case was dismissed, and in the remaining three, convictions were followed by a fine in one case, and suspended sentences in the other two. Upon that record of achievement, District Attorney Crain predicated his assertion that he was responsible for the improvement of conditions in the Magistrates' Courts. In the District Attorney's inquiry not a policeman was indicted, not a bondsman sent to jail, no question raised as to the conduct of any Magistrate on the Bench or an attorney at the Bar. In the Appellate Division inquiry five Magistrates were removed or resigned from the Bench, five or six of the Vice Squad were sent to jail, and the whole Squad dissolved. A former Assistant District Attorney testified that he had been bribed by upwards of fifteen lawyers. Most important of all, the Referee submitted a constructive report which goes to the heart of the problem in these Courts.

Another charge against District Attorney Crain arose out of the scandals in connection with the Board of Standards and Appeals. Investigation into Doctor Doyle's activities consisted simply of writing letters requesting Doyle to waive immunity and testify. This invitation was refused and there the matter dropped.

The Commissioner in his report concluded that the evidence then before him did not sustain the charge of incompetency.

The last charge was based on District Attorney Crain's prosecution of stock dealers against whom charges had been made. The evidence showed that the people of New York City are annually defrauded out of a sum in excess of $50,000,000, through the sale of bogus stocks. These frauds are in the first instance investigated by the Attorney-General of the State. After an injunction has been secured against repetition of the particular activity complained of, then, if the evidence indicates the commission of a crime, the matter is referred to the District Attorney for further action. Many of these matters present the most intricate question of accounting, and such cases are seldom presented to a Grand Jury and rarely brought to trial. It is a saving of public time and money to accept a plea of guilty to a lesser offense than that charged. As the Commissioner said in commenting on District Attorney Crain's handling of the Partos-Cornell Drug Corporation case:

> "The fact is that the case was intricate, the papers in the matter voluminous and it was allowed to slumber in the District Attorney's office without being effectively handled."

Subsequently, and after the Commissioner's report, Partos was tried, convicted and sentenced to prison for a period of from five to ten years. The Commissioner's comment on the inquiry into the Prince and Whitely failure was much the same:

"It is only fair to say that the labor involved may have accounted somewhat for the inertia which in this respect seemed to characterize the action of the District Attorney. However, that can not be deemed an adequate excuse for inaction."

In addition to the foregoing particulars the Commissioner admitted in evidence, charts, prepared by Professor Raymond Moley, designed to disclose the administrative tendency in the District Attorney's office in the handling of cases. He also admitted charts prepared by the defense. It is important to note that he refused to admit them for the purpose of comparing Crain's administration with that of the more forceful, able and courageous administrations of Jerome and Whitman. The charts revealed a practice prevailing in the District Attorney's office, that of disposing of felony indictments by the acceptance of pleas of guilty to lesser offenses. The Commissioner concluded:

"In view of the fact that the practice revealed by these charts is approved by the Judges of the Court of General Sessions, no inference adverse to the respondent can be drawn as tending to establish incompetency."

While the Commissioner was unable to find proof of competent and alert action in many cases under the jurisdiction of the District Attorney, he did not find that

"...the incompetency has been so general in scope and so gross in character that it requires the removal of the incumbent."

In his opinion wherein the Commissioner recommended to the Governor the dismissal of these charges, he said, in part, as follows:

"The fact that the people of the County do not elect the best man to the position, or one who acts in the most efficient manner, is not ground for his removal. In such cases, the people must suffer the consequences of their conduct.... Popular government can be no better than public opinion and the public conscience insist upon ...

"The people who elect a public official are entitled to absolute honesty on his part, and reasonable diligence, and efficiency. ... Where, however, there is no suggestion of dishonesty or wilful wrong-doing on the part of an elected official, he should not be lightly removed from office...."

He had previously pointed out

"... that the charges originally filed, the specifications served in amplification of them and the proof that was adduced at the hearings before me contain no suggestion of dishonesty or wilful wrong-doing on the part of the Respondent."

On the whole case, however, the Commissioner concluded:

"The question whether an elected public official should be removed is not to be determined by individual opinion as to what may promote public interest. Proof, not opinion, is the standard which must be applied in solving such a question. Public interests are to be served, but such interests cannot be truly served at the expense of injustice to an individual.

"Under these circumstances, it is my conviction, that on all the proof before me the Petition for the respondent's removal from office should be dismissed."

CHAPTER XIII

EVENTS PREFACING THE CITY-WIDE INVESTIGATION

SHORTLY after the murder of Arnold Rothstein in 1928, W. Kingsland Macy, the Republican leader, demanded an investigation into the Police Department and its activities in that case. There were others who, even then, demanded a general city-wide investigation into all departments. Nothing came of this demand, but then and there was planted the seed which found its full fruition three years later in the Investigation which disclosed the events described in the following chapters.

It was not until the fall of 1929 that the Rothstein murder was heard of again. Mr. LaGuardia, the Republican candidate for Mayor, resurrected it. He charged that Rothstein had been a friend and money lender to Tammany officials and particularly to Magistrate Albert Vitale. He made other charges, adding one or two each day of his campaign. To help counteract the charges that political influences had thwarted the solution of the Rothstein case, Supreme Court Justice Thomas C. T. Crain ran as Tammany candidate for District Attorney on the promise to bring Rothstein's murderer to justice within fifteen days after taking office. Crain was elected, but by the time he took office, the only person whose indictment for that murder the public knows anything about, had been tried and acquitted. District Attorney Crain has done nothing since, so far as the public knows, towards the effectual solution of that murder. A host of other events happening about the same time as the Rothstein case, appertaining to the city administration, caused rumors of corruption to arise.

The activities of Doctor Doyle, a practitioner before the Board of Standards and Appeals—The Pathé Film fire—the actions of William E. Walsh, Chairman of the Board of

Standards and Appeals,—the Ewald case and others gave rise
to a demand for a general investigation. When the Legislature
convened in January, 1930, Senator Knight and Speaker Mc-
Ginnies announced that they favored an investigation by a
legislative commission to be appointed by the Governor.
Assemblyman Hamilton F. Potter suggested a joint legislative
committee. The net result of these two proposals was that in
March, 1930, the bill, creating the Commission suggested by
Senator Knight and Speaker McGinnies, was passed. It was
proposed that this Commission investigate the Magistrates'
Courts, the Police Department and the Board of Standards
and Appeals. This measure the Governor vetoed, saying in his
message:

> "... Its defiance of precedents; its attempt to add unheard of
> duties to the executive function; its creation of a new precedent
> which if logically pursued would compel future Governors at
> one time or another to meddle in the affairs of every county and
> city in the state—all of these compel an obvious disapproval."

Shortly after the convening of the 1930 legislature, the new
District Attorney of New York County, Thomas C. T. Crain,
undertook a Grand Jury Investigation into the Magistrates'
Courts. This proceeding lasted but two months and then adjourned without having achieved any really useful purpose.

After the 1930 Legislature adjourned, the cry of scandal
still persisting, Senator Knight and Speaker McGinnies demanded that the Governor call a special session of the
Legislature in order to enact some measure leading to an investigation of the conditions alleged to exist in New York
City. This the Governor refused to do.

At about the same time Charles H. Tuttle, the Federal
District Attorney, began to take an active part in these mat-
ters. He was then investigating the passage of $10,000 from
Mrs. George Ewald's bank account into that of a Tammany
District leader, Martin Healy. It was rumored that this was
the consideration paid by George Ewald for his appointment

as a City Magistrate. A little later District Attorney Crain also undertook to investigate this subject. No recommendations having been made by him to the Grand Jury and no indictments having been returned, the matter was taken out of his hands by the Governor who appointed the Honorable Hamilton Ward to supersede him as prosecutor. The Governor also designated Justice Philip J. McCook to preside at an Extraordinary Term of the Supreme Court called to try persons indicted by the Special Grand Jury then convened to investigate the Ewald affair. Later, the persons indicted were tried. Each trial resulted in a disagreement of the jury.

Charles H. Tuttle was nominated for Governor by the Republican party. In his campaign he used the alleged corruption in New York City as his major issue. Governor Roosevelt was renominated by the Democrats and later reëlected. In one of his closing speeches in that campaign Governor Roosevelt said:

"... I, and the members of my administration, do not yield place to any Republican candidate or editor in abhorrence of a corrupt judiciary. We do not yield place to any one in indignation against any holder of public office who is recreant to his trust. We do not yield place to any one in the sincere and honest desire to punish those judges who have or who may prostitute their positions...."

When the 1931 Legislature met, Mr. Macy, who had succeeded to the State Chairmanship of the Republican Party, again demanded the general investigation he had been advocating since 1928. Mr. Macy now had all the events, as above detailed, to strengthen his plea for the investigation, as well as the facts being exposed day after day in the Magistrates' Courts Inquiry. He had had none of these examples of corruption in 1928 when he first demanded an investigation. In addition he used the daily stories developed by the Investigation into the District Attorney's office then being conducted by Judge Seabury as the Governor's Commissioner.

The cumulative effect of all of the rumors and stories of

scandal of the past two years was that on March 23, 1931, at about one o'clock in the morning, over the violent objection of all the Democrats, the Republican majorities in both the State Senate and Assembly passed the Joint Resolution under which authority the events about to be related were disclosed. The time had come at last when the people of New York City were to find out the truth of Mayor Walker's statements to the effect that those who desired an Investigation were mere slanderers of the City's fair name and whether or not, "The people of New York, where Tammany rules, are satisfied with it."

CHAPTER XIV

DOCTOR DOYLE

THE Board of Standards and Appeals is a local city tribunal with discretionary jurisdiction to permit variations from the Building Zone Regulations. A favorable award from this Board may increase tremendously the rentable space of an office building. Pursuant to its edict a district could be changed from residential to business purposes. Obviously its edict might have the converse effect of diminishing property values; for instance, it might permit the erection of a garage or filling station in a strictly residential neighborhood. The Board consists of five members—four of them political appointees of the Mayor and the fifth a member of the Fire Department. By exercising their discretion in favor of a particular applicant his pockets might be lined with gold.

Theoretically this Board serves a very useful purpose. Its jurisdiction lends the necessary elasticity to the prescribed regulation. Its practice and procedure are simple. There is no reason why any one should have to employ any specific person to plead his case. There is not a lawyer, architect or any one else in the city familiar with the Building Codes and Zoning Regulations who could not adequately present to the Board the facts necessary to its decision.

In practice, however, the law creating the Board vested discretionary power in Tammany appointees to grant or deny such applications as were made to it. In fact, its practice fell into the hands of a very small group of men—some laymen, some lawyers. When favorable awards were made large sums of money were sometimes paid in fees to those appearing for the petitioner.

Early in the summer of 1930, District Attorney Tuttle began an inquiry into the tax returns of William F. Doyle, who enjoyed a most lucrative practice before this Board. During nine years of practice before this Board Doctor Doyle had deposited over one million dollars.

His metamorphosis from the profession of veterinarian to that of special pleader before the Board of Standards and Appeals came about in the following way. Back in the early 1900's he was appointed to guard the health of the city fire horses, becoming after years of service Chief Veterinarian to the Fire Department. Subsequently he was appointed by Mayor Hylan to membership on the City Bureau of Fire Prevention. About 1917 he left that employment to begin his practice before the Board. While practicing before this Board he developed the custom of taking part of his fees in check and the rest in cash. He admitted splitting his fees but refused to name the recipients. Inquiry was made to ascertain the persons with whom he had split fees and whether or not any part thereof had reached a city official or political leader. When he was questioned about the matter, at first he declined to name these persons with whom he had split on the ground that to do so might tend to incriminate or degrade him. This refusal blocked Mr. Tuttle in this line of inquiry. District Attorney Crain thereupon extended an invitation to Doctor Doyle to waive immunity and tell all that he knew to the County Grand Jury. Doctor Doyle did not consent to this request. District Attorney Crain then let the matter drop. Doctor Doyle was tried but after the Federal Jury disagreed on one count and acquitted him on the other he retired to Deal, New Jersey,—beyond the reach of the Legislative Committee's subpœna.

George Z. Medalie, who succeeded Mr. Tuttle as Federal District Attorney, has, even with his limited authority, done more for the cause of civic decency than many city and state officials with their greater powers. While Doctor Doyle was in New York in connection with a pending federal indictment he was subpœnaed to appear before the Legislative Committee the next day, July 21, 1931.

This was the first public hearing. Senator Samuel Hof-

stadter, the Chairman of the Committee, opened the proceedings by reading into the record, first, the Joint Resolution
creating the Committee, and then Judge Seabury's letter to
him, as Chairman, accepting the post as Counsel to the Committee, which expressly stipulated that:

> "This acceptance is based on the assurances which I have re-
> ceived, and which I have no doubt expresses the wishes of every
> member of this Committee that, in the discharge of my duties
> as Counsel, I shall have an absolutely free hand. This freedom
> of action is to leave me entirely unembarrassed in the presenta-
> tion to the Committee of such evidence as I deem to be per-
> tinent. . . ."

The necessary formalities over, Doctor Doyle took the stand
in response to Counsel's call. Everything went smoothly for
the first few minutes while the Doctor rehearsed his political
history. As soon as he was asked whether or not it was his practice to take his fees partly in cash and partly in check he became uncommunicative. To answer that he said might tend to
incriminate him.

The Joint Resolution under which the Committee acted by
its terms empowered it to grant immunity. The statute relating
to bribery also afforded immunity to a witness testifying to the
giving of a bribe which was accepted. On Doctor Doyle's refusal to answer, the Committee immediately went into executive session and resolved that in "the public interest" Doyle
should not be excused from testifying and therefore it granted
him immunity from prosecution and directed him to answer.
Again the question was put and again he refused to answer.
Then arose the first storm within the Committee with Assemblyman Cuvillier and Senator McNaboe leading the vociferous
obstruction. Finally when things quieted down Counsel passed
to the following questions:

> "Q. Dr. Doyle, did you, in reference to cases pending before
> the Board of Standards and Appeals, bribe any public official?
> "A. You are alluding to the Board of Standards and Ap-
> peals? No.

"Q. Now, you did not bribe any member of the Board of Standards and Appeals?

"A. No.

"Q. Did you bribe any other public official?

"A. I refuse to answer on the ground that it might tend to incriminate me.

"Q. Dr. Doyle, did you give any part of the proceeds of those fees to any political leader in the County of New York?

"A. I refuse to answer that question on the ground that answering might tend to incriminate me. . . ."

After a series of these questions dealing with Doyle's disposition of his fees, all of which he refused to answer, the Committee cited him to the Supreme Court for contempt. Doyle was then theoretically placed in the custody of the sergeant-at-arms and taken a little later before Mr. Justice William Harman Black, who held him in contempt and fixed his bail at $25,000.

At the insistence of Samuel Falk, Doctor Doyle's attorney, further argument was postponed until the next day when the Court again committed him for contempt, dismissed his writ of habeas corpus, but admitted him to bail, until 2 :00 P. M. the following day. The argument closed with the following request by Counsel and the following order by the Court:

"Mr. Seabury: May I have your Honor's direction that if any application for a stay is made by counsel for the relator to any Court or Judge, I may have notice of that application?

"The Court: Yes, I think that is fair."

Out of Mr. Falk's disregard of this mandate arose the now notorious telephone call from John F. Curry, leader of Tammany Hall, to Mr. Justice Henry L. Sherman of the Appellate Division, in response to which call Mr. Justice Sherman agreed to hear Doctor Doyle's application for a stay of the order committing him to jail, at his home in Lake Placid, New York. But more of that in the following chapter.

Then began a most remarkable series of events. Due to Doctor Doyle's refusal to answer, the two highest Courts of the State of New York and the Legislature itself were convened in Special Session,—all at great inconvenience to members of these bodies and great expense to the taxpayers. After the smoke had cleared away, Courts, citizens and legislators found themselves the victims of a hoax. When he was finally recalled Doctor Doyle stated that he had never bribed any public official.

Before he granted the stay, Mr. Justice Sherman had been informed by Mr. Justice Finch that he would convene the Appellate Division on Monday, July 27, to hear Doctor Doyle's appeal from Mr. Justice Black's order. Thereupon and after hearing the argument the Court unanimously affirmed the order dismissing his writ of habeas corpus and directed the Sheriff to take him to the County jail.

To the surprise of all Doctor Doyle was not in Court nor within the jurisdiction—he was at his home in Deal, New Jersey. So Court and counsel had to wait for three hours until Doctor Doyle could get back to New York. When he finally arrived he was given into the custody of Deputy Sheriff Rosenberg, who took him to dinner in the Hotel Pennsylvania on the way to jail.

Mr. Falk applied to Chief Judge Cardozo of the Court of Appeals for a stay. The Chief Judge determined to hear the argument immediately. This application was heard under different circumstances. No political leader intervened and both sides were heard.

Judge Cardozo denied the application and allowed Doctor Doyle to go to jail forthwith.

On August 1, the Court of Appeals met in special session to hear Doctor Doyle's appeal from the Appellate Division and to determine finally whether or not Doctor Doyle should answer the questions propounded to him. Counsel argued the case on behalf of the Committee. Mr. Orleans, Mr. Falk's partner, argued the case on behalf of Doctor Doyle. Counsel urged that, especially in view of the statute giving immunity to the bribe giver, the constitutional provision, the statute and the joint resolution should be fairly and not tech-

nically construed and pointed out that such an interpretation
was of public importance. In part he said:

> "There are in the state, and in this country, hundreds of thou-
> sands of young men and women whose character has not been
> warped; whose high purpose and public spirit has not yet been
> deadened by cynicism; who still believe the fight against bribery
> and corruption is not a futile battle."

He closed his argument, saying:

> "They believe that in taking part in public office they may
> do something to eradicate the bribery and corruption that per-
> meate the government of some of our great cities. Will you by
> your decision, tell them that this is an illusion; that they can do
> nothing; that bribery and corruption stand entrenched behind
> the barrier of the Constitution?"

There was one question of major importance involved. The
decision of the Court can be understood only in the light of the
actual facts. Both houses of the State Legislature by a majority
of its members, passed this Joint Resolution. The Governor
signed the accompanying and necessary appropriation bill. The
only practical difference then, between this Resolution and a law
is that a law is submitted to the Governor, who, if he approves
it, signs his name at the end thereof. In this case he approved
this Resolution in effect, as is evidenced by his signing the
appropriation bill which was vital to the Committee and the
thing that gave it life. The majority of the Court concurring
in an opinion by Chief Judge Cardozo, that has as its basis
the doctrine of *stare decisis,* held that immunity can only be
granted by a law and not by a Joint Resolution.

Judge Cuthbert W. Pound, who years ago had been a member of the Lexow Committee appointed to investigate the
Police Department of New York City, dissented, saying in
part:

> "When the Legislature acts in its own concerns, in a strictly
> legislative inquiry, some provision of the State or Federal Con-
> stitution must be indicated which stands in the way of the exe-

cution of its purpose to get at the facts for its future guidance by granting full and complete immunity to those who testify before it."

The result of the decision of the Court of Appeals was that the Court affirmed Doctor Doyle's commitment for contempt on the ground that the bribery statute gave him immunity should his answer disclose that he had bribed a public official; that, until the Legislature enacted further legislation sufficient to give him immunity from prosecution for crimes other than bribery, as defined within the limited scope of the statute, he could still claim his constitutional privilege. Chief Judge Cardozo suggested that the Legislature might, when it next convened, pass some kind of a bill under which such a witness who testified would gain immunity.

Even before the Court of Appeals directed Doctor Doyle to answer the question as to whether or not he had bribed a public official, the press had prophesied that he would say "no." No person saw how he could make such an answer and expect to be believed. Everybody awaited his next move with interest. It came in the form of an order to show cause why the Committee should not immediately convene to hear Doctor Doyle's answer. Mr. Justice Carew seemed critical of the Committee and its Counsel for not immediately convening to give Doctor Doyle his chance to purge himself of his contempt. Counsel replied that the Court could not fix the date when the Committee was required to convene, and that the extent of its authority was to vacate the order of commitment and further, that as a matter of fact, the question was academic because the Committee was to meet the next day, when Doctor Doyle would be called on to answer. Mr. Falk withdrew his motion and moved to vacate the commitment. Mr. Justice Carew then adjourned the argument until the Committee had an opportunity to convene, which it did on the following day—August 14.

On that day Doctor Doyle was recalled and questioned as follows:

"Q. You remember that I then asked you whether you had given any bribe to any other public official and you answered that you declined to answer because to do so would incriminate you. Do you recall?

"A. I do.

"Q. Will you now tell this Committee whether or not you gave a bribe to any public official, and if so, to whom?

"A. I did not give a bribe to any public official. The answer is No."

The answer he then gave raised the question as to whether or not he had purged himself of his contempt. It seems that only a truthful answer should have the effect of purging oneself of contempt. Doctor Doyle by his previous refusal to answer, on the ground that it might tend to incriminate him had given rise to the inference that the only truthful answer to this question was yes. He had set the standard by which the truth or falsity of this second answer to the same question was to be judged. The Committee accepted his standard—refused to credit his second answer and declined to attest to the Court that Doctor Doyle had purged himself.

Chairman Hofstadter thus summed it up in the following announcement of the Committee's ruling on this question:

"Will you stand up a moment, Dr. Doyle? (Dr. Doyle rises.)

"The Chairman: On July 21st, the question relating to the bribery of public officers was first put to you; were you then able truthfully to respond in the negative, clearly there was no warrant in law or in good morals for you to decline to answer. The reply could not have incriminated you.

"The conclusion derivable from your refusal to answer must be that the only response which you then contemplated could be truthfully made by you, would be an admission which would incriminate you, and you professed to believe, and in the ensuing litigation in the courts you persisted in so professing, that you would be without immunity from prosecution. The highest Court of the State rejected your contention.

"We do not accept your present denial as credible. If it were, you have been trifling with the Committee and the Courts, and we are unwilling to yield to the suggestion that the processes of

Government are so flabby, and the servants of the people so help-less that you can flaunt your contempt for the State and defiance of its agencies, with utter impunity."

It might be well to compare this statement, based upon the facts, with the loud noises of Senator McNaboe upon the same occasion when he said:

"There is innuendo, presumption and suspicion. There is a forceful attempt to keep a sick man in jail until he does talk. If that is the spirit of these United States, if that is the spirit of this State, if that is the spirit of this legislative committee, I say it is high time for somebody to rise up in great protest and stop placing feeble persons in jail because they didn't give you the answer that you expect to get.

"I say, Dr. Doyle, if I were in your place, I would remain in jail until hell freezed over."

Immediately after the morning session that day, Mr. Falk sued out another writ of habeas corpus which was sustained by Mr. Justice Edward S. Dore. On the application of Counsel the Justice stayed the execution of his own order sustaining the writ of habeas corpus, pending the determination by the Appellate Division of the whole matter, and fixed bail at $20,000.

The Appellate Division affirmed the order releasing Doyle from custody, and on March 3, 1932, the Court of Appeals in a *per curiam* opinion affirmed the decision of the Supreme Court saying in part:

"Upon the record now before us, the untruthfulness of the answer may be a possible inference, but a necessary one it certainly is not."

Nothing so well indicates the difficulties encountered by the forces of law and order in dealing with those elements in our society who obey and disobey the laws at will as does the Doyle case. Some of these difficulties were foreshadowed in the opinion of the Court of Appeals where it was said:

"True, indeed, it is that at an earlier stage of the inquiry the witness had declined to answer a like question on the ground that the answer might tend to incriminate him. We are asked how such a claim of privilege could have been genuine if the witness could truthfully have answered 'No.' But to put such a question is to ignore the character and the limitations of the proceeding now before us. . . . Enough for present purposes that whatever contempt may have been involved in his deceitful claim of privilege must have redress in some other proceeding and not improbably in another forum."

It may not be that our "processes of government are so flabby," and it may not be that "bribery and corruption stand entrenched behind the barrier of the Constitution," but the fact remains that Doyle's defiance has gone unpunished save for eighteen days in the County jail.

CHAPTER XV

MR. CURRY'S TELEPHONE CALL

WHEN, on July 22, 1931, Mr. Justice Black committed Doctor Doyle to jail unless he procured a stay before two o'clock the next day, the rumor was rife that unless Tammany kept him out of jail he would blow off the "lid."

Tammany exerted itself to keep him out of jail, and for a time succeeded.

At 7:30 P.M. on July 22, 1931, occurred the phone call from John F. Curry to Mr. Justice Sherman at Lake Placid. Pursuant to this call from the Leader of Tammany Hall, the Justice agreed to hold himself available to hear an application for a stay of the execution of Mr. Justice Black's order of commitment. That night Ilo Orleans, Mr. Falk's partner, boarded a train for Justice Sherman's home in Lake Placid—three hundred miles away. All of this time Counsel had waited for Mr. Falk to give him notice whether or not he had secured a Judge to hear the application for the stay, in accordance with Mr. Justice Black's order—but none came.

At 9:30 the next morning Counsel telephoned to Mr. Falk who told him that he was still looking for a Judge. At 10:35 that same morning Mr. Falk informed Counsel that the application for the stay would be made before Mr. Justice Sherman at Lake Placid and that he could be heard upon it if he called the Justice on the telephone before eleven o'clock. Counsel immediately ascertained from the Appellate Division in New York City that Mr. Presiding Justice Finch would be at his Chambers all that day and would hear the argument if both Counsel would come before him. He then again telephoned Mr. Falk and suggested that they go before Mr. Justice Finch

and argue the matter before him. Mr. Falk declined to do
this or withdraw his application to Mr. Justice Sherman. Finally, at seven minutes after eleven, Counsel reached Mr.
Justice Sherman by telephone. He protested against all this
"trickery and deceit" which had been resorted to in making
the application. Although Counsel advised him that Mr. Presiding Justice Finch was in town and was ready to hear the
argument if it was submitted to him, Mr. Justice Sherman said
he would act upon the application.

When the matter came on the second time before Mr. Justice Black, Counsel said in regard to Mr. Falk's actions:

> "I charge here, on my responsibility as an officer of this Court,
> that in the application for a stay that was granted, I was denied
> an opportunity to be present by trickery and by deceit. . . . There
> have been days when practices of this kind have been resorted to.
> Attorneys during the Tweed régime and during the Erie Rail-
> road litigations did not hesitate to resort to like methods; but I
> thought those methods had gone out of fashion."

Up to this time there was no information as to who had
made the telephone call to Lake Placid. Almost daily for the
next three weeks the press called for information as to how
the appointment had been made.

While no one questioned Mr. Justice Sherman's right to
grant a stay, there were those who questioned the propriety
of his hearing and granting this stay under the existing circumstances, especially in view of the fact that the Presiding
Justice of his Court was available and ready to hear the application for the stay here in the city under circumstances that
would permit both counsel to be heard.

Later, the whole matter was considered by the Bar Association of the City of New York. Its report exonerated Mr.
Justice Sherman and with a gentle rebuke to Mr. Curry closed
the incident.

On the subject of the Bar Association's resolution, the
Evening Post said, editorially:

"As shocking in its way as was Curry's telephone call to Justice Sherman is the action of the Bar Association to that unsavory incident. While condemning Mr. Curry's part in it as an 'intrusion which could not fail to produce in the public mind a suspicion that political influences were being resorted to to influence the course of justice,' the report adopted by the Bar Association states that its executive committee has failed to find 'anything which reflects upon the impartiality, integrity or judicial conduct of Mr. Justice Sherman.' It is, then, an 'intrusion' for the leader of Tammany Hall, acting in that capacity, to make a request of a judge, but there is nothing which 'reflects' upon the 'judicial conduct' of a judge who listens respectfully to such a request, gives no sign that he regards it as in the slightest degree improper and ends by granting the request of the 'intruder.'"

After the incident, and at the same open hearing at which Doctor Doyle purged himself of contempt Mr. Curry was called as a witness and asked if he had made the call to Mr. Justice Sherman. He admitted that he had made the call.

As Counsel said in his intermediate report to Chairman Hofstadter:

"From the start Tammany Hall has done everything within its power to obstruct and interfere with the exposure of the conditions brought out in the testimony. There can be no question about the participation of Tammany Hall in the legal proceedings which have been taken in the attempt of some of the witnesses to avoid interrogation. Curry's action in springing to the defense of Dr. Doyle, as well as his subsequent testimony, establish it. Not a single one of the miscreants has been repudiated by Tammany Hall, or even criticized by it, for the official wrongdoing which has been shown....

"It is perfectly apparent that what these men did is part of the system upon which Tammany Hall exists and expands; that Tammany Hall approves it and is ready to extend its arm to the utmost to protect and perpetuate its sordid traffic in political influence."

Mr. Curry's testimony must be read in full to be appreciated. Some parts of his testimony are here reprinted:

"By Mr. Seabury:

"Q. You have known Dr. Doyle heretofore?

"A. Known Dr. Doyle possibly twenty years. I don't know how long."

One would have thought this long acquaintanceship might have made Mr. Curry anxious to do Doctor Doyle a favor, but not so, as the following questions and answers show:

"Q. I understood you to say that your only interest in Dr. Doyle is because of the fact that you are interested in any Democrat in the City of New York.

"A. ...I am not particularly interested in Dr. Doyle any more than I would be in Brown, Jones, Smith or any other man.

"Q. When you met in Tammany Hall was it merely a social meeting?

"A. Yes, that is all."

Counsel, not satisfied that Mr. Curry's statement that his interest in Doctor Doyle was only because Doyle was a Democrat, asked him the following question:

"Q. All you were interested in was to challenge the power of the Committee?

"A. ...This is a crucification, if it can be had, of the Democratic Party of the City of New York. The Democratic members of this Committee attempted to go through the State and have this a fair investigation. They were voted down. It is nothing but a prosecution of the dominant party of New York that this Committee is doing at this time."

The fact is: the Legislature refused to vote for a roving committee that might go anywhere in the State when they were given the opportunity.

The Minority, up until Mr. Curry's appearance, had tried to hoodwink the public into believing that they were not obstructing the Investigation. Curry, the Leader himself, exposed them. The fact is, they had been waiting for just such a favorable opportunity when they might accomplish their purpose of obstruction under the guise of raising a Constitutional question. This is the way that Mr. Curry expressed it:

"Yes, because we were expecting, the Democratic... I as representative of the Democratic organization of the City of New York was expecting some one to test the constitutionality of the Committee's powers to grant immunity and therefore when the request came for my aid, I was glad to be of service."

After much quibbling Mr. Curry told his version of his telephone call to Mr. Justice Sherman. It seems that Alfred J. Talley, a former judge of the Court of General Sessions and Doyle's former counsel, had called Curry and asked him if he could locate a judge. This call came to Mr. Curry at his apartment 2K in the Park Lane Hotel. Counsel, to identify this apartment as Mr. Curry's, asked him the following questions:

"Q. Is that where you live?
"A. No, sir. . . .
"Q. Chiefly, it is the place where you have political conferences?
"A. I would say political. . . .
"Q. If there is any throne room, that would be the room that would be the throne room?
"A. I would not say so, Judge. The throne room is at Tammany Hall."

The fact being established Counsel led him back to why he was so interested in Doyle:

"Q. As soon as you heard there was somebody somewhere that was going to test the power of the Committee, your heart was enlisted?
"A. Absolutely.
"Q. And not only your heart, but your sword; that is right?
"A. If you can word it that way, Judge, it is all right. . . ."

Then, in order to show that Counsel, himself, had done him a favor, Mr. Curry put the following question:

"Might I say, Judge, in answer to that, you know me a long while. You know that I have gone to you for favors in the old days, is that correct?

"By Mr. Dunnigan (one of the Minority members):

"Q. And did you get them, Mr. Curry?

"A. Yes, both in the City Court and Supreme Court."

The audience sat up and seemed interested in what this favor was that Mr. Curry had prevailed on Counsel to do. Counsel, not remembering what the favor was, asked Mr. Curry to specify it. To which he replied:

"A. The favor consisted of a jury notice.

"Q. You asked me to excuse a juror?

"A. A juror.

"Q. And I excused him?

"A. You complied with it and I was thankful for it.

"Q. Have you and I ever had any other relations that you can recall?

"A. Not that I can recall."

That episode over, Counsel returned to the subject of the telephone call and Mr. Curry's answers concerning his part in it.

"Q. You seem to be averse to answering my questions directly. Is there any reason for that? I am perfectly willing that you should make any explanation you wish.

"A. I put in a call for Judge Sherman. . . . I thought it was 6:30 but according to the record it is 7:30.

"Q. You did talk to Judge Sherman?

"A. Yes, sir. . . .

"Q. And did you ask Judge Sherman to come down to New York . . . to hear the application . . . of Doyle's lawyer for a stay?

"A. Yes, sir. He then called me back and told me that he had appointments or engagements for the next morning, but that he would be available that morning . . . for anybody that cared to make an application, he would be glad to hear it.

"Q. Did you tell him who would call to make the application at that time?

"A. I wouldn't say that I did, Judge. I think I did. I think I said Judge Talley."

After the call Mr. Curry communicated with Judge Talley who told him that "possibly Mr. Falk" would go up to Lake Placid. When Counsel asked Mr. Curry whether or not he was anxious that Doctor Doyle should refuse to speak, the Minority, as usual, rose in violent objection.

The questioning continued:

"Q. When you learned, Mr. Curry, that charges were made against Dr. Doyle that he had split his fees and when you learned that he was declining to answer, what was there in that intimation that led you to think that it was any part of your duty as the leader of the Democratic Party to try to help him in his pending lawsuit?

"A. I didn't interfere. I didn't do anything at that.

"Q. You knew this, did you not, Mr. Curry: That this case of Dr. Doyle's was in the courts of justice and was there pending, did you not?

"A. I knew that.

"Q. And you knew that Dr. Doyle had competent counsel?

"A. I did.

"Q. Able to protect his legal rights?

"A. I did.

"Q. Now, what business was it of yours as the leader of Tammany Hall to interject your personality into the situation?

"Mr. Cuvillier: That is not a fair question, Mr. Chairman.

"Mr. Seabury: I want an answer to that question.

"A. I did not care whether it was Dr. Doyle or Brown or Smith or Jones or whoever else it was that was going to test the constitutionality, I was glad to coöperate with him because I wanted to test it. That is my answer. It wasn't a question of Dr. Doyle or any one else.

"Q. Now, knowing that his case was pending before the court and that he had able and distinguished counsel, what I would like you to tell the Committee, if you will, is what business it was of yours to interject yourself into that case?

"Mr. McNaboe: I think the witness has already answered that, that he was trying to locate a Judge.

"Mr. Seabury: I heard what he said.

"Mr. McNaboe: Why do we have to sit here and hear this all over again?

"Mr. Seabury: You are not required to sit here, if you do not wish to, Senator.

"Mr. McNaboe: Oh yes, I am required to sit here.

"Mr. Seabury: That is the thing of importance in this whole thing. . . .

"Q. Now, I want you to tell the Committee, did you consider that any part of your political duty?

"A. I would say yes.

"Q. In other words then, that was not a matter of good fellowship merely, that was a matter of interest to the Democratic party?

"A. The Democratic party, absolutely.

"Q. And when you were acting in that way in trying to get a judge to hear the application, you were acting in your political capacity?

"A. Yes, sir. . . .

"Q. Now, just one or two more questions and then I am through: Don't you believe that when a case has come into the courts of justice, you as leader of Tammany Hall ought to keep your hands off?

"A. I do.

"Q. Don't you think it is a great piece of impertinence for you, simply because you are the leader of Tammany Hall, to undertake to find for a lawyer in a litigation pending in the Supreme Court, a judge before whom an application may be made?"

To which Mr. Curry answered:

"A. May I answer you? That is the first time since I was leader of the organization that I have done such a thing."

After that Counsel gave Mr. Curry an opportunity to make any statement that he wanted to, in order, as he said: "To put your position more fairly than it had been put," and then resumed his questioning as follows:

"Q. If you thought the case was important and affected the interests of the organization of which you are the head you would not hesitate to try to get a judge who would hear some application?

"A. I would step on the gas wherever it would be of help to the Democratic party of this City."

Chief Judge Cardozo in concluding his opinion in the first Doyle case said:

"The way to compel disclosure as to conspiracies and attempts is not obscure or devious. A grant of immunity similar to the one contained in the resolution, may be embodied in a statute. The Legislature, when it convenes, may pass an act of amnesty with the approval of the Governor, an act of amnesty co-extensive with the privilege destroyed. The appellant as well as other witnesses will then be under a duty to declare the whole truth, irrespective of the number or nature of crimes exposed to view. . . ."

This was a clear call for a Special Session of the Legislature. The next day the leading editorials called upon the Governor to act. His admirers predicted that he would take the initiative, but they were disappointed. He took no action until receipt of the Committee's resolution on the subject and Counsel's letter.

The Tammany Minority had constantly based their numerous objections to questions propounded to witnesses upon the ground that the Committee could not constitutionally grant immunity. It was now proposed to remove this ground of objection by asking the Legislature to enact an immunity law. The insincerity of the Minority members was demonstrated by the active opposition which they made to the enactment of such a statute. In urging the Governor to call the Legislature into Special Session and recommend the enactment of an immunity law Counsel wrote Governor Roosevelt a letter in which, among other things, he said:

"My dear Governor Roosevelt:

"I have no doubt, from such investigation as has already been made that corruption in the government of New York City is widespread. . . . In the performance of its task the Committee has met with every obstruction which it has been possible for the beneficiaries of this vicious system to throw in its way.

"I deeply regret to say, but the truth compels the statement, that a faction of our party now in control of the government of the City of New York has expressed its opposition to such a statute. The motive which actuates this opposition is not now important, and in my judgment, is not obscure. However this may be, the opposition put forward by this faction ... is a direct challenge to the public spirit and sense of decency of the people of this State.

"If immunity from prosecution is given to certain of these witnesses the last excuse for permitting malefactors to prostitute constitutional provisions to the furtherance of their base purposes will be removed."

Governor Roosevelt called upon the Legislature to meet in Special Session and in his message urged the adoption of an immunity law. There is, however, in his entire message, not a single word of indignation or condemnation of the conditions disclosed by the Committee, nor one word of objection to the obstructive tactics of the Minority members, men of his own Party. The message was "icily regular" and "splendidly null." It did not as the New York *Times* hoped, "give vent to what must be his indignation at the betrayals of public trust by nominal Democrats who are undermining confidence in their party." He did not "flame out in wrath against plunder."

In response to the Governor's call the Legislature met in September, 1931. Nevertheless, after a flood of insulting oratory directed at Counsel to the Committee the immunity bills passed both houses. In each house but one Democrat voted in favor of their passage—Langdon Post in the Assembly and William Lathrop Love in the Senate. The bills were signed by the Governor and became laws.

CHAPTER XVI

THE BI-PARTISAN JUDICIARY DEAL

PRESIDING JUSTICE LAZANSKY of the Appellate Division of the Second Department was one of the speakers at the annual dinner of the Brooklyn Bar Association. He voiced the hope that the Legislature would pass a bill creating additional Supreme Court Justices. That was toward the end of January, 1930. Mr. McCooey was present representing the Tammany Hall annex, the Brooklyn Democracy. Meier Steinbrink, the Republican leader, seated himself at the Democratic leader's table. The newspapers reported him as saying to Mr. McCooey, "We ought to get together on this and see what we can do." Such was the beginning of an arrangement which in effect culminated in denying to the electorate of the Second Judicial District any freedom of choice in the selection of their judges.

Nobody has ever questioned the necessity for some additional justices. The Presiding Justice did not suggest any given number. Mr. McCooey thought six sufficient and so did Mr. Steinbrink. Senator Kennedy, a Democrat from Queens, introduced a bill for eight new judges. However, toward the end of the session Mr. Steinbrink called Mr. McCooey and told him the bill would not go through. Mr. McCooey received the news with silent stoicism. Thus ended the 1930 incident.

At the Bar Dinner in 1931 the Presiding Justice again made his appeal. This time Mr. Fred L. Gross, President of the Bar Association in Kings County, got busy. After a visit to Mr. McCooey by Mr. Gross, the Bar Association passed a resolution urging eight new justices. Mr. Gross reported back to Mr. McCooey, who said, "I will call a meeting of the county leaders, and tell them to get after their Bar Associations." Shortly thereafter, Messrs. Krug of Nassau, Rasquin of Suffolk, Rendt of Richmond, and Theofel of Queens, conferred with Mr. McCooey. Later, while on the witness stand during the Investigation, Mr. McCooey naïvely related how "We discussed the eight and how we should apportion the eight," one for Richmond, five for Kings and two for Queens; these leaders took it as a matter of course that all were to be Democrats.

It must be remembered that at this time the Legislature was Republican, whereas in Kings, Queens and Richmond the Democratic machine controlled the votes. The conferees recognized that the Republicans would not pass the necessary legislation if all the places were to go to the Democrats. With only eight, as Mr. McCooey said, "there wouldn't be enough judges to go around and give the Republicans recognition."

The problem raised by this political exigency was solved by increasing the number to twelve, thereby increasing the annual cost by $100,000 in salaries, for the four additional justices. There was, of course, no justification for such an increase in the budget unless there was an actual need for the justices to take care of the public business. Mr. McCooey's justification for this action, and increase was as follows:

> "We ought not to be the dog in the manger any longer. Let us give the Republicans recognition. I said, for example, if we get twelve, why shouldn't we give the Republicans in Queens one, in Nassau one, in Suffolk one, and in Kings two. I says that would be fair. That would be five Republicans and seven Democrats. . . . I will speak to Steingut, and I will ask him to do what he could to put it through."

Everybody realized that the Democrats had to make a "deal" with the Republicans to put through this legislation. Only one witness was frank enough to call a spade a spade, and that was John Theofel, the Democratic leader of Queens, who testified:

> "Q. How did you propose to get this Legislation?
> "A. Well, we had to make a deal with them."

Others more sensitive to the popular feeling that this was an outrage—a mere patronage grab, characterized it as a "gentlemen's agreement" or an "understanding." It was, as Theofel said, a "deal" and the leaders of both parties worked for it. Not only was it agreed that the division was to be "fair" —five Republicans and seven Democrats, but it was further agreed that the Republicans were to endorse the Democrats and vice versa. Character, ability and those other qualities essential to the good judge were not specified as necessary to be considered. Any one the Democrats or Republicans might name was to be endorsed by the other party. Obviously any reservation of the right of veto by either would have left the whole thing in the air. If such had been the case the Democrats could have rejected the five Republican nominees, put a full ticket in the field and elected them all. As a matter of fact, on August 7, 1931, six weeks prior to the nominating conventions, the Queens Executive Committee of the Republican party passed a resolution "that we endorse candidates recommended by the Democratic Executive Committee for the two Supreme Court Justices." Furthermore, the lists of candidates were not exchanged until two hours before the two conventions assembled and nominated the candidates.

The bill was passed in the Legislature on April 2, 1931. On April 3, and 18, 1931, respectively, the following excerpts were printed in news articles in the *Times:*

"Choice of men for the posts is to be made on a bi-partisan basis under an agreement between the leaders of the two parties. . . .

"Meier Steinbrink, present Republican leader of Brooklyn, is expected to step out of that post to receive one of the Republican nominations for Justice which is to go to his home county. Mr. Steinbrink would have the endorsement of Mr. McCooey for such a post under the arrangement. . . .

"Under the agreement reached between the Democratic and Republican leaders in the Second Judicial District, Brooklyn is to receive five of the new justiceships, Queens three, Nassau County two, and Richmond and Suffolk one each. The Brook-

lyn judgeships are to be divided by three Democrats and two
Republicans, Queens is to get two Democratic judges and one
Republican. The two judges from Nassau are to be Republicans.
The judge from Suffolk is to be a Republican and the one from
Richmond a Democrat."

The "deal" had been made. The Bill had been passed. The
division of the spoils was agreed upon. The public press fore-
told with accuracy the ultimate result. It was common knowledge. Civic organizations urged the Governor to veto the bill,
instead he signed the bill, saying:

"It has been suggested by more than one person that some
agreement or deal has been made between political leaders representing both major parties by which unfit candidates will be
nominated by agreement between leaders to fill these places this
Autumn.

"If the Governor of the State were to undertake to enter this
controversy in any way, he would be usurping the privilege of
the electorate to choose Supreme Court judges, and he would also
be interfering with the rights of parties or groups to nominate
their own candidates under the election law."

As it was evident then and as it developed, the "privileges
of the electorate" were to vote for the candidates selected for
them by Messrs. McCooey, Steinbrink, et al. Of course, this
selection was ratified by the conventions. There was but one
result—the practical disfranchisement of the electorate.

But, continued Governor Roosevelt, if there be a deal, "The
remedy is with the electors themselves to nominate independ-
ent candidates by petition." Not even the Governor suggested
that the "remedy" recommended by him could be effective.

The conventions met on September 26, 1931. The whole
City was startled then by Mr. McCooey's gift of one of the
justiceships to his son Jack. When Mr. Gross and the Brooklyn Bar Association rallied from its surprise it rejected the
report of its judiciary committee which had opposed any
"deal" and endorsed young Jack McCooey.

There were, however, some men with courage enough to

try Governor Roosevelt's "remedy." Immediately following the "rubber stamp" endorsement by the Bar Association, the "No-Deal" party was formed. Their candidates were James E. Finnegan, George D. Friou, Frank L. Tyson and Gerald Morrell.

As the election drew near the two great Bar Associations of Manhattan—the New York County Lawyers and the City Bar—held their meetings. Both recorded their unqualified disapproval. The bitterest struggle was at the County Lawyers meeting when former Judge Daniel E. Cohalan tried to amend a resolution introduced by Judge Seabury. The amendment was designed to embarrass Judge Seabury by putting him in the position of attacking Governor Roosevelt by placing the principal blame on the Governor. After sharp debate Cohalan's amendment was defeated. The resolution was carried by acclamation. It read in part:

> "Resolved, that the New York County Lawyers Association denounces the bi-partisan deal ... as a conspiracy against the administration of justice which in effect disenfranchises the electors. By bargain and barter ... the legislation creating an unnecessary number of judges was enacted and by equally odious methods the conspiracy has been consummated. ... The whole deal is a direct and dangerous assault upon the honor and integrity of the Supreme Court of the State of New York. ...
>
> "Resolved further, that in the opinion of this Association, the law should be changed so as to provide for the election of judicial candidates at a separate judicial election and by a separate ballot upon which the names of judicial candidates shall appear without party designation."

It will be remembered that early in April it was rumored that Mr. Meier Steinbrink would resign his leadership to run for a judgeship. The prevalence of this report caused him to say:

> "I shall not become a district leader or officeholder; to become the latter would be to subject my every act, no matter what it might be, to the inference that I was guided by the effect that it would have on my job."

A review of the march of events runs—his talk with Mr. McCooey at the Bar Dinner—his other activities looking to the necessary legislation—the passage of the Bill in April— his resignation of his leadership in June—seeking the nomination from Commissioner Kracke, his successor—his nomination at the "deal" convention in September—his election in November. Overwhelmingly eleced to one of the jobs he helped create.

Jack McCooey was also elected.

There was one result of the election that shows people can be aroused from their apathy—that upon occasion, even though hopeless, they can exercise the "privileges of the electorate," even though it be but a protest and not a "remedy." One hundred thousand people cast their vote for the "No-Deal" candidates.

Inextricably interwoven in this story of the deal is the story of John Theofel. He was a man of varied interests. The Borough and County of Queens has a population of some two and a half millions. The vote is overwhelmingly Democratic— it is cast for the candidates nominated by Theofel. From 1919 to 1930 he held the office of Deputy County Clerk. Prior thereto he had been a hotel-keeper. As Leader he modestly admitted he had been influential in making the late Mr. Newcombe, Surrogate of Queens County. It seems that while riding in a wheel chair at Atlantic City one day Surrogate Newcombe offered him the job as Chief Clerk of the Surrogate's Court, he saying, to quote Theofel, "You are the man that put me in politics, and this is the first opportunity that I have had to do something for you." Theofel demurred at accepting the job, saying on the witness stand in explanation of his refusal, "I didn't think it was good politics for the Leader of the Democratic party to take the first job that came along."

Times changed; Surrogate Newcombe died. Surrogate Hetherington succeeded to the office. Theofel accepted the office he had declined from Surrogate Newcombe. He admitted also that he had been instrumental in the appointment of Mr. Hetherington. With his acceptance came an increase in salary —as Deputy County Clerk he had only received from the tax-

payers six thousand dollars a year—as Court Clerk he was
to cost them eight thousand dollars per annum. He took office
July 14, 1930, and fourteen days later, on the 28th, the Surrogate asked that his (Theofel's) salary be raised to ten
thousand. In the Investigation, Counsel inquired as to the
basis for this increase after an incumbency of only two weeks.
Modesty overcame Theofel and he suggested that that was a
question for the Surrogate to answer, testifying:

"Q. You can't think of any good reason for it, can you?
"A. No, sir. . . .
"Q. On what ground did you oppose it?
"A. Because I didn't think it was good policy at the time.
"Q. It wasn't because you didn't think you deserved it?
"A. I got enough notoriety through this Committee, and I
didn't want any more through a raise in the salary."

In return for this salary Theofel is entrusted with the very
responsible duties of Chief Clerk of the Surrogate's Court
about which he could give no definite idea as to their nature
and extent while he was on the witness stand. As Counsel said
in his Intermediate Report to the Committee:

"Some idea of this man's unfitness for his office is indicated
by the following testimony given by him:
"Q. Well, now what other departments have you been re-
quired to supervise? Speak a little louder if you will.
"A. We have the Guardianship Department.
"Q. And the Probate Department?
"A. Yes, sir.
"Q. Now what else?
"A. I can't just recall offhand, Judge, the different depart-
ments.
"Q. There are other departments?
"A. Yes, sir.
"Q. But you don't offhand just recall what they are?
"A. No."

Some idea of how justices are created may be gleaned from
his testimony in regard to the elevation of District Attorney
James T. Hallinan:

"Mr. Hallinan is a friend of mine, and he would like to be a judge, and I suggested the promotion for him."

The potency of Mr. Theofel's suggestion is evidenced by the fact that Mr. Hallinan is now Mr. Justice Hallinan.

These two had been old friends. Theofel visited him when he became District Attorney to talk over the selection of the Assistant District Attorneys. He testified:

"Q. So that as a matter of fact, Mr. Theofel, with the exception of the Assistant District Attorneys that had previously been in the District Attorney's office, you recommended all the Assistant District Attorneys and all those appointees, except only the District Attorney's secretary...."

As it worked out it seems that Hallinan had no choice as to his assistants, except to agree with Theofel. This is deducible from the delicate answers he made to the following questions:

"Q. Then you remember this question being put to you: And Mr. Trainor, the private secretary?
"A. That is Mr. Hallinan's personal friend.
"Q. He did not have to consult anybody about him?
"A. He spoke about it, but I believe if a man wants somebody personal as his secretary he should have his choice.
"Q. But he did talk it over with you?
"A. He asked if the man was agreeable."

Another activity which Mr. Theofel admitted was an interest in an automobile agency run by his son-in-law under the name of Wilson Brothers, Inc. He was in fact the largest stockholder. This company had phenomenal luck in selling Pierce Arrows to men who were about to become or had just become public officials. In fact, it seemed that no official was complete without one. The County Clerk bought one. The District Attorney bought one. The Borough President bought one. The Sheriff, a Magistrate, etc., etc.

Between 1918 and 1928 Theofel was Treasurer of the Queens County Campaign Committee. In 1928 the Committee received $123,699.75 in campaign contributions. Out of these funds, Smedley, the Chairman, gave his secretary Kissling $6,000, and then said to Theofel,

"John, take a thousand for yourself."

After a recess, which interrupted his testimony, Theofel testified that Smedley had told him to take it "for your expenses."

CHAPTER XVII

PROFESSIONAL GAMBLING IN POLITICAL CLUBS

NEW YORK has long been known as a safe town in which to conduct a gambling establishment if one only knows the right people. Herman Rosenthal, a professional gambler of an earlier day, knew Lieutenant Charles E. Becker of the New York City Police Force. Becker owned a chattel mortgage on some of Rosenthal's properties. Differences and disputes arose. Rosenthal, due to a plan evolved and worked out by Becker, took a very sudden leave of life. While everything between the two was friendly and the city was quiet, Rosenthal, under Becker's guiding eye, had securely operated his gambling joint. The storm of public opinion against professional gambling, which had been brewing for a long time, gathered and broke. It became necessary for Becker to raid Rosenthal's place. Hence the ensuing disputes and the resultant death of Rosenthal.

Arnold Rothstein, of later days, ran a gambling game at times, among his other accomplishments such as the smuggling of narcotics and liquor. Such activities cannot and do not long go on in New York City without protection. It was at, or as a result of, a gambling party that Rothstein, too, met his death. Among the friends of Rothstein, although there is no proof of his presence at Rothstein's final party, was one Arthur "Baldy" Froelich. Froelich is well known to the New York police as a professional gambler, as is another friend of Rothstein known as Billy Warren. These two ran their gambling game at one time, in a place, disguised as a cigar store, known as Billy Warren's Club at 133 Third Avenue. For a while this "club" operated under a protecting injunction which restrained the police from interfering with or raiding the place. Over many another club, too, was the protecting arm of an injunction

against the police. This was all before 1927, at which time
George V. McLaughlin became the Police Commissioner. Mr.
McLaughlin was a strong and upright man and one fiercely
honest. Above all he eschewed politics and politicians. He was
not of their ilk. He would not do business with them.

Shortly after he took office he formed a confidential squad
whose duties, among others, according to his most trusted
lieutenant, Lewis J. Valentine, was to relieve the Commissioner himself "of investigating allegations of crime or mis-
conduct or corruption against members of the Department."
Another duty was the enforcement of the morals law and the
suppression of professional gambling. As to this last, Valentine says, "It was my particular duty to report to him on what
the situation was, to supervise them and do everything in my
power to suppress the gambling by professional gamblers in
the clubs" and to "suppress professional gambling anywhere
they found it." This squad, comprising some fifty or sixty men,
had as its head Captain Lewis J. Valentine and to him alone
they reported. He in turn reported directly to the Police Commissioner. The men on the Squad were unknown, of course,
to the other men of the Force.

At the time Mr. McLaughlin became Commissioner, rumors
that professional gamblers were operating throughout the
city were prevalent. Rumors of where they operated led him
to suspect that not only in "dives" did they carry on, but in
the political clubs as well. The suppression of this latter evil
was what Commissioner McLaughlin aimed at. He was not
a puritanical fanatic. He cared not a whit how much decent
respectable people played for in their games at home or in
their own clubs. The professional gambler was his mark, for
such was either a confirmed or an incipient criminal and, as
such, dangerous to the welfare of the inhabitants of the city.

In carrying out its duty the first step of Valentine's Squad
was to ascertain the number of big professional games there
were, where they operated and also whether or not they operated under an injunction. Applications made to the courts
resulted in the vacation of some of these injunctions. Com-

missioner McLaughlin had some of the other gambling clubs that were protected by injunctions watched and caused those who frequented them to be subpœnaed to appear at the District Attorney's office. This last named expedient had a discouraging effect upon the attendance of the "club members" or customers. In many cases those who controlled the clubs preferred to consent to the vacation of the injunctions and take their chances on further interference by the police. The number of big games was found to be around eleven. The list of names of the big time gamblers had such well-known persons on it as George McManus, Cokeley, Johnny Baker, Arthur (Baldy) Froelich, Billy Warren, Nigger Rue or Jack Price, Dollar John, Al Levy, and Gus Mayo. Their protection having thus been taken away, these people could no longer operate in any one known and fixed location and so they scattered to all parts of the city to lofts and other unknown places. Some conducted itinerant or floating crap games. Some located in the district clubs of the two major political parties. Among such clubs where these men were found, according to the testimony, were ex-Sheriff Farley's, City Clerk Michael J. Cruise's, and City Court Clerk Harry Perry's.

Valentine's men, having located the operators in these clubs, were directed to observe and watch and see who went in and who came out of these places. One of the first clubs watched was Thomas M. Farley's club on 62nd Street near First Avenue.

For some time prior to May 26 or 27, 1926, this place had been observed and all of the people going in had been watched. Finally, Keller, one of Valentine's men, on the 26 or 27 of May, 1926, decided to raid the club. It had been rumored that George McManus's game was going full blast somewhere on the east side. It was thought it might be here. As he (Keller) approached the club building, he noticed "the lookout which was generally in front of the Baldy Froelich game at 133 Third Avenue, . . . in fact, he was sort of a sign post."

Evidently the inside lookout had seen Keller, for as he neared the club a great commotion and scurrying began. After giving the inmates of the club time to run upstairs the door was opened, according to Keller, by Alderman O'Leary who, upon questioning by Keller as to the type of crowd in there, denied that they were gamblers. Keller, nevertheless, went upstairs to the top floor where he found all this crowd buzzing with excitement over their domino games which they were then busily playing. There was nothing Keller could do. All this was innocent enough. But before leaving he said to O'Leary, "I guess you have got me licked this time. I'll come back and I'll take you out with the patrol wagon if you don't keep this crowd of gamblers out of here." He asked O'Leary who the "boss" was and on being shown a large picture of Thomas M. Farley, now ex-Sheriff of New York County, on the wall, he looked it over carefully and then left saying, "Bear in mind, I am coming back." He did come back and that very soon.

On May 29, 1926, about two in the morning, Keller returned. He found the same lookout on the street and one by the name of Harry seated in a window on the second floor, with a clear view in all directions. Knowing he could not possibly get in through the door he left, and returned to First Avenue. Into some house he went, upstairs and out on the roof, over the adjoining roofs until he reached the club. There he lifted the covered skylight and descended into the clubrooms. He found there a pool table converted into a "craps" table with the odds posted on its sideboards, card tables and other gambling paraphernalia. These, of course, were disordered and scattered about due to the great rush that followed when those present found out that an officer was in the house. A gun was found on the floor, although its owner was never discovered. The interior of the place was found to be changed from the way it had been at the first raid, in that the windows were barred, and covered, heavy or "ice box" doors had been installed making the place almost raid proof. Farley denied that these improvements existed and said that such iron bars as existed in front of the windows were there merely to keep the kids of the neighborhood from "petty pilfering."

As Keller was about to take the prisoners out, he first met Fred L. Hackenburg, who was then Farley's attorney and represented Farley's district in the Assembly. Hackenburg protested but to no avail. Just then, according to Keller, Farley came up and said, "If I was here, I wouldn't let you do that." To this Keller replied, "It isn't too late yet. We haven't started yet. Just try to stop me. Now listen, you may be the executive member here, but upstairs! Keep out of my way until I am finished, or you will go into the patrol wagon with the rest of your gamblers from Third Avenue." Hackenburg and Farley stepped back and Keller loaded some twenty-six men into the patrol wagon and took them to the station house.

The next that Keller saw of Farley was at the station house where he (Farley) appeared and bailed out all of the prisoners. Of the twenty-six arrested and bailed out Farley knew nothing about them, so he said. Among these prisoners were Arthur (Baldy) Froelich, the friend of Rothstein and a well-known professional gambler; Gus Mayo, another gambler, who had had eight previous arrests under different aliases and had been convicted. These were the people for whom he put up bail, the amount of which, as to its sufficiency, has been questioned. Apparently he (Farley) made no effort to ascertain anything about these characters for whom he was willing to put up bail, for he agreed with the following question put by one of the Minority members: "I just want to ask at this point, . . . Mr. Farley, isn't it the custom of the executive members of the Democratic party, where there are arrests in the official clubhouse of executive members of those clubhouses, to bail out any one who is arrested in there with other members of the club?" His answer was, "Right."

This question by Assemblyman Cuvillier and Farley's answer thereto typifies the Tammany spirit of helpfulness to its members, whether or not the members are or associate with professional gamblers or any other type of criminal.

On the stand Farley said of all these men, and the list included Froelich, Mayo and Brown, that all they were doing there at two o'clock in the morning, "... was busy packing baseball bats, skipping ropes and rubber balls. ..." He also contradicted the testimony of the police officials and of his own former attorney, Hackenburg. Two or three weeks after the raid Hackenburg talked to Farley and protested against the continuance of gambling at the club.

At this point Counsel asked Hackenburg, who had taken the stand, if he referred in that conversation to the gamblers being present there, to which Hackenburg answered, "I didn't say that. We understood each other. I didn't need to specify."

It was in this conversation that Hackenburg complained to Farley about the structural changes that had taken place such as the peep hole and the heavy reinforced doors. His remarks fell on deaf ears, for all that Farley said, according to Hackenburg, was that if he didn't like the way the club was run he (Hackenburg) knew what to do as there were others who would like his place in the Legislature. Disgusted, Hackenburg turned and walked away. He is no longer in the Legislature. The close of his testimony shows he knew what Farley meant for he (Hackenburg) says, "Unfortunately politics in New York City is a great deal different than the philosophy underlying Thomas Jefferson. ... I started in life thinking politics was a mission. After a while I thought it was a profession, and now I discover it is not even a trade. In a good many places, Judge, it simply amounts to distributing the loaves and the fishes to those who are waiting for them."

Thereupon Judge Seabury put this question to him:

"Q. ... you believe that in your district, at least, Mr. Farley had something to do with its distribution?
"A. All of it."

The same type of raid was made on other political clubs, the same construction of the building to insure safety was noted, the same denials by the district leaders were made and the same games were played. In the McGuiness club, a departure from the usual raid was found, in that in the safe of the executive member or leader, Peter J. McGuiness, Alderman of the City of New York, were found the computations of the gambling profits. These are called the Play and Pay-off sheets. These showed that in Alderman McGuiness's club between January 1, 1927, and March 11, 1927, that $114,112.00 had been bet, $99,378.53 had been paid out and that the profit to the club was $14,733.47. Alderman McGuiness, however, denied any knowledge of the contents of the safe which bore his name. Another slight difference in the raids on the various clubs was noted in the fact that different professional gamblers were found. One great common and uniting feature of all the raids on all of the clubs was that, with perhaps two or three exceptions, all of the prisoners were invariably discharged.

There was one other political club infested with professional gamblers which merits a little space. This is the Harry Perry Club at 364 Bowery, New York City. Perry is at present the Chief Clerk of the City Court of New York.

On January 5, 1926, two confessed holdup men made affidavits to the effect that the money that they had stolen in the Donnelly Red Book Company holdup had been lost in gambling at Perry's and Farley's clubs. On January 24, 1926, a murder was committed in Perry's Democratic district club. Blood stains were found on the sidewalk adjoining the door of the club, blood stains were found on some of the inside doors of the club. The red trail of blood which led into the clubhouse was followed up the stairs into the large room used by the gamblers. In this room were found more blood stains. On the floor and tables seven empty .32-caliber shells, a fully loaded Smith & Wesson revolver covered with blood were found. Bullet holes in the walls on which hung the picture of the genial leader of this purely social and political club, Harry C. Perry, were also discovered. The murder is as yet, six years after its commission, unsolved. Perry, the district leader, testified that he knew nothing of the matter until subsequently informed of it by the police and that those who occupied the club on that occasion did so without his authority.

One of the frequenters of this club was the notorious Johnny Baker. He was one of Rothstein's men. The only time that Rothstein ever approached Keller was when he asked Keller to give this man, Johnny Baker, protection. What Keller said is not reported. From reports, his expressions on that occasion are not in the vocabulary of any stenographic reporter.

Thus there is seen another side of the Tammany System, the liaison between the political leaders, professional gamblers and other criminals. These men could not exist, nor have they ever done so, without the protection of the politicians. Keller summed it up in answer to Assemblyman Cuvillier's question as to who was interested and who protected these men by saying, "Certain politicians in whose bailiwick or district the game might be operated."

Before Counsel dismissed this subject he called the attention of several witnesses who had been district leaders to their bank accounts and asked them to explain the source of the money deposited therein.

The first is Thomas M. Farley, ex-Sheriff of New York County, of whose later financial activities more will be heard. Farley testified that between January 1, 1925, and September, 1931, he had no gainful pursuits other than his official jobs, the salaries of which in these years ranged annually from $6,500 to $15,000. He later qualified this by saying that he had made some $20,000 as real estate commission. Assuming, therefore, that he received $15,000 for these six years nine months and assume, further, that he actually received these commissions, the total amount he could legitimately have received would be about $120,000. Nevertheless, his total deposits over this period from January, 1925, to September, 1931, amounted to $360,660.34. His explanation was as remarkable as was mysterious the acquisition of the money.

He kept his money at home in a "tin box." Whenever he needed money he would take it out. Later he would replenish the box. This was his practice and habit. Senator John J. McNaboe, one of the Minority members of the Committee, asked him this question:

"Q. In your account you had a revolving process, is that what I understand?
"A. Put it in and take it out."

Counsel summed up this whole unexplained amount by asking Farley the following questions:

"Q. Where did that cash come from ... ?
"A. Well, that came from the good box I had.
"Q. Kind of a magic box?
"A. It was a wonderful box."

At the conclusion of Farley's examination the next day, Mr. Cuvillier, in one of his partially inaudible but incessant interruptions, said that this line of questions should not be allowed as it was purely private business and therefore without the scope of the Committee's jurisdiction. To this Counsel replied in substance, that the total amount of Farley's deposits far exceeded his admitted or known sources of income and further, that Farley had no explanation except the "tin-box" story. Therefore, because Farley was a public official it was within the scope of the Committee's jurisdiction to find out how these moneys were acquired.

Michael J. Cruise, present City Clerk of the City of New York, was another of the district leaders whose club had been raided. He described himself in the following terms: "I am clear as— Q. Clear as what? ... A. Clear as crystal; honest, upright life, all my life." Prior and up to 1909 he had been in the liquor business. Since 1921 he had had no income other than that derived from his official positions. Like Farley, his salary was comparatively small. Nevertheless, in his six-year period, during which time these gambling raids were made, he had by some mysterious process deposited a total of $217,246.91. He had discounted notes to the amount of $73,488.15 which left him net deposits of $143,758.76. Of this amount all that he could have deposited as salary would be $63,000, leaving him some $80,000 to explain. His explanation had not the crystal clearness of his own character. He said that it was savings or money given by his own club to him for "Charity or any other purpose I saw fit to use it for." He had no records of any kind to substantiate any part of his story. It was typical of all the stories these people told explaining the acquisition of their money. One thread, however, ran through all their stories. Whenever the transaction was a legitimate one, no matter when it happened and no matter how unusual it may have been, these people always produced every bit of documentary evidence. All their other transactions were wrapped in a dense cloud of obscurity and mysteriousness and always incomprehensible and unintelligible. Cruise's story was like the rest.

James A. McQuade followed Cruise on the stand to tell his pathetic tale. He is now Sheriff of Kings County, although at the time of his testifying he was Register of that County.

At the time of the raid on his club, he testified, some of the men who were arrested were up in the library reading books. However, he never registered a single complaint to any one about this unfair and unjust arrest of members reading books. He just let it go.

Register McQuade was shown to have deposited in six brief years the sum of $510,597.35. He explained this by saying that everything over his comparatively small salary was borrowed. The necessity for this continuous borrowing amounting to some $400,000.00 was because, through a series of pathetic and untimely deaths and other circumstances he had had cast on his shoulders alone, the entire support of thirty-three other McQuades. His charitable nature was boundless, for not only did he so manfully accept the burden of thirty-three McQuades, but he used to bail all the neighbors' children whenever they got into trouble. He even bailed out the man who wrecked McQuade Brothers brokerage firm by stealing $260,000.00.

His method of support of the thirty-four McQuades was unique. He would borrow from A, and when A would call for his money, he would borrow from B to pay A. Then when B would request his money he would borrow from C to pay B and so on down the alphabet. He took no account of the fact that this process would keep his balance at exactly the same level, for as soon as he deposited a certain amount he withdrew an equal amount. He kept no records of any kind to substantiate this story. He was asked: "Have you any data or writing that will enable you to designate the persons from whom you borrowed these sums?" to which he answered: "A. As the money was paid off, it was off my mind, and I thanked God for it and destroyed anything I might have." Counsel then asked him: "Q. Why do you give thanks to Divine Providence?" To which he replied: "A. I give thanks to Divine Providence for permitting me to pay those people who were kind enough to loan me the money." His explanation ended there.

Harry C. Perry in whose club the murder above mentioned occurred was the last of these district leaders to tell his story. In four years and nine months he managed to deposit $135,061.50, of which $21,366.17 was salary. The balance was accounted for by inheritance to his wife from his mother- and father-in-law, by bets, by money left on the mantelpiece and borrowing and then borrowing again to pay back the original lender. Captain Valentine testified that in a conversation Commissioner Warren had with Perry about the gambling in his club that Perry said to him (Warren), "When the organization takes care of my captains, I won't have to run a crap game in my clubhouse."

Charges were later preferred against Perry on the ground that he was unfit to be Chief Clerk of the City Court. He was tried by three Democratic Judges of the City Court. He was defended by Jeremiah T. Mahoney, an ex-judge and a power in Tammany circles. All of the charges filed against him were dismissed after the trial and he was retained in office.

These, then, are the stories of three district leaders in whose clubhouses raids were made by the police for running gambling games and harboring professional gamblers.

CHAPTER XVIII

THE Counsel and the Majority of the Legislative Committee had been honestly and industriously at work trying to clean house since the first of August. The Minority had been equally industrious in endeavoring to prevent the disclosure of the truth. It took no intelligence to see that the Tammany Organization could sweep its municipal candidates into office. Organization would inevitably win over apathy. The old cry rang out once again, "We've got the votes; what are you going to do about it?" Tammany, confident of victory, was delighted to make the continuance of the Committee an issue and then when it got out the regular organization vote and elected its candidates, to hail it as a vindication, because every election that Tammany wins is hailed as such.

What little there was left of the Republican Organization, hoping to capitalize politically the work of the Committee, deliberately made it an issue.

None realized more fully than Judge Seabury that the Tammany Organization would win. Support of the Committee and its work, while highly gratifying, was of no political consequence because it was not organized. From a lawyer's viewpoint he was not ready for the verdict of the jury. He had not finished putting in his proof. He was determined that the Republicans should not seek partisan advantage at the risk of impairing the usefulness of the Committee. He called Colonel Edward C. Carrington, the Republican nominee for Borough President, to the stand, to prove that the Republicans were just as bad as Tammany Hall when given the chance to do business with the City.

Colonel Carrington's activities linking him to the City dealt

with Pier 32—the same pier which David Maier, ex-convict
and friend of Mayor Walker, in conjunction with William
Hickin, President of the National Democratic Club, secured
for the North German Lloyd.

Carrington, who introduced himself to the Committee as
"the next President of the Borough of Manhattan," had
formed a syndicate which had purchased the assets of the
Hudson River Navigation Company. Prior thereto and in
1926 his corporation had employed the law firm of Gibboney,
Johnston & Schlechter to protect its interest in the condemnation proceeding which the City had instituted to acquire
Pier 32. Although Colonel Carrington was very quick to
assert that everything was above board, he was just as quick
to seal the lips of those who were the Company's attorneys
at the time, under the claim of privilege between attorney and
client.

After the Company was reorganized, Mr. Carrington took
an active interest, as was natural, in fixing the lawyer's fees.
He rejected their first proposal that was based on a sliding
scale of 1% of the first $1,100,000 obtained in condemnation;
4% of the next $400,000, 6% of the next $500,000, 25% of
the next $500,000, and 50% of everything in excess of
$2,500,000. He wrote to another member of the syndicate
the following: "Gibboney has submitted a sliding scale proposal in the matter of the compensation of our legal friends
in respect to the pier." He added that it was "grossly unfair
and inequitable" and that he hoped "to see a member of the
law firm" and get the matter adjusted satisfactorily. At no
place in the correspondence was the attorney's name mentioned. Why? It may be that in the custom of Judge Olvany's
firm, as discussed later, to hide its identity in reference to
certain city matters the answer will be found. Colonel Carrington continued: "It is unnecessary for me to impress upon
you ... the importance of the connection that we have made
in this matter." Counsel questioned him as to the importance
of this firm. His testimony on that subject was as follows:

"Q. What was the importance of the connection that 'we had made with that firm'?

"A. Judge Olvany was President of Tammany Hall, the leader of Tammany Hall, a very important connection (laughter). We had the property that the City was about to condemn. . . .

"Q. You surprise me, Colonel, do you mean that Judge Olvany, by reason of his bossship at that time, might have influence with the Dock Department and others that would facilitate you in getting a higher price from the City of New York for this pier than you otherwise would have gotten if you had depended upon your strict legal rights?

"A. As a simple-minded man I would think that the leader of Tammany Hall would not stand in the way of a citizen getting a fair price for his property from some of the institutions and departments of the City of New York. . . .

"Q. In other words, you wanted the political influence of the head of Tammany Hall in your business proposition, didn't you, frankly?

"A. I didn't want him but I approved of their selection.

"Q. So that we have it this way: that you personally did not want the benefit of the political influence of the boss of Tammany Hall, but since the corporation had made that selection you approved of it, is that right?

"A. That is right.

"Q. Now don't you think, Colonel, that you are somewhat in error in saying that you did not want this political influence? Didn't you want it?

"A. Well, we wanted all influences that would enable us to get a fair price for this property."

Carrington, endeavoring to evade Counsel's questions as to the "importance of the connection" with Olvany's firm, said the importance of this connection was merely to get the Corporation Counsel's office under way. Counsel then suggested that perhaps the Dock Commissioner who at that time had before him the appraisal of one James R. Murphy (who had been retained by the company), that the property was worth $3,177,000, was an important factor. It appears that after Commissioner Cosgrove had received this appraisal, Mr.

Murphy suggested that Colonel Carrington have the Hudson River Navigation Corporation purchase, for $65,000, a piece of property in Sunnyside, in which the same Michael Cosgrove, the Dock Commissioner, had an interest. Murphy, so Mr. Carrington said, represented that it could be resold for about $125,000. Colonel Carrington testified that when the proposition was first offered to him, he immediately rejected it. In this testimony he was contradicted by one of his attorneys, John J. McManus, who later testified, in substance, that he and Mr. Carrington discussed this proposition in November, 1927, while they were at lunch. Mr. Carrington told him at that lunch that Mr. McKenzie, the General Counsel, had refused to participate in it. After lunch they went back to Colonel Carrington's office. As to their discussion there he (McManus) testified as follows in response to Counsel's questions:

"Q. Well, let us come to the Long Island property.

"A. Carrington laid down a paper in front of me and asked me to O.K. on the top of it if it was in shape as a legal document as to form.

"Q. Now what was the paper?

"A. It was a contract for the purchase of real estate, contract of sale.

"Q. The real estate being in Long Island City?

"A. That is right. . . .

"Q. What did you say in reference to that suggestion by Colonel Carrington?

"A. I asked him if this was the same matter he spoke to me about at lunch, and he said yes. I then told him I would O.K. it as to form if he would put one clause in there, and that clause was that I understood it was inland property in Long Island City which the night line had no use for, and was being bought for the purpose of inducing the approval of the purchase by the City of New York of Pier 32, North River. We all signed our names as witnesses, so that in the event of any claim coming along in the future by the City, we could all very easily and inexpensively be indicted.

"Q. Indicted for what?
"A. I assume bribery, from my conversation with Carrington."

Later when Colonel Carrington was recalled, he denied everything that Mr. McManus had testified to except the one essential fact that while this transaction was pending, he was offered a piece of property, in which Commissioner Cosgrove had an interest, for $65,000.

Mr. Carrington was very zealous in giving people to understand that he, the candidate for Borough President on the Republican Ticket, had not, in this transaction, personally retained Judge Olvany. Indeed he had gone to the Committee Headquarters to deny a statement to that effect which had appeared in the public press. This denial he reiterated while on the witness stand. To this denial he added the statement that he had no desire to conceal Olvany's connection with this transaction. Again there was a conflict in the face of which Carrington drew the following subtle distinction, "I simply was not advertising the fact; was not concealing it."

On June 24, 1927, he telegraphed Mr. F. J. Lisman, a well-known banker in New York, the following message:

"Had satisfactory interview G. Will see Judge Blank next week.   Carrington."

Colonel Carrington testified that "G" referred to Gibboney;

"but," inquired Counsel, "who is Judge Blank?
"A. Judge Olvany."

Mr. Carrington had testified that from the time the syndicate was organized up to June, 1927:

"I think my entire activity was confined to dealing with Mr. Gibboney's firm and one visit I paid to the office of Olvany, Eisner and Donnelly up to that time. I think that is the lone activity that I showed in the whole ... anything connected with the Company. That particular time I had personal matters of my own that took up all of my time."

The events described below will test the accuracy of this testimony:

On July 1, 1926, he received a wire from Mr. Gibboney to the effect that he (Gibboney) had made an appointment for him (Carrington) to see Judge Olvany the following week. For some reason Mr. Carrington could not kep this appointment and so the next day he wired Mr. Gibboney to make it for Monday, the 12th, which was done. On the 9th, Mr. Gibboney wired him "cannot see Judge Monday," to which Mr. Carrington answered: "Make appointment next Wednesday. Must see Judge."

To sum up his testimony thus far: As early as the first of July, 1926, he had sought an appointment with Judge Olvany. This date had been changed several times, and the last postponement was secured at Colonel Carrington's request and insistence that he "must see Judge." In fact, he came all the way from Chicago to see Mr. Olvany. Counsel asked him, then:

"Q. And you discussed this whole matter with him, didn't you?"

to which he replied:

"A. I discussed nothing with him except tarpon fishing."

although on the very next day he wrote Mr. Lisman:

"I had a satisfactory talk today with the party whom you understand I was to see in person."

It was, as appears from the following letter, at this very conference that he (Carrington) personally retained Judge Olvany's firm. It is written to Mr. Lisman and dated June 30, 1927.

"On July 14th last I had a conference with Messrs. Olvany, Eisner & Donnelly in respect to handling Pier 32 for the Hudson River Navigation Corporation, and employed this firm to represent the Company in the matter of the sale of the pier to the City...."

This he said was not employment; "I ratified the appointment of Gibboney's firm and Olvany's firm as his associate." Wasn't it the other way round, Counsel suggested, Gibboney the figure-head and Olvany's firm the real attorneys? Mr. Carrington replied: "I can't answer yes or no to that," whereupon Counsel continued reading from this same letter:

> "Gibboney was merely selected as a figure-head in the matter. . . ."

The Colonel was still doubtful so Counsel continued reading:

> "I don't think that any real progress has been made in the matter of the pier, and I place no credence and have no faith in the statement. . . ."

Counsel then resumed questioning:

> "Q. Wasn't the man in whom you placed faith and credence, Judge Olvany?
>
> "A. Judge Olvany's firm. . . .
>
> "Q. Do I understand now that the only reason that led to the selection of Judge Olvany was your knowledge of his legal ability?
>
> "A. He had political influence and his firm had legal ability. . . .
>
> "Q. A happy combination, isn't it? (laughter).
>
> "A. A happy combination, that is it exactly."

After those questions and answers Counsel went on reading from this letter, as follows:

> "A conference has been arranged next Tuesday with the Dock Commissioner, which I understand was suggested by Judge Olvany (such is Mr. McKinnon's statement to me), and both Mr. Gibboney and Mr. McKinnon have expressed the wish that nobody except themselves represent our Company at this conference."

By Counsel:

> "Q. Now don't you think that this letter shows pretty well that you were the reason for bringing Olvany into the situation?
>
> A. The letter speaks for itself, Judge."

From the negotiations up to the date of the letter, it looked
as though a private sale to the City, without condemnation,
would be put through for $2,534,412.20. Such a price was
satisfactory to Commissioner Cosgrove, in fact he had signed
a contract to buy the Pier at that price. The Sinking Fund
Commission did not approve this contract. On motion of Commissioner McKee, on June 6, 1928, it was referred back to
the Commissioner. As to this series of events, Colonel Carrington testified:

> "They sent it, as I recall, back to the Dock Commissioner,
> after I had agreed to an abatement of $100,000 at the suggestion
> of Mayor Walker."

Another contract was then entered into for $2,400,000 but
that also was never approved. Thereupon condemnation proceedings were instituted by the City which later resulted in an
award of $2,000,000 to the owner. Prior thereto the contract
with Gibboney's firm as to the fee to be paid had been changed
to a straight 6% on whatever amount was recovered. On the
basis of the award, this agreement would entitle the attorneys
to $120,000, which, according to Mr. Carrington, was to
include Judge Olvany's fee. Just how much the "figure-head"
retained and how much went to Olvany's firm was not sus-
ceptible of being shown.

At the fall election the Tammany machine, as was natural,
actively aided their upstate allies in an effort to elect a majority of the Assembly—the lower house of the State Legislature. This—so that having control of the Assembly they
could kill the Committee and stop the Investigation. That
effort failed as did their effort to defeat Assemblyman Abbot
Low Moffat of the Fifteenth District in New York City, who
was then a member of the Committee and up for reëlection.
Into this District Tammany sent its "floaters" and "re-
peaters." Evidence of this illegal practice was presented to
the Counsel by The Honest Ballot Association. When the
Committee convened on October 29, 1931, Counsel an-

nounced his intention to present the evidence to them. Assemblyman Cuvillier and Senator McNaboe showed their insincerity and their efforts to prevent these disclosures by objecting to this line of evidence. The Joint-Resolution specifically empowered the Committee "to investigate all matters and things affecting the methods and practices relating to the ... election ... to public office. ..."

After the turbulent Senator McNaboe had been silenced, Counsel called Frank C. Keen of 56 East 59th Street, the day clerk in the Hotel Nassau. He testified that fourteen people had falsely registered as living at that hotel. Not one of them was a resident therein. Upon the registration list two had said that they occupied room 26, two room 14, and others gave numbers in the twenties to thirties. The obvious falsity of this registration was disclosed when it was shown that the room numbers started at 201 and went to 223, then 301 and 323 and so on up to 801 to 823. Five of the group had gone to the booths together and registered one after another, then two and then the other seven. Senator McNaboe recorded his resentment at these disclosures by saying, towards the conclusion of this evidence:

"What is going through my mind is this, what does all this mean? ...

"I am trying to find out. It doesn't mean anything to me."

The next witness was Carmine Schafer Ciapetta, Superintendent of an apartment house at 65 East 96th Street. Ten people had falsely registered as living there. Eight of this group registered one right after the other. Two of this group, a man and woman representing themselves to be husband and wife, registered together. Not one of these registrants was a tenant. Four out of the nine apartments were vacant.

Four people registered from 1408 Madison Avenue. Two of them said they lived together in Apartment 2-A, the other two also said they lived together in Apartment 2-C. Both of these apartments were vacant. First, one pair registered together and shortly thereafter the other two.

This same procedure was followed by another group of four, only this time the first pair said they lived together in Apartment 6-A of 19 East 98th Street, and later when the other pair registered they said they lived together in 6-A of the same house. As a matter of fact, this was also a vacant apartment.

These two election districts where this group of four registered are within two blocks of each other. It is not at all unlikely that these "floaters" took advantage of this proximity of these booths and registered in both places.

The recapitulation presented to the Committee strongly corroborates this theory. In one district James Kennedy registered from 56 East 59th Street, age 27, twenty-seven years in the State and County and last voted from 100th Street and Broadway in 1928. In another district William Kennedy registered from 65 East 96th Street, age 27, twenty-seven years in State and County, and last voted from 100th Street and Broadway in 1928. In a third district James Regan registered from 1408 Madison Avenue, age 27, twenty-seven years in State and County and last voted from 100th Street and Broadway.

Herman Glick registered from 56 East 59th Street, age 32, last voted from 204 Manhattan Avenue, business address 342 Greenwich Street. In another district Samuel Berger registered from 65 East 96th Street, age 32, last voted from 204 Manhattan Avenue, business address 342 Greenwich Street. In a third district Henry Gold registered from 1408 Madison Avenue, last voted from 204 Manhattan Avenue, no business address given.

Jack Weber registered from 56 East 59th Street, age 31, last voted from 209 West 118th Street. In another district Joseph Singer registered from 65 East 96th Street, age 31, last voted from 209 West 118th Street. In a third district Samuel Cohen registered from 1408 Madison Avenue, age 31, last voted from 209 West 118th Street.

There was, of course, no fact to indicate whether these people enrolled as Democrats or Republicans. The result of the facts proved before the Committee was notice to the "floaters" that they had been discovered so they absented themselves from the polls on election day. Tammany concentrated its attack on Moffat, the Republican Assemblyman from this district. Notwithstanding this attack, his (Moffat's) majority over his Tammany opponent was some 3,000 —three times greater than his majority in 1930. When the returns were in, it was found that Assemblyman Moffat, from the 15th District, was the only Republican Assemblyman elected throughout the entire City.

The new Democratic leader in that district was John F. Sheehy. He had been chosen personally by John F. Curry and, with his support, had been elected over the former leader, Frank Briarly, who had been censored by Mr. Curry for permitting the election of Assemblyman Moffat and Senator Samual Hofstadter in 1930. Evidently something more than changing personalities was necessary to change defeat to victory. Tammany needed in this district a leader who occupied an official position, one who could distribute patronage to Tammany workers. When, therefore, Governor Roosevelt was forced to remove Farley, Curry seized the chance to strengthen the organization and suggested the appointment of Mr. Sheehy. Accordingly, the Governor gave this "plum" to Tammany. Fraudulent registration was only one of the methods used to win the election for Tammany.

A still more despicable device was the manner in which they used the money raised for unemployment relief to further their campaign. The exposé of this situation before the Committee was a blow at the very foundation of the Tammany system. If it were shown that Tammany deprived the needy of relief funds, it was very serious for the Organization.

The facts developed in relation to this situation are as follows:

By means of a Charter amendment, the City appropriated a fund of $10,000,000 in April, 1931. This was to be distributed through the offices of the Department of Public Welfare. Only those were eligible who were "legal residents of the City and voters therein for at least two preceding years" and then only if the applicant was "head of a family with dependents." Each applicant was, by the terms of the law, required to produce a certificate to the effect that he had voted for at least two years. Registration began April 21 and stopped May 2. During that period 19,757 had registered. That was as many, if not more, than could be cared for under this appropriation.

Rumors of scandal in the administration of this fund had arisen and had been given wide currency in the public press. The *World-Telegram* went further than most, especially in connection with its administration in Staten Island, ruled over by Borough President Lynch. It was, therefore, to the Borough of Richmond that Counsel first turned for investigation. For intensive study the week from June 1 to 6 was selected. The total amount paid out during that week was over $41,000. This sum was distributed to approximately 2,250 persons. Of this number, the political affiliation of some 1,247 were all that could be determined. Of these 1,247 persons, 1,134 were enrolled Democrats, 109 were enrolled Republicans and 4 were Socialists. Expressed in percentages, of the total number on the payroll for that week, 90.9% were Democrats, 8.7% Republicans and .4% were Socialists. It is significant to note that the ratio of enrolled Democrats to enrolled Republicans in the Borough of Richmond was four to one.

The district leader is the backbone of the Tammany system. He is continuously urging his claims for a share in any patronage available for distribution. The more people he can provide with city jobs the stronger his hold on the district vote. This $10,000,000 fund was just so much more for them to distribute judiciously. As appears from the percentages given above, the leaders took care that most of this money, when distributed, should secure a new vote or insure the continuance of an old vote. During the time of registration the

district leaders practically lived in the five Borough Halls.
The statutory requirements were a dead letter where the
applicant was one who could be used in building up the organization. Witness after witness took the stand and told a story
substantially the same: That he registered but didn't get a
job—that he then went to the district leader, who took him up
and introduced him to the Commissioner, which resulted in his
getting the job, because he was an enrolled Democrat. He had
no dependents, but that prerequisite was conveniently over-
looked. Some witnesses testified that they even lived with
their parents in their own homes; that their families had one
or more automobiles; that the money they earned and received from this fund was not used to help support the family
but merely as personal pin money, and lastly that they were
not even qualified to vote, which, in itself was a distinct violation of the law under which this fund was appropriated. It
was developed that many of these young men who obtained
this relief came from families having five or six prospective
voters. Perhaps that, too, was coincidence. Thus, while the
needy suffered, young men such as these were made beneficiaries of these moneys in violation of the clear requirements
of the law.

Bad as that was, Tammany did not stop there. In the one
week investigated by the Committee, it was found that 123
people, as said above, received pay whose registration cards
could not be found. The amount thus paid out to these persons
in this one week was approximately $2,000.

In Manhattan, Samuel Levy was elected Borough President. The fact is, he had more money to distribute than any
other Borough President of the City. Another fact is, that he
received one of the greatest pluralities ever recorded in an
election to that office. Prior to the elections, Mr. Delaney,
Secretary to the then Borough President, distributed many of
these cards to local Democratic political clubs. The local
leaders had to keep their "vote" contented, which at this
particular time was tantamount to getting them on the relief

fund payroll. The leaders solved the problem presented by the fact that although registration had closed in the preceding May, they back-dated these cards to April. Various witnesses assured the Committee that the only purpose of this dating back was "to keep the thing in uniform." Obviously this business was irregular—the club was not a designated place of registration—the registration had closed months before, and further no one, save a Tammany leader, checked to see whether or not the applicant fulfilled the requirements for employment.

The Yucatan Democratic Club in the 26th Election district of the 19th Assembly District, whose leader is Martin J. Healy, sent out a letter to the voters, reading:

> "It is the purpose, aim and object of the Yucatan Democratic Club to strive to foster the welfare of its members; with special emphasis on the relief of those who are unemployed, and special efforts towards securing for them positions in the city government; the appropriation recently made by the Board of Estimate in which the sum of $20,000,000 was made available for the unemployed, is positive proof that the City Government under the Tammany Hall Administration is determined that no deserving member of the Party shall suffer acute want."

No one could have summed up the Tammany viewpoint better or more concisely. Tammany used the fund for the benefit of its members—it used it as a campaign fund—it was distributed from the local clubs and through the local leaders to "deserving" members of the party—through its manipulation of this fund it gave to those with means of their own, and kept it from the needy.

Immediately after the Committee's hearing on this matter, Charles F. Kerrigan, acting under Mayor Walker's order, endeavored to refute the proof which had been offered before the Committee in relation to the 123 people receiving pay from whom no registration cards could be found. To repel the attack was the Administration's first thought, and not, as one might expect, to punish the offenders. The seriousness of this matter was evident in the very violent session held in relation to these 123 people and in the statements then made by Mr. Kerrigan in his attempt to confuse and confound the proof offered. However, after the battle on this subject ended and the noise died down, only the facts as had been proven before the Committee remained. Tammany had deprived the needy and used the fund for campaign purposes.

CHAPTER XIX

THE LEASE OF A CITY PIER

WHAT do you do if you want a lease to a City pier?
You hire Special Counsel. Why? Not because there
are complicated questions of law, but because of
political connections. How much does it cost? Fifty thousand
dollars at least. What does Special Counsel do for this fee?
Goes "uptown" to "Fourteenth Street" to "Tammany Hall."
Does Special Counsel keep all of this "legal fee"? No. There
is testimony in the record that Hickin (William H. Hickin,
President of the National Democratic Club) "was very definite with respect to the fact, that a part would have to be
passed on." The record contains no denial of this statement
by Hickin himself.

William H. Hickin was called to the witness stand and given
a chance to explain his side of the story, but he refused to
testify unless he was granted immunity from prosecution for
any crime which might be disclosed by his testimony. To sign
such a paper, would leave him open to the possibility of criminal prosecution, and would, he said, be a "tacit admission"
and carry an "implication" of wrongdoing.

In lieu of any testimony from Hickin, it was proven by other
witnesses and canceled vouchers that the North German Lloyd
paid him $50,000 by check dated May 13, 1931. This check
was deposited in his personal account on June 2, 1931. On
June 15, he drew a check to bearer for $10,000. This check
he then endorsed and cashed. On June 24, he drew another
check to cash for $35,000. This too, he endorsed and cashed.
These two checks accounted for $45,000 out of the $50,000
paid him. Where did it go? Was part of it "passed on"?
Hickin could have told the Committee what happened to this
money. He chose not to, however.

In 1930, Mr. Hickin renewed a bank loan for $50,000 at six per cent interest. In July, 1931, the bank pressed him for payment. Hickin said, according to the bank's employees, that he was not in funds and, therefore, not able to make any reduction. By October he had reduced it to $44,000 when it was again renewed. At this time there was another conversation between the manager of the bank and Hickin. The former testified:

> "Q. Well, what did he say about his financial resources or assets by comparison with what they were a year ago?
> "A. He said there was no change....
> "Q. ...And did he tell you, that since that time he had received a fee of $50,000?
> "A. No, he did not....
> "Q. Did he make any statement to you as to his estimate of his income for the year 1931?
> "A. Yes, ...$35,000."

In his Intermediate Report to the Committee, Counsel thus characterized this payment:

> "A review of the situation makes it perfectly clear that the 'legal fee' was a subterfuge, under the guise of which a large sum of money was extorted from the Steamship Company as the price of political influence, without which the lease would not be granted."

The North German Lloyd is a financially responsible company. It had its own general counsel, one Edgar W. Hunt, and it was also represented by the law firm of Cohalan & Stanley.

Theoretically all that one has to do to procure a lease in New York City is to apply to the Dock Commissioner and if he approves the application, it then comes before the Sinking Fund Commission. If he disapproves, application may be made directly to the Sinking Fund Commission. So far as the procedure and proof are concerned, the matter could, to all appearances, easily have been handled by the company's counsel. Whatever may have been the appearances, the fact is that the company made its application to the Dock Commissioner. Nothing ever came of this.

It was at this point that one David Maier, an ex-convict and a politician of seeming influence, assured the North German Lloyd Company that he could get the desired lease. It would, of course, cost two or three thousand dollars for "lawyers' fees." Yet, in spite of Maier's assurances that he would try to keep the cost down, the "lawyers' fees" finally rose to $50,000.

The testimony discloses that Maier was the principal factor in this business. However, when he took the stand, he was very deprecative of his part. He was very free in denying statements attributed to him by other witnesses. He was hesitant and evasive in all of his testimony. To impeach his credibility, Counsel put into evidence his conviction for bribing a witness to give perjurious testimony. This, then, was the man that the North German Lloyd Company was driven to in order to obtain a lease in New York City.

The Mayor was instrumental in the granting of this lease in that he gave his approval to it so that it might come on for a hearing before the Sinking Fund Commission. Mr. Schuengel, the resident director of the company, testified that he talked with the Mayor about it.

In his private examination, Maier was asked this question:

"Q. And you never had any part in any negotiations with any steamship companies of any interests, that is what your testimony boils down to?

"A. None whatsoever. . . ."

Because this testimony was shown to be untrue, he withdrew it in the public hearing and substituted this answer:

"A. . . . Up to the time that Mr. Hickin entered into it, I was the only one negotiated. From the time that Mr. Hickin entered into the case, I absolutely had nothing to do whatsoever with the lease proposition. . . ."

Thus was raised an issue of veracity between David Maier and every other witness who testified on this matter.

In July, 1924, Mr. Schuengel went to Europe. During his absence Mr. Hunt, the attorney, managed the company's affairs. Both he and Mr. Weber, secretary to Mr. Schuengel, were instructed to keep the latter informed of the progress made in the application for the lease.

On July 11th, Weber cabled Mr. Schuengel:

> "Saw M. in the evening. Total now 25,000. Reason collision 250,000 party...."

Weber testified that this meant that he had seen Maier who told him that to procure the lease it would cost the company $25,000. The next morning it seems that Maier and Hickin called on Mr. Weber and repeated the demand for $25,000. The excuse given for thus raising the price was that another lawyer had assumed to represent the company in securing the lease in return for a fee of $250,000. From the cables between the North German Lloyd offices here and in Bremen, and other circumstances, there arose the inference that Mr. Herbert Smythe was interested in this negotiation. However, after this matter was developed at a public hearing and discussed in the press, he issued a statement to the effect that he did not recall the circumstances. Certainly such excerpts from the testimony, as the following, indicate that the company was alarmed because of his apparently unauthorized intervention. It was reported in messages to the head office in Germany: "He" (Maier) "also stated definitely that Mr. Smythe would not be in a position to cause any difficulties whatsoever"; "inform 250,000 party are not interested any more."

Another excerpt from one of the letters, showing the fears of the North German Lloyd officials, reads as follows:

> "For the moment we consider it best not to say anything to Hickin about the Smythe application, ... if we told him of it, there is always the possibility that he and Smythe will get together and combine their interests to our detriment, giving us a further squeeze. In a word, we must not assume that anybody concerned will act honestly and in good faith."

In the face of these statements was the relationship between Hickin and the company really that of attorney and client? Generally, clients who have not a hundred per cent faith in their attorneys, terminate the relationship. The reason for the continuance of this association is found in the wisdom in having political influence. The company, apparently, didn't retain Hickin because they knew him or because of his outstanding legal ability, but because, under existing conditions in New York City, they found it wise to do so in order to have even a chance of obtaining the lease they sought.

When Hickin and his associates had been assured that the Company would pay $25,000, they endeavored once more to increase their fee. One Captain Jarka, who had handled the stevedoring for the Lloyd Company for years, testified that Maier came to him sometime in 1924 and told him that he would have to give up his profits under his contract as part of the consideration for the Lloyd Line getting the lease. Jarka thereafter, in a conference with Mr. Hunt, offered to contribute $10,000 if he could continue to handle the stevedoring for the Company. This new move made Lloyd increase their offer to $30,000 provided there would be no attempt to "muscle in" on Jarka's contracts. This conference was followed, a few days later, by a cable from Mr. Hunt to the Bremen office, reading:

"Talked with Doozl" [Maier], "lawyer's fee cannot be less than 20,000 [dollars]. Paying 15,000 additional will eliminate Jarka...."

to which the Bremen office answered:

"Suggest you authorize utmost $20,000 lawyer fee plus addition to same amount if necessary to eliminate Jarka."

Mr. Hunt then had a further talk with Maier, after which he again cabled Bremen that Maier had assured him that $40,000 would cover the whole thing, that is both the lawyer's fee and elimination of participation in Jarka's profits. In spite of these assurances Maier did not procure the lease for the $40,000 and so Mr. Hunt had to wire Bremen again the following cable:

"Lowest figure obtainable including everything is $45,000."

During the testimony in regard to this pier lease, the Minority were pursuing their customary course of turbulent interruption. In one of his speeches, Assemblyman Cuvillier, in an unguarded moment, showed that he was really not so insensible to existing conditions as he consistently pretended to be, for he said:

"You know, the matter of securing a pier in the City of New York is a Herculean job; that it takes a considerable lot of work, and I may say political influence...."

When Maier first came into the picture, he assured both Mr. Hunt and Mr. Schuengel that "he stood in a good position with them," i.e., City officials. In July, 1924, when Maier and Hickin demanded $25,000, Mr. Schuengel wrote to Mr. Hunt protesting that Maier had repeatedly asserted that it would only "cost us a few thousand; that under no circumstances would more enter into question." Further testimony showed that

"... he [Maier] repeatedly emphasized that the T. group... was under obligation to him...."

Both Mr. Schuengel and Mr. Hunt were led to believe that the people back of Maier and Hickin were the Tammany group.

Mr. Hunt testified that he first met Hickin in July, 1924. At that meeting, Hickin told him, according to his testimony, that "he had had considerable experience in negotiating pier leases; he had acted for several companies in that connection." Mr. Hunt further testified that he was not persuaded to accept Hickin because of "any information about Mr. Hickin's outstanding legal ability," but that "assurances as to political connection" influenced his selection. The retaining of this Special Counsel was, as Counsel to the Committee characterized it, "... just a cover and a disguise ... under which this money was to be paid to this group." The Company's main reliance was on Maier—even though Mr. Hickin was their attorney for securing their lease and the one to whom they paid the fee.

Throughout the testimony of the North German Lloyd representatives, it was Maier who was referred to as the "go-between." It was Maier who was to be "active in fixing the terms of the contract." When it was first intimated that some other stevedore was going to "muscle in" on Jarka, the North German Lloyd looked to Maier to make a counter-offer of a cash payment in lieu of the elimination of Jarka as stevedore for the Line. The Company's memorandum on this subject bears this out and reads, in part, as follows:

"Maier will submit this but thinks it will not do."

It was to him he said that Tammany was under obligation. It was his political affiliations that counted with them. His were the "assurances" upon which they placed so much reliance. Maier's position with the new leader, George W. Olvany, was alleged to be good. He backed up those "assurances" by saying that this lease was the "reward due and promised him for thirty years of service, and that nobody can take it from him." It was Maier in the beginning, it was Maier in the middle, and it was Maier at the end.

As promises and "very good assurances" went unfilled, and as the price unceasingly rose, Mr. Hunt experienced disgust. Both Mr. Hickin and Mr. Maier had told him that "everything was in good order and that the matter would be put through" quickly. Hunt reported to Mr. Stimming, the General Director of the Company:

"... With regard to such assurances from such sources, I can only confirm what Mr. Schuengel has no doubt already told you, that inasmuch as we are dealing with intermediaries, not principals, we are compelled to take what they say ... and wait a reasonable length of time to see how their promises work out. ... I very much fear (because of what I have heard of other cases), that intermediaries are always a necessary evil in such matters and that we can scarcely expect to be able to deal with principals...."

The intermediaries were David Maier, and the lawyer, William H. Hickin. The principals back of Maier were the political people, the "T" group, which was alleged to be Tammany Hall. The confidence which the North German Lloyd had in their necessary lawyers is expressed by the following quotation from the same letter from Mr. Hunt to Mr. Stimming:

"As to the increased demands for compensation, I was not surprised...."

Even after an agreement had been reached at $45,000, Mr. Hunt wrote to the Bremen office:

"In fact I had difficulty to obtain agreement to any sum less than $50,000 and am shivering now with fear lest a report come in that the reduction to $45,000 will not be approved."

Mr. Hunt testified that the Lloyd Line had piers in many different cities of the world, but that in no other port in the world had they "had to employ a lawyer or undergo any special expense of any kind in hiring a pier anywhere, except in New York City."

The year 1924 passed and still the Company had no pier. In 1925, through the negotiators, they came closer to the "T group." President Heineken of the North German Lloyd, had "a confidential conversation with the Secretary of Tammany Hall, Mr. Eagan, and with Mr. Hickin, during which conversation both gentlemen assured him that the pier was assured for the Lloyd." On that subject, the testimony is as follows:

"Q. You didn't think you got the pier from the Secretary of Tammany Hall?
"A. No....

"Q. But you did understand, did you not, that it was a good as well as a comforting thing, to have the assurance from Mr. Eagan, the Secretary of Tammany Hall?

"A. Yes."

The Lloyd's two new boats, the "Bremen" and "Europa," were due to arrive in the spring of 1929. The need for a pier was desperate. Finally, over the heads of the "intermediaries," an attempt was made to establish direct communication with George W. Olvany, the leader. This is shown by Mr. Schuengel's answer to Counsel's question:

"A. And I tried all means and every purpose at my disposal to get a pier and therefore I thought in addressing such a letter to the Leader of Tammany Hall, and too, I think I have addressed a similar letter to Mayor Walker, it would bring matters along."

This, then, and the testimony following, demonstrated clearly who were the real people controlling the granting of a pier lease in New York City. To them Mr. Schuengel was finally driven. His testimony showing such to be the case follows:

"Q. What did you think Mr. George W. Olvany had to do with aiding you in getting a pier . . . ?

"A. Well, having the understanding that the City members —the City Officials are members of Tammany Hall, that he might ventilate the question to the club there. . . .

"Q. You believed Mr. Olvany would have influence with the officials of the City who would have to pass upon the granting of the lease?

"A. Yes.

"Q. Therefore you wrote him to ask him to use his influence with those City Officials?

"A. Yes."

Mr. Schuengel testified that he did not leave it all to Mr. Olvany, but that he himself talked to the Mayor. It was to the Mayor, also, that Mr. Schuengel prematurely wrote in September, 1930 (approval of the lease was not given until November 12, 1930), in part, as follows:

"... I was informed that the Sinking Fund Commission has passed on our lease.... This was indeed good news for me, and as I feel that the action of the Commission at this time was largely due to your personal interest in the matter, I wish to express ... my ... sincerest thanks and appreciation...."

Thus, after these vicissitudes, the North German Lloyd secured their lease for a pier, demonstrating that what it requires in New York City today to procure one is political influence and a lawyer's fee, a part of which "is to be passed on."

CHAPTER XX

WHEN George W. Olvany became Leader in 1924, he was hailed as the Leader of a "New Tammany." When John F. Curry succeeded him in 1929, it was lamented as a return to the old Tammany of Croker and Murphy. After the public had seen them both on the witness stand in 1931, it concluded that, though Leaders change, Tammany itself never changes. It stays the same with the people of the city its perennial victims.

Judge Olvany—a title he had earned by six months' service on the Bench of the Court of General Sessions—had known William E. Walsh, the then Chairman of the Board of Standards and Appeals, for a period of approximately fifteen years. In his capacity as Leader, Olvany admitted that he felt free to make "constructive suggestions" to city officials. Chairman Walsh sometimes would drop off at Tammany Hall on the way home. He and Olvany would then discuss some complaint that had been made to Olvany about the Board's action. Counsel summed this situation up, thus:

> "Q. Have we got it this way: That the only occasions in which you ventured to interject your personality into the situation by getting in touch with the Chairman of the Board, was where you acted in what you believed at least was in deference to your sense of duty, to help some one that needed help?
> "A. As a good Samaritan."

These discussions, of course, dealt with decided cases—properly reviewable only in the courts—and pending cases other than Olvany's.

The firm of Olvany, Eisner and Donnelly was at the time interested in cases pending before the Board. Success in these cases meant large fees, failure brought little or nothing. Judge Olvany testified that they never discussed the cases in which he was interested—that he never played the part of the "good Samaritan" for his clients. Nevertheless, the method of Olvany's retainer in some cases—his unwillingness to testify or produce his firm's books and records—and finally his own statement that to do so "might do us very serious damage and the client very serious damage"—are facts to be considered in determining the accuracy of his statements.

There are in force today certain building and zone regulations, designed to promote the general health and safety. These are promulgated by the Board of Estimate and Apportionment. In recognition of their inelasticity, the Board of Standards and Appeals was created with power to permit variations therefrom. These variations range from permission to build a wall without set-backs, to a change in the use of a given plot. Only the Board of Estimate has power to re-zone a given district, so as to permit the erection of a business building, in a district theretofore limited to residences. The practice and procedure before the Board is simple. Its practitioners are not limited to lawyers. Indeed, a layman, Doctor Doyle, was its most successful pleader.

The five members of the Board are appointed by the Mayor. In rendering their decisions they possess wide discretionary powers. If this is exercised in favor of the applicant, it may substantially enrich him. A Tudor City may arise where stand the homes of the poor. Thirty thousand square feet of rentable space, capable of producing an income of one hundred and fifty thousand dollars a year, may be added to a Fifth Avenue office building.

As Leader, Judge Olvany had influence in the selection of the members of this Board. To the appointees he made "constructive suggestions." His law firm was much sought after in connection with matters before the Board of Standards and Appeals.

Fred F. French—best known as the builder of Tudor City—wanted permission from the Board to depart from the established regulations in such a way as to add more rentable area to the French Building, at 551 Fifth Avenue. Acting on the suggestion of a friend he retained the firm of Olvany, Eisner and Donnelly, on a contingent fee,—this being as he said: "a habit of my own. I always do that if I can." He spoke with Mr. Donnelly, one of the partners, over the telephone, and then being busy, he asked an old friend of his —John N. Boyle—to look after it from that time on. When Mr. French first took the stand he made a great show of defiance to Counsel, but finally was driven to admit that one of the factors leading to the selection of this firm was the knowledge that Judge Olvany had political influence. In making this admission he stated quite emphatically, as was most natural, that he did not employ them to exert any improper influence.

Although the Olvany firm had been retained and it was to them that Mr. French looked for results, the retainer agreement was made between the 551 5th Avenue Corporation and Mr. Boyle. While the contingent fee was a habit of Mr. French, this acting through an intermediary—which had the effect of disguising their interest in the matter—seemed to be a habit of Judge Olvany's firm. Perhaps the reason for this method of being retained may be found in the following testimony of Mr. Olvany on the subject of his firm's taking business in which the city was involved:

"We avoided City matters as much as we possibly could. We took very few matters at all. I didn't think it was right for us to take them.

"Q. You mean because of your position in the organization?

"A. Yes. . . .

"Q. And the natural influence you would have over commissioners and heads of departments?

"A. Exactly so. We could have had all the business we wanted, but I refused to allow this business to come into the office."

In addition to the fact that the retainer agreement was in Mr. Boyle's name and not that of the firm, it is also true that the name of Olvany, Eisner and Donnelly nowhere appears on the official record of the proceeding. Therefore, unless one knew that Mr. Boyle was acting for Olvany's firm, one could never have known that they represented Mr. French before the Board. In spite of the statement of Messrs. Olvany, Walsh and Donnelly's, it must be obvious that the firm did not appear "openly" in this case.

Apparently all of the correspondence in regard to this matter was carried on by Mr. Boyle. In reporting the progress of the matter to Mr. French, Mr. Boyle said:

> "We have very good assurances that what we want will be granted."

When he was pressed as to who gave him these assurances, Boyle answered that Mr. Donnelly had so reported to him.

> "Q. Did he state to you the sources from whom he had received these very good assurances?
> "A. He did not and I never asked him."

Mr. French did not know what was meant by "assurances," but he thought they might have received some cheerful news from "the head of the Building Department." Mr. Donnelly testified, "I never gave any assurances except to say to him my opinion of the problem."

Even though the fee was contingent upon success, Mr. French had at the very outset given Boyle a check for $35,000 to be held in escrow. This Boyle deposited in a "special account." When the case was finished and it came time to pay, Boyle drew his check to cash, cashed it and turned over the currency to Mr. Donnelly. Boyle says this was at Mr. Donnelly's suggestion; the latter contradicted him, however. Boyle supported his statement by saying that he wanted a receipt, some "evidence to prove the payment." Donnelly himself admitted that he wanted the cash, but insisted that he merely acquiesced in Boyle's suggestion. Here follows the reason why he wanted cash, given for the purpose of show-

ing that there was no intent on his part to conceal his firm's
identity in this matter:

"Q. It would have been entirely agreeable to you if he paid
you the amount by check?

"A. No, we had reached a policy where I did not desire,
where moneys were received by other lawyers, and they were to
make the payments to us, to have any checks outstanding with
our endorsements on, which might be capitalized or exploited,
and I was perfectly willing, in accord with that policy, to take
the cash. . . .

"Q. Wasn't the purpose of asking that the payment be in
cash, in order to keep your identity and connection with that case,
or the connection of your firm with that case, from being disclosed?

"A. It was not."

It is not known whether or not the firm of Olvany, Eisner
and Donnelly still adhere to that unusual practice today.

Before Mr. French could build Tudor City he had to get
favorable decisions from both the Board of Standards and
Appeals and the Board of Estimate. Having in mind his recent success in regard to 551 5th Avenue, his thoughts
turned once more to Mr. Donnelly. After several appointments to discuss the matter, the following terms were agreed
upon: If all the relief sought was granted the fee was to be
$100,000. However, in this case French deviated from his
habit in regard to contingent fees and it was stipulated that
there was to be a payment in advance of $20,000. French
testified that he understood Olvany, Eisner and Donnelly
were to represent his interests and to "openly appear as of
record, of counsel." Donnelly had a different idea and "for
convenience" he invited one Frederick J. Flynn, a lawyer, to
come into the case. In spite of French's understanding, it was
Flynn who appeared openly on the record and not Olvany,
Eisner and Donnelly.

Although Flynn had not been retained, the contract was
made in his name. There was no indication thereon that he
was to hold any part of the fee in trust or that he was to

give one cent thereof to Olvany's firm. Within a month, however, the firm had taken an assignment. Oddly enough the assignment was in blank. The fear of Flynn's untimely death was the explanation for this assignment. Both Flynn and Donnelly tried to have it appear that this arrangement served some useful purpose in the practical handling of the case. However, both were driven to admit that nothing was done that could not have been done just as well had the retainer been taken in the firm name, rather than in Flynn's, and then assigned to them in blank.

The first payment made under the contract was by a check to Flynn's order in the sum of $20,000. He first deposited this, and then drew and cashed his own check for a like amount. Flynn, who said his bank was only three blocks from Mr. Olvany's office, stuffed the bills in his pocket and delivered them to some one there. This, he said, was pursuant to a "practice on a prior transaction."

When the second payment fell due, the firm, of course, held the assignment from Flynn, but for some reason did not notify the French interests of this fact. Again, this payment was a check to Flynn—a deposit—a check to cash—a withdrawal in bills, and then the long trudge of three blocks from bank to office. Although it was an established, it was, nevertheless, an unusual custom! Forty thousand dollars paid by French through Flynn to Olvany's firm without a receipt from them and without a scrap of paper evidencing their retainer. There was nothing except a verbal retainer of the firm—a written retainer with the firm's nominee—and then an assignment in blank of the fee from their nominee to them. It does seem a difficult method of employing a lawyer.

It once looked as though the firm was going to receive a check for the third payment which they would have to endorse. Not so, however. When Flynn got the check for $10,000, he simply endorsed it in blank and delivered it to Olvany, Eisner and Donnelly. To have merely deposited this in their firm account would have been a departure from the usual way of doing business, so to pursue their usual method,

they took the check to the National City Bank and bought
with it a cashier's check for a like amount. This check, without endorsement, was deposited in the firm account. Not even
Mr. French or his corporation was to have a check with their
endorsement thereon. Perhaps they felt that this was one of
the occasions on which their firm name might "be exploited
or capitalized."

These first three payments, totaling some $50,000, were
made while Judge Olvany was Leader of Tammany Hall.
Forty thousand in cash, and ten thousand by the cashier's
check above described. This case was in his office during the
period when Mr. Olvany said in reference to his firm's
handling City matters, "I wouldn't allow this business in the
office"—"I didn't think it was right for us to take them"
because of his position in the organization and the natural
influence he would have over heads of departments. However
that may be, the fact is that after he ceased to be Leader of
Tammany Hall, his firm acknowledged to French the existence of the assignment and took the last payment—$25,000
—not in cash, but by a check made out to the order of Olvany, Eisner and Donnelly. This was in settlement of all
claims by reason of their services under this contract.

In regard to the No. 1 Wall Street matter, we again see
the hand of George W. Olvany, the Tammany Leader. To
build it, as envisioned by the architect, it was necessary to
secure favorable action by the Board of Standards and
Appeals. Employment of special counsel was considered at
a conference between the principal officers of the Corporation, the architect and counsel for the Corporation. The
Counsel for the Corporation is a well-known and established
firm and there can be no doubt of its competency to prepare
the necessary papers and argue the matter before the Board.
At the conference, however, some one suggested Olvany's
firm as "experienced and successful in that line," and it was
agreed that they should be retained. The member of the
firm in this conference knew that Olvany was "head of Tammany Hall," and he "had it in mind" as he testified:

"Q. You knew he was the head of Tammany Hall, didn't you?

"A.　I knew that, certainly.

"Q. Well, that is an important consideration. Did the fact that you knew he was the head of Tammany Hall, did you have that in mind when you agreed to the suggestion that that firm should be retained?

"A.　Why, certainly, I knew it and had it in mind.

"Q. Was it in your judgment one of several factors which worked contributory to that selection, so far as your vote was concerned?

"A.　I don't know that I can tell that."

This gentleman then set out to effect the retainer on satisfactory terms. He interviewed one of the firm's associates, Mr. Ostreicher of Judge Olvany's firm, as follows:

"I asked him if his firm would act as counsel with us ... he stated that they would and we discussed fees. He then stated that they desired to act through Mr. Rorke."

Again the retainer was taken in the name of the firm's nominee. The payments on account were made to the nominee. Their share was delivered to them by a cashier's check payable to a member of Olvany's firm. This retainer called for a fee of $25,000, but for some reason an extra $5,000 was added on at the end, bringing the total amount up to $30,000. This sum was paid by two checks—both to Rorke's order— one for $5,000 and the other for $25,000, which he (Rorke) deposited in a "special account." Here again in paying Olvany's firm, resort was had to the purchase of a cashier's check—this time to the order of Mark Eisner in the sum of $27,000.

The 257 Madison Avenue Corporation wanted to change the zone in which their property was situated so as to permit the erection of an office building in the block on Madison Avenue between 37th and 38th Streets in New York City. According to Alexander Rorke, the lawyer employed to handle this matter on behalf of Olvany, this application was opposed by "the Murray Hill Association, the Morgans, the Bakers, the Delafields, and the Foxes and the Tiffanys" who wanted the district to remain a residential one. Previous owners of this property had made the same application through such reputable members of the Bar as Rudolph R. Loening and the firm of Taylor, Knowles and Hack. In April, 1925, the Board of Standards and Appeals had unanimously denied this application. In this the Board was sustained by the Supreme Court in April, 1926.

The corporation, however, was not disposed to accept this defeat. Mr. Alfred B. Jones, acting for the corporation, sought to retain Mr. Thomas E. Rush, who was at that time the President of the National Democratic Club, to carry the matter on to the very end. For one reason or another, Mr. Rush did not accept the retainer. Upon Mr. Jones' request for advice, Mr. Rush directed him to Olvany's firm. At the first conference, as was testified to, Olvany told Mr. Jones that his firm could not take the case because it did not practice before the Board of Standards and Appeals. Later, Judge Olvany told him they would take it provided they could select the associate counsel. To this Mr. Jones assented. Mr. Alexander Rorke was selected by Judge Olvany's firm. The fee as finally fixed between Mr. Rorke and Mr. Jones was $25,000, although at Jones' first conference with Judge Olvany a different amount had been suggested.

With Olvany behind him, Rorke got to work and where other perfectly reputable and capable lawyers had failed, he won. The Board reversed its position and was again sustained in its action by the Court.

Once again the passing of bills took place, but this time Mr. Rorke did not base it on custom or precedent. He swore that the suggestion that cash payments be made "came from somebody in the [Olvany] firm." But his memory failed him at that point and he could not identify the person who had made this suggestion. The total cash fee paid to the firm in this case was $16,500.

There may have been other and similar instances of Olvany, Eisner and Donnelly's legal practice before City Boards, but further inquiry was blocked. It seems that records that took up too much room when the firm had moved had been destroyed. The other records could not be checked because of Judge Olvany's refusal to produce them. His reason, he said, was not because he or his firm had anything they wished to hide, but because he was forbidden by law so to do unless the clients would sign a waiver of their privilege in having their matters kept secret. Although Judge Olvany professed a desire to coöperate in every way, he admitted that he had not asked his clients to waive their privilege against his disclosure of confidential communications. The names and addresses of the firm's clientele who had retained him in City matters Judge Olvany placed within that category.

In ten cases before these City Boards, and one condemnation case hereinafter described, the aggregate fees paid by the clients were $251,706.28; of this the Special Counsel, Rorke, Flynn, etc., received eighteen per cent or $45,237.50, while the firm itself received $206,468.78 or eighty-two per cent. Of their share they received $120,000 in cash, $35,-937.50 in cashier's checks, and one check for $24,931.28 made out to one of the partners. The only payment made by check to the order of the firm was the final payment of $25,000 in the Tudor City matter. This, however, was paid after Judge Olvany had ceased to be Leader of Tammany Hall.

From the testimony of Messrs. Donnelly and Olvany, it is evident that some of the payments for services rendered by the firm never went into the firm account—payments as high as $20,000 went into the individual account of one or other of the partners. Nevertheless, from January, 1925, until November, 1931, the deposits in the firm account reached the total of $5,283,032.19. The Leader of Tammany Hall gets no compensation from the organization, nor is it necessary.

In the excellent report of Mr. Leonard Wallstein on the condemnation "racket" he says:

"The existing method of valuing land acquired by condemnation by the City of New York is extravagant, wasteful, unfair to the City, frequently unfair to the private owner and beneficial to nobody except favored and profiteering real estate and political interests, or a combination of both, with their supporting staff of specialists, lawyers and expert witnesses."

Judge Olvany's firm conducted these condemnation cases, too. This is one case: A corporation bought a piece of property. It paid $25,000 in cash and gave a purchase money mortgage of $185,000. James F. Donnelly of Judge Olvany's firm was originally the attorney of record. A little later, however, Flynn was substituted in his place. From that time on, the firm name of Olvany, Eisner and Donnelly nowhere appears on the public record of the proceeding. Within ten months after the purchase the land had been condemned. From the award the client received $634,601.25 as principal and $120,891.54 as interest, a total of $755,492.79.

Under the original retainer Judge Olvany's firm would have been entitled to

"two per cent upon any award and interest obtained herein up to and including the sum of $360,000 and twenty per cent of all of said award and interest whatsoever the same may be in excess of said sum of $360,000."

Due to some reason not necessary to go into here, the firm of Eagan and O'Reilly had been retained, so the fee had to be split. Therefore, instead of receiving some $86,000 for their services the firm got but $33,000. Once again the firm worked through special counsel in a City matter and once again the fee went not to the firm account, but into one of the accounts of one of the partners.

Thus closed the story of George W. Olvany, who so well characterized himself as the Good Samaritan, for has Tammany not been, since its inception, a charitable institution—with no beneficiary of its charity specified?

CHAPTER XXI

HOW BUSES CAME TO STATEN ISLAND

STATEN ISLAND lies about two or three miles from the southernmost tip of Manhattan, known as the Battery. From the City proper it is reached only by ferryboat. It is quite large, about seventeen miles from the northernmost point to the southernmost boundary and for the most part three and a half to four miles wide. It is very hilly and rather sparsely settled save at St. George where the ferry docks.

For many years its only transportation facilities were the trolley lines and a railroad. Of course, as population has grown inland and spread, these facilities have become inadequate to meet the consequent needs. Hence, the necessity for more trolleys and railroads or buses. The cost of supplying trolleys and railroads was prohibitive; therefore transportation by motor bus was the only method of solving the problem of transportation.

Into this picture as early as 1925 came one Minthorne T. Gordon. He was later to become known as the "pioneer" of buses on Staten Island. By turn he had been a broker on the Curb Market in New York, a stock salesman, an insurance broker and finally a bus operator. Prior to his arrival on Staten Island, pursuant to talk with McGinley, the then Democratic leader, Gordon had operated a line of buses on Chambers Street in New York City under a permit from the Department of Plant & Structures. For this operation he had purchased six buses, paying $15,000 in cash by borrowing it, and leaving some $30,000 due thereon. This purchase was made by and through the Tompkins Bus Company which had been formed sometime early in 1925.

In about March or April of that year Gordon took his company and buses over to Staten Island and began to operate under another and distinct permit from the Department of Plant & Structures. This permit was merely a temporary license and was in no sense to be construed as giving him a permanent right to operate a bus system, as does a franchise. Nevertheless, he operated. He had no permit nor franchise from the Board of Estimate which is absolutely essential to a legal operation, nor did he have a Certificate of Convenience and Necessity from the Transit Commission which, too, is absolutely essential. It is seen therefore, that Gordon started his bus operations on Staten Island without the necessary legal permissions. Later on in 1925 he obtained two successive short term permits from the Board of Estimate both of which were illegal because the provisions of the Charter requiring prior publication of notice of the application had not been met. In violation of the permit illegally granted on July 31, 1925, which provided that the rate of fare should be five cents, the Tompkins Bus Company on November 22, 1925, raised its fare to ten cents. The excuse given by Gordon, while on the witness stand, was that if that had not been done there would have been no bus operation as far as he was concerned in Richmond County which is the same thing as Staten Island. He was asked:

"Q. That was just a permission that the company conferred upon itself by reason of what they deemed the necessities of the case?
"A. Absolutely."

This permit expired on December 31, 1925. Nevertheless, the Tompkins Bus Company ran without any kind of permit or franchise until it was granted its franchise on July 28, 1927. In attempted justification of this procedure Gordon testified about the payments made by his Company for license plates, pretending that these license plates in themselves gave some sort of authority to operate. Another violation by the Tompkins Bus Company of its permits was its failure to pay the amounts required to the City as compensation. These defaults continued until shortly before it was granted its franchise and then made up, because, under the provisions of the Charter it could not be granted a franchise while in arrears, so it is quite apparent why these defaults were then made up. The checks of the Tompkins Bus Company in payment of its employees had been dishonored for insufficiency of funds. At the time the franchise was granted the Company was about $300,000 in debt to the bus manufacturers and other creditors. It ran on a hand-to-mouth existence. Unless it had a very good business on Saturdays and Sundays it could not even buy its gasoline to run the buses. It paid its current obligations with borrowed money. As late as March 6, 1928, on one of the numerous hearings on its application before the Transit Commission for a Certificate of Convenience and Necessity, Commissioner Godley in his opinion rejecting the application, said:

> "Although the applicant promised from time to time to produce responsible people who would undertake this financing and although numerous adjournments were granted to enable it to produce such proof, the evidence was never offered and the applicant finally rested with the production of its balance sheet as of November 15, 1927, to which reference will be hereafter made. ... In short, the proof adduced shows that the applicant has no funds with which to finance the operation which it has undertaken under its franchise and has no definite plan of procuring such fund.
>
> "In my opinion, no certificate should issue unless the applicant show financial ability and resources as will give some assurance that the operator will furnish efficient service commensurate with public needs.
>
> "I, therefore, recommend that the application be denied."

On the other hand, the Staten Island Coach Company, Inc., which had an application before the Board of Estimate and Apportionment at the same time as the Tompkins Bus Company, was a much stronger company financially, as appears from the Reports of the Board of Transportation to the Board of Estimate, which read in part:

"Financially, this petitioner has the support of the Richmond Light & Railroad Company and other interests affiliated with that Company. It also has an experienced staff of employees accustomed to handling traffic on a major basis. The petitioner has evidenced a readiness to meet any reasonable demand of the City as to requirements of bus equipment and operation and further the Company (Staten Island Coach Company) states it prefers a ten year franchise grant, but would accept an eight year franchise grant. It justifies its preference for a ten year grant upon the ground that it plans to buy equipment so as to take title thereto, necessitating an investment upwards of one million dollars, that the immediate returns on this investment, if any, would be small, and that to realize anything at all on its bus project requires several years for development."

It is apparent from a reading of these reports which was the better company. These were official reports and were before the Board of Estimate and Apportionment of which Borough President Lynch was a member, when it voted the franchise to the Tompkins Bus Company. Earlier in the history of the granting of this franchise to the Tompkins Bus Company, Mr. Lynch had voted against such action. According to the testimony, Mr. Lynch made no protest against any of the violations of the permit of the Tompkins Bus Company, nor did he protest against the raising of the fare by that Company without lawful reason. As to this last, Gordon testified that, if Lynch had dared protest, he would have been "run off Staten Island." There were still further reasons why the Tompkins Bus Company should not have been given the franchise and the Staten Island Coach Company should have been granted it. It is merely necessary to enumerate, not elaborate them.

The first concerns the routes and mileage to be covered under the terms of the franchise. The routes of the Tompkins Bus Company will be first considered. Its routes purported to cover some eighty miles. In fact, its routes covered only fifty or fifty-one miles according to Gordon's own testimony. This is due to two things. First: Certain routes paralleled existing trolley routes. For this type of bus route the Transit Commission has never granted a Certificate of Convenience and Necessity. The reasons for this are obvious. Second: The inaccuracies in the description of the routes to be covered by the franchise. For these misdescribed routes the Transit Commission refused to grant the Certificate of Convenience and Necessity except in one instance, and in this case the misdescription evidently was not called to their attention. Although the certificate of Convenience and Necessity had been granted in error as to this route the Bus Company did not operate it and when an attempt was made to force it to operate over this route the Tompkins Bus Company refused, and refused successfully to operate over this route on the ground of the misdescription in the application. On the other hand it was operating without right over routes for which the Transit Commission has refused its Certificate, nor was it paying a single cent to the City for such use, nor had Borough President Lynch nor any other City agency objected. As to the non-payment aspect of the question Gordon was asked:

"Q. So far as these routes that you are operating but which have not been certified or sanctioned by the certificate, how much do you pay to the City of New York?...

"A. We pay no tax on those particular routes....

"Q. As to the operation of those particular routes do you consider that you are conferring a favor upon the people of the City?

"A. I most certainly do.

"Q. Even though they get nothing?

"A. Certainly."

The second reason concerns the rate of fare. The Tompkins Bus Company had divided the Island into eighteen routes for which it sought the franchise, and further, had divided these routes into zones for which it charged five cents per zone. Of the eighteen routes, thirteen had two or more zones and one had four zones so that unless one rode only in the first zone the fare was more than five cents. The average fare was between seven and eight cents.

The final reason why the Tompkins Bus Company should not have been granted the franchise in preference to the Staten Island Coach Company lies in the comparison of the amounts to be paid to the City as compensation under the terms of the franchise. Under the Tompkins Bus Company arrangement, that concern was to pay to the City a minimum of $25 per month per bus operated; there was, however, no guarantee as to the number of buses which it would operate each month. As it worked out, even after the franchise was granted, the Bus Company was in arrears to the City.

On the other hand the Staten Island Coach Company was preferable for the following reasons: One: Its routes were to cover actually seventy-six miles as against fifty-one of the Tompkins Bus Company. The Board of Transportation reported to the Board of Estimate and Apportionment that these routes: "... will obtain for the more populated section of Richmond a reasonably comprehensive system of transportation for the Borough's present surface needs." Two: Its fare was a straight eight cent fare without zones and was no higher on the average than the fare of Tompkins Bus Company. Three: Its guarantee to the City yearly, as minimum compensation, was $12,000.

Therefore, looking impartially at the two corporations it is apparent that the Staten Island Coach Company was the better and stronger company. The question therefore arises, why did Lynch propose the franchise be granted to the Tompkins Bus Company, the same Company whose application for a franchise Lynch had previously voted against; the same Company which had been disapproved by the Board of Transportation, and the same Company which had been refused Certificates of Convenience and Necessity by the Transit Commission.

First, one indisputable fact is that Lynch and Gordon, the controlling interest in the Bus Company, had been intimate friends of long standing. Second, Lynch's specious claim that the Staten Island Coach Company was merely a "paper company." Gordon also used these very words. Lynch's testimony as to this was that for about a year previous he had endeavored to get Bertram G. Eadie, the President of the Staten Island Coach Company, to reduce the fare to five cents. If that were so he must have then thought the Staten Island Coach Company more than a "paper company." Third, a newspaper. This was the *Staten Islander*. This was at first a semi-weekly paper. Later it was changed to a daily under the name of "The *Staten Islander,* Inc." From time to time, so it was testified, Lynch had put money into it so that by July, 1926, he had invested some $60,000 and had come to the end of his financial rope. He had to get out. Since January, 1925, the applications of the two Companies had been pending before the Board of Estimate and Apportionment. From time to time, on Lynch's motion, final action on these two applications was postponed, the last occasion being on June 30, 1927, when action was again put off until July 27, 1928, the day on which the Tompkins Bus Company was granted its franchise.

Within a week prior to July 27, 1928, Gordon, Lynch's friend and the controlling interest in the Tompkins Bus Company took over, according to the testimony, the *Staten Islander,* Inc., agreed to run it, support Lynch politically, and finally, give him a note for $30,000 in payment therefor. All this, of course, Lynch indignantly denied, though his earlier denials had been evasions. The agreement was testified to by one Evan Taylor, reputed to be and admitted by himself to be Lynch's dummy on the *Staten Islander,* Inc. Further, a perfectly disinterested witness, one Godwin, testified from a memorandum made shortly thereafter, that he said to Gordon shortly after he had heard of the deal, "Well, I suppose you took over Borough President Lynch's interest in the paper with the understanding that the Board of Estimate would take care of the franchise when the time came"; and that Gordon answered, "Yes, that is right." Mr. Godwin also testified that Mr. Gordon denied that he had made that statement. He also said that Mr. Godwin had misunderstood him.

CHAPTER XXII

THE LIQUOR BUSINESS IN QUEENS

SINCE the time of the Triumvirs of Rome and Dumas' "Three Musketeers," men have banded together on innumerable occasions in bodies of three, to perpetrate some act or carry out some scheme, noble and chivalrous in its conception or ulterior and illegitimate in object. Nor has Prohibition overcome this human propensity, as the story now to be told will show. Two such sets of men are here dealt with.

The first triumvirate was made up of three men, by name Meyer Oxhandler, Max Hoberman and one John Doscher, Jr. The second, of one Peter deVito, who used the name of Marino; Donnelly, who used Wilson as his alias; and the third member, as was testified to by various witnesses, was one Thomas Mullarkey, a vanished Inspector of Police in New York City.

Some time in August, 1930, the first group organized themselves for the purpose of manufacturing and selling liquor. Each man of the three had different functions. Oxhandler was to supply the tanks and barrels, Hoberman was to be the financial agent and supply a still, and Doscher was to supply the "locus operandi." All three were then to work together for their common well being. Oxhandler in answer to this direct question put to him by Counsel

"Q. And the purpose of the partnership was to manufacture this liquor and sell it, I suppose?"

answered

"A. Yes, sir."

Each man carried out his bargain. The still, a five hundred

gallon one, was set up in operation at 182nd Street and Jamaica Avenue in Queens County, New York. The location
was in the rear of a building belonging to Doscher's father,
the front of which was used as a paper warehouse.

One day in September, 1930, very shortly after operations were begun, young Doscher happened to see two men
looking over the place quite thoroughly. He suspected them
and reported the fact to Oxhandler, telling him they looked
like prospective tenants or police officers, he didn't know
which. Oxhandler suggested getting out then, but as they had
no place to go the incident was forgotten and nothing was
done at that time.

Some few weeks thereafter word came to Doscher, through
a bookkeeper, from an alleged police officer, that the "Boss,"
meaning the Inspector, wanted to see him (Doscher) or else
action would be taken. This, as Doscher well knew, meant
one of two things, either money or a raid and the end. It
was thereupon decided amongst themselves that he (Doscher)
should go, and by pretending to be the owner of the legitimate warehouse business in the front, feel out the situation.
He went. He saw the Inspector. He came back and reported.
It seems that when he got to the Police Station he saw the
man he later identified as Mullarkey. In this conversation, he
(Mullarkey) learned that Doscher was not the head man,
whereupon he said to Doscher, as testified to by Oxhandler,
"You tell the boss of the still in the back that I want to see
him, not you. What are you doing here?" whereupon Doscher
left with instructions to send his "boss" back at six o'clock
that evening. It was decided that Oxhandler should go, but
not empty-handed. Then it was that Hoberman came to the
fore and put up some $300 in small bills, which Oxhandler
was to take with him. Promptly at six o'clock Oxhandler and
Doscher arrived at the 168th Street station house. They went
into Mullarkey's office. Doscher was excused and dismissed,
so he waited for Oxhandler in the car about a block from
the station house. Among Mullarkey's first remarks to Ox-

handler were: "What right have you got to set up around here without first coming to see me?" Oxhandler was puzzled. He hadn't known up to then that Mullarkey could be "seen." He didn't respond to the question. Mullarkey went on and told Oxhandler that he had to get out as too many people seemed to know of the place. In reply Oxhandler testified that he offered to try to get him $500 per week in return for his protection. This was unsatisfactory for reasons which will later be developed. Thereupon Mullarkey, according to Oxhandler, said to him ". . . that so far as this particular place was concerned, he would not entertain any proposition, but that if I (Oxhandler) would get some other location, get out of here and get some other location in his division, why, he would talk to me (Oxhandler) on the proposition then." The reasons for that remark, too, will later appear. There was a little further talk as to the length of time it would take to get out and the amounts to be paid as protection for the new establishment (which were to be $500 per week to Mullarkey and $100 to his right hand man), then Oxhandler prepared to go. Before going, however, he once again offered Mullarkey, for past favors, the $300 in cash which he had taken with him. This Mullarkey refused, but Oxhandler insisted that he take it, if for no other reason than that it would be a sign of good faith as to any future proposition. Just before leaving, Oxhandler opened the top drawer of Mullarkey's desk and threw the money in and closed it again. He then left. He was asked at this point by Counsel

"Q. Well, did he [Mullarkey] follow you to the door and insist on your taking the $300 that he had refused?
"A. Oh, no."

Immediately thereafter on the next day this triumvirate got to work, dismantled their place and retired on the eve of Rosh Hashana in September, 1930. From this particular triumvirate young Doscher then retired.

To carry out Mullarkey's recommendations, Oxhandler

and his partner thereupon sought out a new location. With
the help of one Mattthew Greene, Chief Sanitary Inspector
of the Health Department in Queens, a place on 87th Street,
Woodhaven, Long Island, was located. According to Oxhandler, Greene was to get $50 a month. This, of course,
Greene denied. However, he did not deny that he knew what
kind of a place was to be run. He knew that the place, even
though it was rented ostensibly for a legitimate business, was
in fact to be used for the manufacture of bootleg whisky.
His knowledge was proved by the following questions and
his own answers thereto.

"Q. There was a time...that you understood they wanted
it for a still?
"A. Ultimately, yes....
"Q. You understood the ultimate proposition was that they
were going to use it for a still, but first they were going to rent
it to a dummy?
"A. Yes.
"Q. For a legitimate proposition?
"A. Storage warehouse.
"Q. Then it was to be turned over to be operated as a still?
"A. To them or some other crew....
"Q. Who were going to use it for these illegitimate pur-
poses?
"A. Yes.

After Oxhandler and Hoberman had obtained this new
location on or about November 1, 1930, they set up again
with the same five hundred gallon still they had used at the
Jamaica Avenue establishment. This time the location was
behind an old house in a place used as a piano factory. Oxhandler, not forgetting his friend Mullarkey, went back to
see him to tell him he couldn't possibly pay him $500 a week
but that for the present he would pay $200 a week with hopes
for more as business increased. This offer Mullarkey, according to the testimony, accepted. The payments were to be
made on Saturdays at the police station office or at Mullarkey's house. The installation of the still took about one week's

time. The following week, about November 14, 1930, Oxhandler testified he delivered his tribute to Mullarkey's home in the form of two one-hundred dollar bills. The following week, about November 21st or 22nd, according to his testimony, he paid his last fee to Mullarkey.

The following week included Thanksgiving Day. It so happened that that day was bitter cold. This caused the steam from the still which was in operation to vaporize in great quantities and as it was piped to the street, all this steam came out of the manhole there and caused an inspection to be made. This some policeman did, even coming up to the windows and looking in. Oxhandler saw him, which fact made him extremely nervous, so he looked up Mullarkey and told the story to him. Mullarkey told him: "Well, Inspector Kelly's men may have got the report above my head," and "you are going to get knocked off, so you might as well get out." Thereupon Oxhandler's crowd laid low all that Friday, until towards evening, when they started up again. Very shortly thereafter, that same evening, they were "knocked off" by Inspector Kelly's men. So far as has been learned that ended Oxhandler's activities as well as those of the first triumvirate.

The second triumvirate of deVito, Donnelly and Mullarkey had, according to the testimony, come into being even before Oxhandler, Hoberman and Doscher, Jr., broke up and left the Jamaica Avenue property. Peter deVito is well known in and around Queens County. He lives next door but one to Inspector Mullarkey. Donnelly was a friend of deVito's of ten or twelve years' standing. He had met deVito while he was working for a grocery store and later had even worked for deVito himself.

Some time in the summer of 1930, around August, while visiting deVito at his home, according to Donnelly's testimony, deVito said to him "... he thought he would open a still in Jamaica; that police protection, he could get all he wanted from Inspector Mullarkey." Then shortly followed this question and answer.

"Q. And when he gave you this assurance that he could get any necessary protection from Inspector Mullarkey, what did you say in reference to deVito's earlier proposition that you open a still?

"A. I said that would be all right, 'as long as you got police protection.' "

The plan grew and ripened until it consummated in deVito and Donnelly's taking a look at a place on 182nd Street, Jamaica, some time in September, 1930. This place they later took. At this time, however, these two men were using the names of Marino and Wilson, respectively. It will be recalled that it was just about this time that young Doscher reported to Oxhandler that he had seen two strange men looking over the place. It was about this time that Doscher received word that the "Boss" wanted to see him or else he would take action. It was about this time that Oxhandler did go to see Mullarkey who then said to him, as above stated "... that so far as this particular place was concerned, he would not entertain any proposition...." These facts, then, prompt the question, was Mullarkey interested with deVito and Donnelly in running a still at this place? The facts themselves are undisputed and must answer.

First: deVito and Donnelly, deVito and Mullarkey were friends.

Second: deVito and Donnelly in September, 1930, looked over the place which Oxhandler, Hoberman and Doscher had and at which place in November, 1930, Tom Williams, identified as Mullarkey's son, was arrested.

Third: Mullarkey told Oxhandler about this same time that he and his group would have to get out of that particular spot.

Fourth: That later on in September, 1930, there were six or seven men working in and about this place. Their names were given later as, Joseph Miller, Albert Siano, John Cafero, Sabino Ferrigno, Giussepe Amato, John B. DeLuca and John Doscher.

Fifth: There was a man working in about the place known by the name of Tom Williams or McWilliams.

Sixth: By the following questions and answers this same Tom

Williams was identified as Thomas Mullarkey, the son of Inspector Mullarkey, by the witness Donnelly.

"Q. And among the men ... there was one who was known under the name of Tom Williams?
"A. Yes, sir.
"Q. Did you see him working there?
"A. I did; yes, sir.
"Q. Did you recognize him?
"A. Yes, sir.
"Q. And you recognized him as who?
"A. Tom Mullarkey, young ... Tom Mullarkey, Jr., son of the Inspector.
"Q. Son of the Inspector?
"A. Yes, sir."

He also was identified by the witness Cafero.

"Q. Had you learned afterwards who this Tom Williams or McWilliams was?
"A. I knew who he was.
"Q. Who was he?
"A. Inspector Mullarkey's son.
"Q. Who told you that?
"A. Mr. deVito."

Seventh: There was a raid made on November 22, 1930, by Inspector Kelly's men at which seven or eight men were arrested, among them this Tom Williams.

Eighth: That every one was taken to the station house and booked except Tom Williams. The testimony of Donnelly on this is as follows:

"Q. Everybody booked except the Inspector's son?
"A. Yes, sir."

Ninth: That Inspector Mullarkey retired from the Police Department when it appeared that charges might result from this transaction. Although drawing a pension from the City, he disappeared when sought by the Investigation and has not been heard of since. He has been indicted by the Federal authorities for his part in this affair.

There remains but one question in this whole story and that is how the pension check mailed to Mullarkey's home, in payment of his September, 1930, pension, became endorsed on October 7, 1930, when, according to the uncontroverted evidence, Mullarkey had disappeared on September 9th, of that year. The only witness who testified as to this remarkable occurrence was the Inspector's wife, Mrs. Nora H. Mullarkey. She fixed September 9, 1930, as the day on which the Inspector disappeared and September 3rd, as the day on which her son Thomas, Jr., disappeared. She also said she had not since September 9, 1930, heard of or seen the Inspector.

On or about October 1, 1930, the pension check of her husband Inspector Mullarkey was received by her at their home. She took it and put it, unopened, on the bureau in the Inspector's room, where it lay for four or five days. On the evening of October 6th, she arrived home around 11:30 P.M. and on lighting the light at the head of the stairs she noticed that the papers on the Inspector's bureau had been disturbed. She went and looked, and there, much to her surprise, she says, lay the check which had been endorsed by the Inspector and two other people unknown to her, who signed as witnesses to the Inspector's endorsement. The Inspector, she testified, had taken nothing away with him on this visit, clothes or anything else, nor had the only two people in the house heard of his being there. When asked as to any statement in explanation of this extraordinary transaction she replied that what she had said was the truth and that she had nothing else to say. She was then excused.

CHAPTER XXIII

"CRUMBS ON THE TABLE"

FROM November 27, 1913, to June 7, 1929, there was an officer on the New York Police Force by the name of Dennis Wright. His function was for part of this time to suppress the illicit liquor and gambling professions which flourished in the Bronx. Such work is now commonly known as Vice Squad work. Towards the end of his career he was mysteriously transferred from the 8th Division, to which he had been assigned, by a Lieutenant, who was his superior, according to the testimony he gave at his private examination. There, under examination he said:

> "A. ... I got transferred away from there one time about a year before I got retired. I got transferred out of that office and it was Lieutenant ... who was instrumental in having me transferred out of there for no reason that I know of."

At the public hearing when he was confronted with this answer he made a long explanation attempting to show that it was an Inspector and not the Lieutenant who was responsible for his transfer. The point of this change was never made quite clear unless it was that he feared the enmity of the Lieutenant more than that of the Inspector. The theory behind his examination was that Wright, while assisting in the protection of the speakeasies in that Division, in some way had infringed on the Lieutenant's rights and so angered him. Hence, his transfer from the 8th Division. To prove this, Wright was asked

> "Q. You must have treaded on his toes or on the toes of some of the speakeasies he was protecting."

to which he answered

"A. Probably I did but that is what I could never get explained to me. I never could get that explained to me why I got transferred out of there or if it was anything serious, or anything wrong in my action, I would not get back."

Lost in his own contradictions as to his story, he finally gave up and attributed this change of testimony to a mistake on the part of the stenographer in originally recording the minutes. This foundation having been laid, despite his denials, he was next asked by counsel if he, himself, ever did any collecting, to which he replied "never." Asked why he stood silently by and let others be paid, he replied, "I would have to, a cop is only merely the crumbs on the table." A little earlier he had said that by this answer he was not trying to defend his office, because as he said, "It could be paid in there by the hundreds and me not know it."

The next link in the chain tying him to the protection business was the development of the fact that he knew the head of the "Liberty League."

This "League" was apparently a group of ex-bartenders, the ostensible purpose of which was to foster a spirit of good will among its members and also to have social functions and revive the kindly jovial life of the "good old days." It was in fact a protective organization, the members of which would pay "dues," receive a little card which would be conspicuously shown and thereby protect them from raids being made. Not only did he admit knowing this man who was head of the League, but he told the Committee that this same person used to come around to the police station, for a purpose not admitted by any one connected with it, but nevertheless quite clear. Here was his background. The next step to see whether or not he was telling the truth when he denied knowing anything of the business and asserted his complete innocence, was the development of his story of his bank deposits and their source.

Between the years 1921 and the middle of 1929 when he resigned, during which time his salary, except for a short period, was less than $3,000 per year, he managed to deposit some $93,500. This amount he said came only from his salary and "income from my investment." This "investment" was apparently real estate, for he received $170 per month in rents from it; also he received about $100 a year from his dividends. The total of all these amounts nowhere near approximated his known deposited total. The question naturally arose, where did it come from? His answer was interesting.

It seems that in 1918 or 1919 Wright was dispossessed by the landlord because the landlord wanted the apartment for some one else. So he (Wright) went to a "friend" in the Bronx and asked this "friend" to look around. The "friend" looked around, came back and reported to Wright that there was a place at 3233 Decatur Avenue in Bronx County. This was a three-story frame house built on a plot of seven lots. To the back, was a bluff of rocks some thirty-three feet in height. The "friend" said, "There is a floor here." Wright said, "It will suit me." The "friend" said, "They won't rent you the floor. You had better buy the building." So after that, Wright said, "We went and seen the agent," and after some negotiations, Wright agreed to buy the building, land and the rocks. The price was approximately $16,000. The "friend" who showed him this place turned out to be his brother. The agent's identity was never discovered. So here was Wright with a building, land and rock to buy and no money. Thereupon, he went again to his now deceased "friend" and brother, Patrick Wright, who ran a hotel for "gentlemen only" on West Street and said to him, "When you went in the hotel business I advanced some money. . . . I didn't ask anything from you. Now, are you fit to repay me?" To which Patrick replied, "Yes, how much do you want?" However, before divulging the amount he needed, Dennis told Patrick he had better come up and see the building. Just why that was necessary wasn't made clear, for Dennis had just finished explaining that Patrick was the "friend" who had shown him the building in the first place. Nevertheless, up they went again. On seeing it this time, Patrick said, "Well, it is a bargain." Shortly thereafter they decided to buy the whole thing. To help Dennis out Patrick then repaid the $10,000 Dennis had lent him some time before and, "In addition to that, during the years 1919 and 1924 he advanced me $15,000." This totaled $25,000, $10,000 in repayment and $15,000 a new loan, for which new loan Dennis gave a note. The money Dennis never repaid during the lifetime of Patrick, who died in 1924 or 1925, nor have the administrators or executors of Patrick's estate ever demanded payment. It was a peculiar kind of a note anyway, for as Dennis testified even though there was "no limit to the note.... It is past due now." He then explained why no payment was ever demanded, bringing in a new character, "a seafaring man." As to this situation, it was asked:

"Q. Don't you think that was pretty easy to borrow $15,000 on the note, pay no interest on it, and then never have anybody turn up and ask you to pay the note?"

to which he answered,

"I do not, for the reason why, when he advanced me that $15,-000, he said that he would go as a partner with me to construct a building on the property, and he also spoke to a friend of his, Mr. Manning, who he got interested in the proposition also. Mr. Manning advanced me $14,000."

It turned out that this Mr. Manning was a "seafaring man." He must also have been a very secretive one for Wright knew nothing about him; never knew how long he had been a seafaring man, what he did on the boats, what boats he was on, whether or not he was an officer, what boat he was last connected with, when he last went to sea, nor where he now was. The last that Wright ever heard from him, he thinks, was when he got a postal card from Philadelphia. This money which Manning lent him was to build a house, not buy one, and also to get five per cent interest from Wright on his money instead of the three per cent he had been receiving. This transaction took place sometime about 1924. Since then

Wright says he has paid the whole sum back at different times by giving Manning cash and securities when he (Manning) would call at Wright's home on one of his infrequent visits to the Port of New York. In fairness it must be said that the original loan and the repayment thereof are impossible to isolate and trace in the bank transcripts of Wright's accounts. This then was the complete accounting for approximately $39,000 of the $93,500 he had. Another $18,500 came from a loan from the Railroad Building and Loan at 43rd Street and Lexington Avenue. He also received "three hundred pounds in cash for the education of my little girl" from his mother, but unfortunately he had no record of any kind evidencing this gift. Counsel then returned to the loans of his brother Patrick and Mr. Manning, the seafaring man, in an effort to find out if he had used the money for the purpose for which it was lent. It was then learned that Dennis had become involved in a great deal of trouble over the building; that the contractor had gotten hold of about $25,000; that the building itself had gotten tied up in litigation and that the only thing that ever happened in regard to the construction of the building, was the excavation of about three-fourths of the rock behind the proposed site. It was never even learned whether or not he got the apartment he was seeking, which was the opening act of this story.

After this interesting but incredible story, Wright was questioned in regard to certain checks appearing in his accounts coming from Croton, and deposited in Croton, New York. This part of his story is equally interesting and just as incredible. When the question was first put to him he began parrying it and telling a long story about how, after he got out of the Department in 1929, he received some checks from upstate from his immediate family. He was immediately reminded that the check which Counsel had in mind was a 1924 check in the sum of $10,050. This check he had forgotten completely, he could remember no detail of it. It turned out to be a cashier's check drawn on July 29, 1924, to Wright's own order and endorsed by him to one Mabel Moto. He said, after recovering his poise, for up to then he knew nothing of the production of this check, "I don't recall who Mabel Moto is."

"Q. Isn't she your partner in an enterprise at Croton?
"A. No.
"Q. A speakeasy enterprise?
"A. No, I have got no friends in speakeasy business."

The fact is that the place run by this Mabel Moto is called "Moto Inn" and is a well-known roadhouse on the Albany Post Road, and, it is rumored, has all the accompanying pleasures. Wright admitted finally that he had known the place since 1923 or 1924, further than that he would not go. He was then shown a check drawn on July 12, 1926, for $1,500 coming from Croton. All he could say about this particular check was that it came from some member of his family, but he didn't know which one. The record of another check was shown him dated October 8, 1930, which he admitted might have come from Moto Inn and finally one for $1,000 drawn on September 6, 1930, which he said he thought came from his sister. She, it seems, after all, owns the building in which Moto Inn is located. Perhaps he was not quite frank in his answers when he denied knowing Mabel Moto and denied knowing anything about the checks. Who knows? All he would say to Counsel, who put this final question to him

"... Isn't all this money that has been shown in these bank accounts aggregating nearly $100,000 the savings that you were able to tuck away chiefly while you were collecting when you were attached to the 8th Division?..."

was

"You have got the wrong information."

CHAPTER XXIV

THE TRIAL AND REMOVAL OF SHERIFF FARLEY

ON the sixth of October, 1931, Thomas M. Farley, Sheriff of New York County, was called before the Committee to testify. He took the stand and was tendered, as the usual custom is, a waiver of immunity. He protested signing it in the form in which it was submitted on the ground, that although it was signed at a public hearing, it might be used later as a waiver of immunity as to any testimony he might give at a private hearing. He kept on repeating this answer but never once would he indicate whether or not he would sign the waiver. Finally, in answer to the direct question again being put to him by Counsel he replied,

"Well, I thought you understood the English language." This colloquy was interrupted by Farley's counsel, Siegfried Hartman, who then undertook to advise Farley what to do about signing the waiver. Counsel objected to Hartman's interrupting, saying:

> "I object to this kind of interruption, either from Mr. Hartman or any other kind of interruption, whether they be Untermyerisms or otherwise."

Farley was then asked who suggested that he raise this question about signing the waiver, to which he replied:

> "No one."
> By Counsel: "Q. You did not hear Mr. Hartman make that suggestion a few minutes ago?"
> "A. I pay no attention to him."

A little later with the specific date of his testifying interpolated, Farley signed the waiver and told his story amidst the constant interruptions by the Minority members of the Committee.

During the course of his examination, he gave his version of the police raids made on his club. He stated that the men found in his club at about 2 A.M. were not professional gamblers, as was charged, but

> "The members that was there was busy packing baseball bats, skipping ropes and rubber balls, because our May day outing took place on May 29th."

It was here, too, that he explained his duties as Sheriff by being ignorantly vague, enumerating a few and then passing over all the others by saying

> "All the duties that are in the Charter we perform."

There was one section of the Penal Law, *viz.:* Section 997, of which he had never heard, which section makes it the duty of the Sheriff to inform against violators of the gambling law. When confronted with this provision, all that he could say about it was

> "I am not familiar with that."

It was on this day too, that he told of his now famous "tin box."

All other charges he blandly denied despite the documentary evidence produced. At last, he was excused.

The newspapers carried tremendous headlines of his "tin box" story. Editorials were written in ridicule and protestation by practically every paper of the town. The greatest publicity attached to his, the Sheriff's, own story. Many there were who expected that the Governor, having the power of removal, would act. However, the silence from Albany day by day became more ominous and eloquent. It became clear the Governor was not going to take the initiative. Time went by —nothing happened. Finally, on December 30, 1931, Counsel in his private capacity wrote to the Governor, presenting eleven different charges against the Sheriff and demanding his removal. He closed his letter by saying,

"... The present Sheriff of the County of New York is unfit to hold the office of Sheriff and that to permit him longer to do so would be a grave injustice and affront to the citizenship of this County."

Later on, on January 19, 1932, Counsel again wrote the Governor, adding to his previous specifications the charge that the Sheriff had knowingly appropriated the interest on funds which had come into his hands as Sheriff and again demanding the Sheriff's removal.

The Governor ordered the Sheriff to answer by the 1st of February, 1932, which he did.

Before the story of the actual trial is told, it seems best to look briefly at the charges and the answer. The charges, summarized, were: one, that professional gamblers operated under Farley's protection in his own clubhouse; two, that Farley caused structural changes in the house itself to be made, the better to accommodate the gamblers and to obstruct the police in their duty of the suppression of the gambling; third, that Farley falsely denied making such changes; fourth, that after such changes were made, the clubhouse was used by and for professional gamblers; fifth, that the police were twice required to raid the clubhouse on account of the gambling therein; sixth, that Farley bailed out the people there arrested giving inadequate security; seventh, that Farley falsely swore that all the persons arrested were members of his club, engaged, at the time of the raid (two o'clock in the morning) in packing baseballs, rubber balls, May poles and skipping ropes for a May party; eighth, that Farley willfully refused to testify in private, in violation of law; ninth, that Farley deposited between January 1, 1925, and September 22, 1931, $396,503.66 of which his admitted income was not more than $87,000; tenth, that Farley was unfamiliar with the duties of the Sheriff and was incompetent and unqualified to perform them; eleventh, that Farley appointed incompetents in his office and continued them in office and finally, by the second letter, that Farley knowingly appropriated the interest on funds coming into his hands as Sheriff.

As said above Farley in a reply or answer, filed on February 1, 1932, attempted to avoid the charges, and when this method or an absolute denial wasn't possible, resorted to irrelevant remarks and personal abuse of Counsel.

Were this abuse an isolated instance it might well be passed over, but it is not unique nor isolated. It is a part of the scheme of attack which Tammany Hall has used, from the beginning of the Magistrates' Courts Inquiry, when the situation became embarrassing and it was shown what type of politicians it harbors.

As said above Farley's answer falls into three categories. First, denials; second, evasions; third, abuse. They will be treated in this order. First, a flat denial of all charges relating to professional gambling in his clubhouse. Second, the evasions and irrelevancies such as

> "He [meaning Counsel] has deluged the City and County departments with subpœnas. He has combed the public records. He has examined over 4,200 witnesses in secret hearings but has presented in public the testimony of only 173 and only such evidence as in his opinion might lend color to his accusations. . . .
>
> "I came of humble parentage and was forced at an early age to earn my own living. . . .
>
> "For many years practically all of my time has been devoted to public service . . . and to the political and charitable work connected with Tammany Hall. . . .
>
> "Lyons [a police inspector] must be confusing my club with one of his many observations. . . .
>
> "The bars . . . were old iron bars . . . and may now be seen on the basement windows of the residence immediately adjoining the clubhouse, as well as on the first, second and third floors of Judge Seabury's home at 154 East 63rd Street. . . .
>
> ". . . this huge transcript shows that the police, for reasons of their own, went to extremes to establish a case of professional gambling. . . .
>
> "Of course, the whole examination on this subject was designed to entrap me into an admission. . . .
>
> "I determined, therefore, that since it was my legal right so to do, I would insist upon my testimony being given in public

and thereby minimize attempts to garble or distort what I might say. Unfortunately, I find now that not even a public record is sufficient to prevent my detractors from at least attempting to distort it. . . .

"I am not versed in the law or the art of repartee. . . .

". . . I was not disposed to refuse to answer any question however impertinent and offensive. . . .

"I am confident that your Excellency will not mistake Judge Seabury's partisan ridicule for proof, or receive Judge Seabury's biased and distorted version. . . .

"I am not instructed in the law and I can boast only of an education in the public schools and in the school of personal experience. . . .

"Among working people like Flaherty [one of Farley's assistants], substantial sacrifices in adversity by brother for brother, neighbor for neighbor and friend for friend are the rule and not the exception."

So much for the evasions.

The third category of his answer is abuse.

At the outset of his answer Farley starts his abuse of Counsel, saying of the Majority of the Committee

". . . which, under the leadership of Judge Seabury, has been conducting a purely partisan campaign to discredit the government of the City of New York and its individual office holders. . . .

". . . This opportunity to answer Judge Seabury is welcome, particularly in view of the many reckless and unfounded accusations which he has given public circulation. . . .

"He has been uniformly sustained in his every course and policy not only by the Committee but also by the public press, which palliates his continuous failures and insufficiency of proof and broadcasts as facts his unsupported accusations and innuendoes. . . .

"It is therefore, I submit, deeply significant that this exponent of the hypothesis of civic corruption . . . is utterly unable even to formulate a charge which has a relevant bearing upon my right to the office of Sheriff. . . .

"From my observation of the procedure at private hearings . . . I had noted that, notwithstanding the cloak of secrecy which was supposed to envelop the private hearings, the press carried . . .

Judge Seabury's advance predictions as to the subjects ... to ventilate at these private hearings, and after the private hearings had been held, regularly published garbled versions ... versions, which seemed always to stress, in a manner calculated to be as damaging as possible, the incriminating theory, ... but without setting forth the position of the person attacked."

As to his bank accounts and his "tin box" story, he says,

"My accuser's method appears to be to create a wholly inaccurate picture of my testimony and then to attack that distortion as incredible."

In defense of his "tin box" story, Farley through Mr. Hartman, his Counsel, resorted to this:

"Judge Seabury would undoubtedly have been better pleased had I kept all my funds in the Bank of the United States. ..."

This was inserted solely to cast aspersions on Judge Seabury for the appointment of Isidor J. Kresel (after recommendation by the Bar Associations of New York City), as Counsel in the Magistrates' Courts Investigation and who was indicted later on for his connection with the Bank of United States. It was an attempt to link Judge Seabury to that most deplorable bank failure.

Thus it was through the whole fabric of his answer—denial, evasion and abuse.

At last on February 16, 1932, Thomas M. Farley stood in the Executive Chamber at the State Capitol in Albany, before Governor Roosevelt, who, acting in "the historic capacity of Chief Magistrate" was to determine the gravamen of the charges against, and the fitness of, Thomas M. Farley for the position of Sheriff of New York County.

With the Executive Chamber crowded, at one-thirty in the afternoon on that day the Governor opened the proceedings. As the evidence developed it fell into five distinct categories. The first related to the gambling in the Farley clubhouse, the second concerned Farley's refusal to testify at a private hearing, the third pertained to the general unfitness of Farley as evidenced by his subordinates, the fourth dealt with the question of Farley's appropriation of the interest on certain funds in the Sheriff's office and the fifth and last was the explanation by Farley himself of his personal accounts.

As the story of professional gamblers and gambling has been told previously, suffice it to say here that generally speaking the evidence was the same. The evidence adduced as to this charge was not sufficient in the Governor's eyes for him to use it as a basis for his final act of removal. The same is true as to the second and third categories into which the evidence fell. The fourth division as to the appropriation of interest was very fully discussed by both sides. Judge Seabury argued, that stripped of all shams and subterfuges, Farley must have known that this money was going into his personal account. He showed how the title of the account reading

"Thomas M. Farley, Sheriff, special account"

was changed to read

"Thomas M. Farley, special"

and thereby, as he says,

"...the whole funds that had previously been in the official account were by that magic stroke of the pen converted from official funds into private funds of Thomas M. Farley."

He showed that on examination before the Committee, Farley had not mentioned this account among his other personal accounts, even though it had a balance of approximately $10,000 at the time. Judge Seabury also showed that Farley had not mentioned the interest on his accounts as Sheriff as one of the sources of his income. He showed how, as to a certain fund already in the Sheriff's office when Farley became Sheriff, he took that money out of one bank where it was drawing 2% interest and put it into a bank paying 3% interest and further, how he, Farley, then took 1% of the accrued interest leaving the other 2% to be applied to that fund. Judge Seabury then demonstrated how some of the Sheriff's books showed the payment of interest and others did not; how interest was repaid to litigants when demanded out of the personal account of Farley, although he, Farley, says that in the great rush of signing checks he didn't know he was repaying this money.

At this point the Governor said,

> "If your theory is right, Judge, how do you account for the previous Sheriff taking that money?"

to which Judge Seabury replied:

> "Well, I think the reason Culkin (the former Sheriff) took it was ... the same reason Farley took it. I think he wanted the money."

Then, in conclusion of this subject, Judge Seabury addressing the Governor directly said,

> "Isn't it a plain proposition? Can your Excellency say that you will sanction a practice that permits Sheriffs to take interest upon public funds that are in their possession?"

In defense, Mr. Hartman, Farley's counsel, said that Farley was merely following a custom that arose at least as early as Sheriff Griffenhagen and one that had been followed since by all the Sheriffs. He cited, as support, an opinion of Mr. Louis Hahlo, then a Corporation Counsel who held merely that the City had no interest in these moneys, not that the Sheriff was entitled to it. The citation of this was merely to show that the question of appropriation of interest arose openly as far back as 1916. In response to this Governor Roosevelt said to Mr. Hartman:

> "In other words, your claim really is that all of this money, through a succession of Sheriffs, was a lost child—that nobody knew who it belonged to, and after a Sheriff went out of office, he took it himself?"

Mr. Hartman, of course, couldn't admit that, so he proceeded to prove, that not only did the interest not belong to the litigant but even the principal itself did not. To this the Governor replied:

"That is a new one on me. I am interested."

To demonstrate this proposition Mr. Hartman went back to the "old English days" and explained how the Sheriff of a county was equivalent to an earl, and how he (the Sheriff) had control of the county and was the King's representative. Mr. Hartman then developed that when the Sheriff levied on an execution he was acting for the King, the inference being that, as the King was the Supreme Sovereign of the Country, he had title to everything in the Country and that therefore the litigant had no interest nor ownership of the fund. Following this he developed various schools of thought relating to a public officer's custody of funds, which discussion culminated in the conclusion that the title to both principal and interest is in the Sheriff, as a public officer, because he is an insuring debtor. The explanation was long and intricate and the conclusion will be, if true, a source of worry and amazement to litigants who must give their judgments to Sheriffs to levy executions thereon. All they will then have is a hope that the Sheriff will return something to them. After the discussion pro and con on the question of the interest charges the hearing was adjourned by the Governor to the day following.

At ten o'clock, February 17, 1932, the second day's hearings began with the taking up of the last charge by the Governor—that of Farley's bank deposits. As has been explained in an earlier chapter, the charge was that Farley deposited, in the period from January 1, 1925, to September 22, 1931, some $396,503.66, and that as to the acquisition of this amount no credible explanation was given. Farley's answer was a ninefold one. It was as follows: First, that so far as the charges specified a period before he took his present office they were irrelevant; second, that the matters were personal and private; third, that nothing was acquired dishonestly or improperly; fourth, that Judge Seabury dis-

torted his testimony; fifth, that the "tin box" expression was
Judge Seabury's and not Farley's; sixth, that none of the
evidence adduced discredits the Sheriff's story; seventh, that
the Sheriff's average monthly balance was about $1,500;
eighth, that the Sheriff could have resisted testifying as to
these moneys under the ruling of the Barnes case; and ninth;
that it was the Sheriff's lifelong policy to keep his money at
home and not trust it to financial institutions.

In his discussion of these deposits Judge Seabury once
again pointed out what Farley's income was known to be for
the period covered, and further, how when he, Farley, couldn't
explain it, its source always was attributed to his "tin box"
into which Farley said he had started putting money as far
back as 1910. He further pointed out how there was approximately $133,000 to be accounted for, even assuming that, as
Farley said, there was at the beginning of 1925, $100,000 in
the "tin box" and that he had another $116,000 derived from
his salaries and commissions since that date. The difference,
all of it, was attributed to the "box." Now, why do they
make these explanations of these tin boxes, Judge Seabury
asked, and in answering his own rhetorical question he said:

> ". . . Isn't it perfectly evident to your Excellency that the reason
> is that if they said in any other way that is capable of verification,
> it would be possible to show that their explanations fall? And also
> everybody knows who has heard the statement that it is a mere
> cock and bull story told for the purpose of relieving him from
> making embarrassing explanation."

In answer to this Farley again explained the moneys by saying
they were deposits and redeposits of the amounts taken from
the "tin box," some loans and several other classes. As Mr.
Hartman himself said,

> ". . . Sheriff Farley cannot do any more than state to you the
> categories. . . ."

Thus it was that no detailed explanation ever was made.
After listening to Mr. Hartman's general classifications of

the deposits without detailing them in any way the Governor laid down his rule, which in the future will be a guide to the conduct of public officials, saying in part:

> "As a matter of sound public policy, I am very certain that there is a requirement that where a public official is under inquiry or investigation, especially an elected public official, and it appears that his scale of living, or the total of his bank deposits far exceeds the public salary which he is known to receive, he, the elected public official, owes a positive public duty to the community to give a reasonable or credible explanation of the sources of the deposits, or the source which enables him to maintain a scale of living beyond the amount of his salary.... Even if a mere suspicion exists, there falls upon the public official the duty of coming into court with full information as to his personal finances, and that being so ... I still do not believe that a complete and full explanation has been made by the Sheriff as to the total of the deposits that are involved since 1925 in these bank accounts."

The hearing then closed and shortly thereafter, on February 24, 1932, the Governor handed down his decision, upon which he based his determination to remove Farley as Sheriff of New York County. In his decision, the Governor dismissed all the charges save the one as to the bank accounts, and as to this he held that Farley had not lived up to the standard which he himself, the Governor, had laid down and which is, in part, quoted above. Thereafter on the same day the order removing Thomas M. Farley as Sheriff was entered and he became Thomas M. Farley, ex-Sheriff.

Some time later, on the criminal charge of having misappropriated the interest on the deposits in his custody, he, Farley, was acquitted and the whole matter of Thomas M. Farley, Sheriff and ex-Sheriff, was laid to rest.

CHAPTER XXV

A TRAGIC ADVENTURE

ABOUT sixty years ago in the town of Zador, Austria-Hungary, one Louis H. Roth was born. In early youth he came to America in search of a sister who had left home. Whether or not he ever found his sister is not important. The important fact is that he thus came here and has remained ever since. At some period between the date of his arrival in America and 1923, this same Louis H. Roth became known to the world as Louis H. Willard.

The events covered by this chapter begin in the year 1923. The initial fact is the purchase by Willard of certain property at the corner of McClellan Street and River Avenue in Bronx County, New York City, with the purpose of erecting a public garage, as was logical because the land at that time was practically a wilderness. Shortly after his purchase Willard applied for a permit to build this garage. In so doing he first met William J. Flynn, who for many years has been the Commissioner of Public Works of Bronx County and, at times, the Acting Borough President under Henry Bruckner, the Borough President.

Willard's application for this garage was addressed to the Board of Standards and Appeals, this being the proper body to grant such a permission. The application was filed about July 1, 1923. On July 2, 1923, a letter in opposition thereto came to the Board from Flynn, apparently in his official capacity. It was signed "William J. Flynn, Commissioner of Public Works." Though the letter was so signed, Flynn took the witness stand, and swore that it was signed only in his capacity "as a citizen and a resident who had lived for more than twenty years within a stone's throw of these premises." This conclusion he worked out by means of

236

a long and evasive series of answers to the effect that although he had dictated the letter, his stenographer had written it out and signed it after he had left the office for the day. He said, however, "if I had seen the letter after it was written, ... I might have put on there 'Unofficial.' But not having seen it, the letter just went out." Counsel then asked him: "Do you find anything in that letter that would justify anybody ... in concluding that that letter was not sent ... by you in your official capacity as Commissioner of Public Works?" to which he answered, "No, but the intention was as a private citizen." This whole colloquy was designed to negative the inference that he had used his official power to oppose the application of Willard, but that he had used it merely, as he says, "To protect my private property" and "to serve and promote ... my private interest, to protect my private property."

Whether or not the Board could or did infer that the letter of July 2 was a protest by him in his private capacity, even though it bore his name as Commissioner of Public Works, it is clear that his second letter dated July 14, was an official protest against Willard's application, admitted to be such by him. It was signed by him as Acting President of the Borough of the Bronx. The fact that he had a private personal interest in the matter did not dissuade him from acting officially. He stood on his testimony which he had given earlier in the hearing and which he repeated, *i.e.*, that he had never used his official position or station to promote his own private interest as citizen and taxpayer.

The date set for the hearing on Willard's application was July 17, 1923. Flynn showed up at the Board meeting that day to protest. The capacity in which he appeared was doubtful. In an endeavor to make Flynn's capacity clear, Mr. Dunnigan, who represented Willard at that time, asked, "May I interrupt to ask if Mr. Flynn represents himself or speaks for owners within the affected area?" In answering this Flynn said, "... I am qualified to speak for myself." This, of course, still left the question open, so the Chairman of the Board said:

"The Senator [Dunnigan] wanted to determine are you speaking officially or as a taxpayer?" To which Flynn replied: "I didn't say that." Unintelligible as that answer was, the matter was dropped and the Board then proceeded to the substance of the application.

There were two or three arguments urged that day by Flynn against the granting of the application. The first was "The man who gets in and excludes his neighbors, will make a fortune. . . ." The second: "A garage and a fortune for Mr. William Waldorf Astor who renounced this Country and must get money to pay fourteen per cent Income Taxes on the other side, at my expense and at the expense of this little woman who raised a family of six children." The third: "That the building of a public park was in contemplation and therefore the granting of a permit to erect a public garage directly opposite would be detrimental to the interests of the City." The application of Willard was denied.

The next important fact to remember is that in November, 1924, Flynn, through a dummy, purchased the property directly opposite this plot of Willard's with the purpose of erecting a public garage, as his testimony shows. He said:

> "Q. And did you intend to build a public garage upon those premises?
> "A. Yes. . . ."

Flynn planned not to have his name appear in the deed nor in the application contemplated by his neighbors for the erection of a public garage to be made to the Board, because of the opposition which would have arisen had it been known that he was in on the proposition. It was planned also to have the application made not on behalf of Flynn's premises, but on behalf of the adjoining premises, so that if the application to erect a public garage were granted as to those premises, then Flynn himself could also have a public garage on his property.

There are certain important dates to record and remember relating to the purchase by Flynn of this property. The first—

November 5, 1924, the date of the contract for the purchase of Flynn's property from the Astor Estate, by Margaret Carey, Flynn's dummy. The second—February 5, 1925, the date of her deed from the Astor Estate and also the date of the recording of that deed. The third—February 5, 1925, the date on which Margaret Carey deeded the property she had purchased from the Astor Estate to Flynn. The fourth —January 7, 1928, the date on which Flynn recorded the deed from Margaret Carey to him which he had received three years before. Another fact important to notice is that despite all of his remarks Flynn himself purchased this property through a dummy from the same William Waldorf Astor whom he had denounced on the hearing of Willard's application in July, 1923, within two years from the date of his speech of denunciation. There was some evidence, too, tending to show that Flynn had endeavored to purchase this property from the Astor Estate as early as 1918. At his public hearing, Flynn at first denied unequivocally he had had these negotiations, then reversed his position and qualified his answer saying, "I haven't the slightest recollection of ever discussing it. . . ." Another important fact to bear in mind is that when the application to erect this public garage was made by Flynn's neighbors, the park which was merely contemplated when he opposed Willard's application, was then actually in existence. Later the application came on for a determination by the Board of Standards and Appeals and, after a hearing, was denied. This denial was affirmed by the Supreme Court and the Appellate Division. The decision of the Appellate Division ended Flynn's hopes for a permit to erect a public garage. This, however, did not discourage Flynn from obtaining and running, in effect, a public garage even though it was not officially recorded as such. This job was put through as follows: Immediately after the Board of Standards and Appeals had denied this application with the subsequent affirmation by the Courts, which took approximately three years, Flynn then conceived the idea of erecting many individual garages on the plot. He testified:

"Q. Then you conceived the scheme ... of erecting a great
number of individual garages upon your premises?
"A. In accordance with law; that was my intention."

Before the garages could finally be erected there was one
more obstacle which he had to overcome. This was a resolution introduced by the Mayor at the Board of Estimate meeting on December 15, 1927. This provided in substance that
only one garage unit holding five cars would be allowed on
one plot under the same ownership. The purpose of the resolution was to carry out, in definite terms, the spirit of a
former ordinance to the same effect, but which according
to the Court of Appeals did not, by its wording, accomplish
that purpose. This, if adopted unamended, would have killed
Flynn's plans to have enough units to house ninety-one cars
and also would have left him with a large plot of land on
which he could build only one five-car unit. The resolution
as originally proposed by the Mayor was recommended for
passage by the Chief Engineer of the Board of Estimate on
December 21, 1927. Following that approval it was referred
to the Committee on Plans and Public Improvements of the
Board of Estimate. The President of the Borough of the
Bronx was Chairman of this Board. When this Committee
met on January 10, 1928, Flynn, in place of Borough President Bruckner, was in the chair. This resolution came up for
discussion at that meeting. Under Flynn's chairmanship and
at his suggestion it was amended so that it operated only
against plans filed on or after March 1, 1928. This meeting
was on January 10, 1928. On January 31, 1928, Flynn's
plans for his garages were both filed and approved. The resolution, after it had been amended by this Committee, was again
offered to the Board of Estimate on February 16, 1928, by
the Mayor. This Board then ordered it advertised in the
City Record, setting March 1, 1928, as the day for the Public Hearing. On March 1, 1928, the original resolution with
the amendment of the Committee on Plans and Public Improvements was passed by the Board of Estimate and thus
became a law. The records show that Flynn was the first and

only person in the whole of New York City whose plans for such a series of garages were filed and approved before the last day allowed by law. He was therefore in the position he objected to as to Willard, that of being the first and only one to get in and exclude his neighbors. As it turned out he profited individually by his official action in recommending the amendment to the resolution, without which he would not have been able to build his ninety-one garages.

Another situation in which William J. Flynn's official action resulted in advantage to him individually was developed in the story of his activities in connection with the establishment of McCombs Dam Park Extension in Bronx County. The facts in that case are as below detailed.

Some time in April, 1924, William J. Flynn, his wife, Frank Flynn and others petitioned the Local Board of Bronx County to set aside, for the establishment of a public park, certain land situated in that borough. Some time thereafter in June, 1924, the plans for this park were approved by the Board of Estimate of New York City. To pay the cost of establishing this park the Board of Estimate determined that the residents of a certain area surrounding the park should pay twenty-five per cent of the total cost and that the city itself should bear the other seventy-five per cent of the total cost.

In November, 1924, through a dummy purchaser, Flynn purchased certain property fronting on this park. This property, as was said above, was purchased by Flynn with the purpose of erecting a public garage thereon. This plan, it will be remembered, was defeated.

Some time in January, 1926, certain persons petitioned the Local Board to include within the park, the block in which Flynn's property was, for the sake of the uniformity of the park. This petition Flynn denounced as the work of "busybodies" and said that it was signed only by the tenants and not the owners of the property affected.

In the early part of February, 1926, a petition in opposition to this proposition was filed. Nowhere did it bear

Flynn's name nor that of his dummy, despite the fact that he was financially interested in the action to be taken by the Local Board on this petition. About two weeks later and particularly on February 19, 1926, this petition came up before the Local Board for determination. Flynn himself presided over the meeting. The minutes taken by the stenographer record Flynn as being very enthusiastic towards his own activities in procuring the park. Further, they fail to record that Flynn disclosed to the meeting that he was financially interested in the outcome. The action taken by this Board was a denial of the petition filed in January by Flynn's so-called "enemies." This meant that Flynn's property was not to be taken by condemnation, to be included within the park's boundaries.

In October, 1928, Mr. Justice McCook handed down a tentative decree in the condemnation proceedings relating to the land taken for the park. By this decree Flynn was assessed approximately $13,000 as his share in the total cost of the park. This amount was based on the fact that his property was within the area of assessment. Between the date of the decree and some time in December, 1928, some of the objectors, not including Flynn, filed their petitions with the Board of Estimate asking relief from the assessments levied.

The question as to whether or not these assessments were reasonable or excessive had come to the attention of one of the engineers of the Board of Estimate. On November 15, 1928, he filed a report stating that the assessments as levied were reasonable and not excessive. This report was referred to the Committee on Assessments of which Flynn, himself, was a member. This Committee met on December 4, 1928. Flynn was present as a member of this Committee. He argued against the adoption of this report. Even at this date he had not revealed his interest in the property affected. Flynn's position before the Committee that day was that the so-called "fifty-acre rule" of the Board of Estimate should be applied. This rule provided in substance that if a park were over fifty acres in area the cost of its establishment should be borne by the whole borough or the whole city and not by local assessment. The application of this rule, if applied in this case, would inure to Flynn's benefit to the extent of $13,000, the amount which he had been assessed.

The area of McCombs Dam Park Extension was approximately only twenty-five acres. To bring this case within this rule, Flynn argued that the acquisition by the city of the area of this park, and that of the original McCombs Dam Park, should be treated as a single transaction, even though the title to the original McCombs Dam Park had been vested in the city for over thirty years. By this reasoning the two tracts could be considered as one tract of over fifty acres. This Committee on Assessments reported to the Board of Estimate favorably to the petitioners seeking relief from assessment, overruling the report of the Board's own Chief Engineer. The date set by the Board of Estimate for a public hearing and disposition of this matter was January 10, 1929. On the morning of that day Flynn joined in the petition for relief from assessment revealing for the first time his own interest in the matter. On that same day the Board of Estimate granted the petition for relief from assessment, placing the entire cost of the park on the city.

As a result of this action the city was forced to pay approximately $600,000 more than it would have had to pay had the petition not been granted and the original plan of assessment followed, and Flynn was relieved from paying his $13,000 assessment.

There were other matters relating to Flynn into which Counsel to the Committee delved. They showed that Flynn in those other activities had conducted himself in a somewhat similar manner. The testimony on the manner in which Flynn obtained his own "curb cuts" and the way in which he got around a ruling of the Tenement House Department, to his own advantage, is too voluminous to detail here. Even a brief summary must therefore be omitted.

Before this chapter is closed a return to Willard and his relations with Flynn must be made. In his testimony Willard had related how at every point in his activities in Bronx County he was thwarted by Flynn. It seemed that no matter what he tried to do he was invariably blocked by Flynn. This situation, he explained, so affected his financial status that he lost all of the property he had ever owned in the Bronx. He had further testified that, after his final downfall, which he attributed to Flynn, judgments for the first time in his life were filed against him and that these have been increasing ever since so that to this day, because of his condition, he has not been able to pay them off. His whole position and feeling in the matter were summed up in the question Counsel put to him and the answer he gave. The question was:

"Well, then, you were about through, weren't you, as far as your investment was concerned?"

Willard's answer was:

"My investment and everything that I held dear in life. Mrs. Willard, my wife, on this account, took it so much to heart, she said, 'Here, you can't beat that dirty dog,' and she committed suicide, and the one that brought that about, that state of affairs, is that yellow dog sitting over there."

Willard here pointed to William J. Flynn, Commissioner of Public Works of the Borough of the Bronx, New York City.

He then testified that because of his experiences his total pecuniary loss, as nearly as he could estimate it in dollars and cents, was $126,000.

Flynn thereupon took the witness stand. His answers, when they were definite, were, as was expected, simply a denial of any misuse of his discretionary power as Commissioner of Public Works. On his next resuming the stand, all of a sudden he refused to testify further unless he was given a chance to answer Willard's charges then and there. This demand of his and his refusal to answer any questions resulted in his being held in contempt of the Committee. During the proceedings, which resulted in Flynn's being cited for contempt, his attorney, one Abraham Wilson, submitted an affidavit in which some of the most scandalous and indecent statements ever made by a litigant were incorporated. Counsel moved the Court to strike this affidavit from the files. The Court took approximately three weeks to decide this motion. When the Court finally did decide, its decision was a denial of the motion of Counsel together with an attack on Counsel and his motives. The opinion concluded with the remark that New York City is the City of "Sweetness and Light."

An appeal was taken by Counsel from this decision of Mr. Justice Ford's to the Appellate Division of the Supreme Court. On the argument Counsel read to the Court certain of the offensive passages from the affidavit, particularly one which stated that while Counsel was acting as Referee in the Magistrates' Investigation, his counsel on that Investigation, Isidor J. Kresel, had been indicted for perjury and that Counsel himself seemed not to have learned his lesson from this indictment. The inference from this remark was that Judge Seabury, as Counsel, had himself committed perjury. It is well to note that as far as regards Mr. Kresel he was tried upon that indictment and that his trial ended in a directed verdict of acquittal. There were other statements equally false and vicious not necessary to enumerate here. Suffice it to say that Appellate Division unanimously reversed the decision of Mr. Justice Ford, struck the affidavit from the files, and recommended that the Association of the Bar of the City of New York investigate the activities of Flynn's attorney in preparing this affidavit and finally taxed all costs of the appeal upon Wilson, Flynn's attorney.

After a hearing before Mr. Justice Ford, Flynn once again resumed the stand to testify. Finally, he finished. He was then permitted to make the statement he had previously endeavored to make. The statement, as much as was allowed to go into the record by the Chairman, was a very bitter attack on both Counsel and the witness Willard.

The attack by Flynn on Counsel was so outrageous and palpably false that no space will be wasted in demonstrating its falsity.

The attack on Willard will be discussed and refuted. First:
Flynn accused Willard of being a fugitive from justice from
New Jersey. To substantiate this charge, Flynn produced an
arrest record from the Hoboken, New Jersey, police files.
It bore the picture of Willard when he was known as Louis
Roth. This was all he produced. What he failed to produce
and what was vital was a record of a conviction. This he
couldn't produce because after the time of Willard's arrest
in 1907 and the taking of his picture, all of the indictments
found on the charge for which Willard had been arrested,
had been "nolle prossed," or, in other words, dismissed and
discharged on the motion of the Assistant Prosecutor who
had charge of them. Exemplified copies of these indictments
with the "nolle prosse" attached were produced by Counsel.
The first endeavor by Flynn to destroy Willard's credibility
by showing him to be a fugitive from justice was thus destroyed. Second: Flynn charged that Willard had a criminal
record well known to the New York City police. This record,
when produced by Counsel, showed that Willard had two
arrests, the most recent of which was 1896. It further showed
that he had been discharged on both of these charges and that
his picture was taken from the gallery and destroyed on
January 19, 1912, by order of Police Commissioner Waldo.
Flynn produced nothing else, no record of conviction or anything else to discredit Willard's credibility. His attempt in
this respect to discredit Willard was therefore of no worth.
Third: Commissioner Flynn then attempted to disprove Willard's testimony that Mrs. Willard had committed suicide
from an overdose of veronal poisoning. To do this Flynn produced a death certificate from which he quoted in part, to
the effect that Mrs. Willard had died of chronic myocarditis.
Had this been all there was to produce there might have
been some substance to his refutation, but there was more.
Flynn failed to read the very next sentence of the same report
which recorded the fact that this diagnosis was made "...
pending chemical examination of the viscera." Also he failed
to read or make reference to the final death certificate which

had been made after the prescribed chemical examination and which was so marked, reading in part: "... and that the chief and determining cause of her death was veronal poisoning; that the contributing causes were suicidal." When the public doctor first inspected the premises where Mrs. Willard died he took a statement from her husband, which statement has to this day never been disproved, in part as follows: "... on May 10th, 1930, ... the husband and wife went to bed as usual, except she was terribly nervous. This nervousness and intensely melancholy condition was due to financial reverses suffered by the family recently." This statement was embodied in and was a part of the file in the Medical Examiner's office from which Flynn quoted only in part in his attempt to discredit Willard's story of Mrs. Willard's suicide. Thus Flynn failed in his third attempt to impeach Willard's credibility. Fourth: Flynn attempted to prove that Willard, on his financing operations, had actually made a profit instead of losing $126,000. He did this by speculating on what the various building operations had cost Willard. These amounts he added up. Then he took the separate amounts which Willard had borrowed on mortgage. He added these up and subtracted his speculative total from the total of the separate amounts of the mortgages and announced the difference as Willard's profits. What he failed to do, and it was most important, was to figure out how much of each succeeding mortgage loan went to pay off a then existing mortgage. Had he done this, his total, if correct, would have proved Willard's figures, but that is not what Flynn wanted, as is proved by his testimony when he said: "I am here to discredit Mr. Willard..." and also "... He is the biggest crook and swindler that ever came into town." Once more he thus failed to accomplish his avowed purpose of discrediting Willard. Fifth: He accused Willard of having unlawfully practiced law some twenty-five years ago in Rochester, New York, under the name of A. Guy Hirsch. Later on Willard resumed the stand and denied the statement. This finished Flynn's story but not his activities in regard to

Willard. Shortly after he had finished testifying he presented the A. Guy Hirsch matter to the District Attorney. The matter was subsequently presented to the Grand Jury with the result that Willard was indicted for perjury for denying that he was the same person as A. Guy Hirsch and that he had unlawfully practiced law in Rochester. On that indictment he has not yet been tried, but a motion, one which sometimes precedes a dismissal of an indictment, *viz.*: a motion to inspect the Grand Jury minutes, has been made and granted. His Counsel has since made a motion to dismiss the indictment but as yet this has not been decided. There the matter stands.

CHAPTER XXVI

WALKER AND THE EQUITABLE BUS FRANCHISE

MAYOR WALKER rode into power on a campaign platform which included a promise to put buses on the streets within a short time. That was in 1925. Six years later Manhattan and Queens were still waiting for the fulfillment of his pledge.

State Senator John A. Hastings was an intimate associate of Mayor Walker from the time they were in the New York Senate together. He was also a vice president of a bus company in Queens. In the summer of 1925 he went to Kent, Ohio, where he saw Frank R. Fageol and Charles B. Rose, President and Vice President of the Fageol Motors Company, bus manufacturers, and William O'Neil, the President of the General Tire and Rubber Company. These men, seeking a market for their buses and tires, fell in with Hastings' plan to buy out an existent bus company and apply for a city-wide franchise. From letters passing between Fageol and his New York representative, J. Allan Smith, it is evident that this group believed that Senator Hastings had the "ear" of the incoming administration; that he could get a franchise "for any company that he might designate," and that they had the "inside track."

This venture took on a political aspect almost from the start when it was suggested that a campaign contribution would be advisable. Although the following telegrams passing between Fageol and Smith's secretary were introduced in evidence, none of this group would admit making any such contribution.

> "Hastings must have campaign contribution
> Monday Smith gone Wire Commodore"

> "Will wire Hastings contribution Monday"

Shortly after Mayor Walker's election the negotiations to buy out an existing line were discontinued "on the advice of Hastings and political leaders."

Thereafter Fageol, Rose and O'Neil each contributed $40,000 to a common fund and by agreement J. Allan Smith was made trustee. The Equitable Coach Company was incorporated and made its application for a city-wide franchise. Included in the proposed capital "set-up" were 210,000 shares of common stock, one-third of which was to go to the bankers, one-third was to be divided between Fageol, Rose, O'Neil and Smith, and the remaining one-third was to go to the "trustee." This trust agreement recited that this fund was to "secure bus franchises for greater New York," and it recited further that "any residue of junior securities left over after taking care of Hastings" and others was to be divided between Fageol, Rose, O'Neil and Smith. It is admitted that Hastings was to have had a stock interest but the true extent of this interest was never learned. At that time such an interest was considered very valuable. Indeed, a report of the estimated earnings for the first ten years of operation showed $19,000,000 available for distribution to the common stockholders. There was testimony that Hastings and his associates were to receive one-third of this common stock, which would, under this estimate, have yielded $6,000,000 in dividends.

This gigantic return was to result from bus operation alone. However, an even broader scheme was envisioned under which all surface lines would be absorbed in the Equitable, which was also to operate the city subways for a short period. The Equitable was to be the Leviathan of the traction companies. This plan was set forth in a document entitled "Plan for harmonizing and consolidating all the transportation facilities in the City of New York." Fageol claimed authorship of this plan. Hastings denied that he ever saw it. However, it was brought to the attention of some of those to whom the Equitable appealed for aid, viz.: the late Anson W. Burchard, Mr. Charles E. Mitchell, Chairman of the National City Bank, and

Mr. Leroy T. Harkness. The latter testified it was shown to him by Fageol in the presence of Hastings.

These prospects of future riches did not fill the present needs of Hastings, who was described by Rose as their "political contact man," and so they put him on the payroll of the Equitable, as of September 1, 1925, at a salary of $1,000 per month and expenses. Still later O'Neil (who described the Senator as "a typical politician. He was on everybody's side all of the time") put him on his payroll, first, at $1,000 per month and later at $1,500. In addition to that Smith and Fageol each loaned Hastings $2,500, and O'Neil loaned him $5,000. None of these loans had been repaid in May, 1932, although they had been made in December, 1928.

Both Hastings and Walker admit that they frequently discussed the Equitable project, but both of them are very deprecatory of the Senator's usefulness in winning the franchise for his employers—the Equitable group.

When the suggestion of a city-wide franchise was first broached to members of the Board of Estimate and Apportionment, not one of them favored the proposal. Mr. Bruckner, Borough President of the Bronx, wanted to give the franchise in his borough to a subsidiary of the Third Avenue Railway Company. Borough President Byrne of Brooklyn favored some other company for his borough. Borough President Miller of Manhattan favored still another. General Berry, the Comptroller, was also opposed to any city-wide grant. Politically the situation became acute. Olvany, then leader of Tammany Hall, called a conference of the members of the Board and the Democratic county leaders in an effort to harmonize and reconcile the conflicting interests. He made little or no headway and very shortly the Mayor became the outspoken proponent of a city-wide franchise. Finally, Bruckner, and McKee, President of the Board of Aldermen, backed by Edward J. Flynn, the leader in the Bronx, and others, succeeded in getting the separate franchise for their borough. They then backed the Mayor's and Delaney's plan to give the Equitable the franchise for Brooklyn, Manhattan and Queens. Delaney, who, as

Chairman of the Board of Transportation, had previously made an adverse report to giving a separate franchise for the Bronx to the Third Avenue Railway Company, made a report in its favor.

Finally, after all the bargaining was over, at a formal meeting of the Board of Estimate on January 27, 1927, on motion of the Mayor, the Board of Transportation was directed to prepare franchise contracts for the Equitable and the company proposed by Borough President Bruckner for Bronx County. The passage of the resolution effectively removed all rivals for a city-wide franchise.

As a matter of fact, there was pending at that time the application of the Service Bus Company for a city-wide franchise. In every municipal campaign for the past decade Tammany has pledged its candidate to the five-cent fare. And yet here they turned down the Service Bus which had the five-cent fare and took the Equitable which divided some of its routes into zones, and proposed to charge a fare of five cents in each zone. Under this zoning arrangement a passenger might have to pay a fifteen-cent fare. The Mayor sought to avoid the effect of this by testifying that the Equitable "had an initial five-cent fare." Other matters affecting passengers in which the application of the Service was superior to the Equitable was in giving free transfers with twenty-trip books, and in the number of buses to be provided, and in the frequency of service or "headway." So far as the city is concerned the recapture provisions in the Equitable proposal were more favorable. The Service Bus deposited a certified check for $100,000 as security for the performance of its obligations. The Equitable made no deposit. Both guaranteed a $300,000 yearly return to the city. In addition the Equitable offered a return of five per cent of receipts "from transportation" in Brooklyn and Manhattan and three per cent in other boroughs. Service Bus offered a flat three per cent of its "gross operating revenue."

Furthermore, both Delaney and the Mayor admitted that a satisfactory showing of financial responsibility was the *sine qua non* to a franchise. The Service Bus presented an absolute undertaking by the International Harvester Company to supply it with $12,000,000 worth of rolling stock, and in addition thereto, two banking houses of the highest repute, the J. Henry Schroeder Banking Corporation and Edward B. Smith and Company, agreed to underwrite its securities.

Hastings and the other Equitable promoters testified that the only financial commitment in favor of the Equitable was the verbal promise of Anson W. Burchard, who died five months before the franchise was granted.

Mayor Walker, however, testified as follows:

"Q. And you never, in believing,—in forming the conclusion that the Equitable had sufficient financial support to warrant you in granting its franchise, relied upon the belief that Burchard would finance it?

"A. I did not. When I voted for the franchise, I did not believe that Mr. Burchard was financing it.

"Q. Well, even when you considered it prior to that time, before you voted for it, you did not believe that he was going to finance it, did you?

"A. When I considered what?

"Q. The franchise. You see, Mr. Burchard died five months before the franchise was granted. Now, my question is whether, while this franchise was under consideration by you, you considered that Mr. Burchard was going to furnish financial support for the Equitable.

"A. Now, let's please end it. The reason and the financial support that we were led to believe the Company had, came from the J. G. White Company known all over the world."

The Equitable's ability to finance its operations and hence its "prospective financial responsibility," according to the Mayor, rested in two things; first, testimony of the late Mr. Choate, vice-president of the J. G. White Management Corporation, and second, a letter from Mr. Pardee, the president of that corporation, which was "formed to take over the management and operation of public utilities and industrials." Although it sometimes made advances to its clients, it never, by itself, financed a venture. Its business was management not financing. J. G. White and Company, Inc., was the financing company, but neither Mr. Choate nor Mr. Pardee was authorized to nor did they assume to bind the J. G. White and Company, Inc. In fact, there never was either an oral or written commitment binding the J. G. White and Company, Inc. to finance the Equitable. Still further, J. G. White Management Corporation never bound itself to finance the Equitable. Mr. Pardee's letter reads in part, and in the only essential part, as follows:

> "We have assurances of bankers and others that the necessary funds can be provided under satisfactory form of franchise and under such form of securities as may be approved by the Transit Commission."

There is no promise in that binding any company or person to finance the Equitable. There is nothing in the testimony before the Legislative Committee as to exactly what efforts, if any, were made to determine who these "bankers" were or what these "assurances" were. Certainly neither the Board of Estimate nor the Board of Transportation had before it a definite written commitment from these "bankers."

Contrast that with the application of the Service Bus which presented to these Boards written commitments signed by authorized representatives of the International Harvester Company, the J. Henry Schroeder Banking Company and Edward B. Smith and Company.

In regard to the application of the Service Bus, Delaney reported:

> "All financial arrangements are tentative. No unequivocal agreement to finance appears in any of the communications, and the reservations indicate that decision will be deferred until a franchise is awarded."

Had the Equitable's application been subjected to that test after a full investigation it, too, would have been rejected for the same reasons. Indeed, Delaney, while on the stand, admitted that his conclusion that the Equitable possessed the essential requisites of "financial responsibility" was an "error of judgment."

Furthermore, on April 3, 1929, the Transit Commission denied the Equitable's application for a Certificate of Convenience and Necessity. That was the end of the Equitable, for it could not operate without such a certificate. In denying its application Commissioner Godley declared that the Equitable was "not only a financial cripple but is suffering from complete financial paralysis."

First, after the franchise was granted no demand was ever made upon the J. G. White and Company, Inc., or the J. G. White Management Corporation to fulfill this alleged promise. Secondly, at a meeting of the Board of Estimate on March 4, 1929, Mayor Walker made the following statements in defending the Equitable franchise:

"... this Board understood that the General Electric Company was behind this. ... We know it; the unfortunate and untimely death of Mr. Burchard found no General Electric Company behind it. Admittedly it was a moral commitment, but no legal commitment, they refusing to carry on for some business reasons with which we can have no quarrel. ... That is a different situation, but it was unfortunate, that his death deprives this Company of that financial background which it enjoyed when it was voted the franchise. ..."

In this connection it is significant to note that J. Allan Smith testified that at first he would talk with Burchard and then with Hastings, who was in contact with the Mayor, but that subsequently Hastings established his own contact with Burchard and that he (Smith) dropped out of the picture.

Finally, as we have said, Byrne of Brooklyn, went over to the Mayor's side, and on July 28, 1927, the Board of Estimate on motion of the Mayor voted the Equitable franchise. The franchise contract itself was signed by the Mayor on August 10, 1927. The Equitable then applied to the Transit Commission for a Certificate of Convenience and Necessity without which it could not operate.

At one point in his testimony the Mayor swore that he

had never heard of three members of this Equitable group, to-wit: Smith, Rose and O'Neil. He had heard of Fageol, and Hastings, of course, was his close personal friend. Later he said he had heard of Smith but that he never knowingly saw Smith.

The very night after the franchise was voted some one gave an "old clothes" party. While Smith first testified that the Equitable group shared part of the expense for this party, he later changed his testimony. All of the Equitable group who testified in regard to this party denied that it was in celebration of getting the franchise. Nevertheless, among others, it was attended by the Mayor, Hastings, Fageol, Smith, Rose and O'Neil.

The following night O'Neil left for Europe. The Mayor went to see him off. Rose testified that he saw the Mayor in O'Neil's stateroom.

Another circumstance tending to link the Mayor and the members of the Equitable group centers around the disposition of a block of stock in the Interstate Trust Company. Mayor Walker admitted that he was offered a block of this stock, and that he told Hastings, Stanton his secretary, and his friend Senator Herrick about it. Herrick testified that he purchased this block of three hundred shares in his own name, with cash which he received "from the City Hall."

"Q. Well, did you understand that it was money sent to you by the Mayor?
"A. By the Mayor or by Mr. Stanton.
"Q. Well, when you say by Mr. Stanton, do you mean sent to you by Mr. Stanton for the Mayor?
"A. I assumed it was for the Mayor."

The Mayor denied buying any of this stock and, in fact, says he never saw a share of it. Herrick swore that he bought this stock for the Mayor, with money furnished by the Mayor, and further, that he sent three hundred shares, in four certificates, two for one hundred and two for fifty shares each, to the Mayor.

After the Mayor gave his testimony in regard to this matter, Herrick read it and said, "It rather shook my recollection," and further, "The question is, either my recollection is wrong or the Mayor's is wrong, I don't know which."

The two one hundred share certificates next appear as collateral for a loan of $23,000 to J. Allan Smith. The bank drew its check in this sum to J. Allan Smith, who then deposited it in the Equitable "Trustee Account." No one could explain how this happened. The Mayor denied that he ever received or saw these certificates. Eventually, one hundred and fifty of these shares were sold to pay off the loan. After the repayment of the loan there remained a balance of $9,194.17, which Smith turned over to Hastings, who had also received one of the fifty share certificates of this stock. Of the remaining one hundred shares, Smith retained fifty, his wife twenty-five, and Fageol twenty-five.

A few years later, when the Interstate Trust Company was merged into the Chase National Bank, Herrick testified that he asked the Mayor whether he still had this stock, to which he says the Mayor replied:

"No, I put it up for collateral and it is all gone."

The Mayor, however, testified:

". . . I never at any time told him that I had hypothecated or pledged the stock or put it up for a loan."

Inasmuch as this stock actually was pledged, Herrick's testimony is quite persuasive.

It has been seen how the Mayor argued in favor of giving a franchise to this Equitable group during the Manhattan Club conferences, and how its competitor, the Service Bus Company, was excluded by the Mayor's proposal that a franchise contract be prepared for the Equitable Company in January, 1927, and how in the following July, he moved that a franchise be awarded to it, and, how finally in August, 1927, he signed that franchise.

His efforts on their behalf, however, did not end there. He, himself, endeavored to secure the financial backing by companies other than the J. G. White Management Company, which company was alleged to have once promised to undertake the financing of the Equitable Coach Company. He went first to Mr. Charles E. Mitchell, Chairman of the Board of the National City Bank. Mr. Mitchell testified as follows:

"Q. What was the subject of conversation between you and the Mayor?

"A. The subject was the possible financing of the Equitable Coach Company."

Following this conversation with the Mayor, Mr. Mitchell ordered a study of the subject. Later, after the conclusion of this study, Mr. Mitchell, by letter dated January 28, 1927, advised the Mayor that his bank could not undertake to finance the Equitable.

Even before his conversation with Mr. Mitchell, the Mayor had talked with Mr. William H. Woodin of the American Car and Foundry Corporation about "the financing of the Equitable Bus Company."

Furthermore, the Mayor made attempts through Judge Appleton and Mr. Owen D. Young to have the General Electric Company fulfill the alleged personal and moral commitment of Mr. Burchard. But all to no avail.

On March 17, 1928, Smith wired Fageol,

"No answer yet your suggested financing stop He [*Hastings*] advises War Board [*Tammany Hall*] notified boy friend [*Mayor Walker*] time limit [*for commencement of operations under the franchise*] was April 15th stop Have made progress upstairs [*General Electric Company*] and arranged meeting late yesterday between Judge [*Charles W. Appleton*] and boy friend [*Mayor Walker*] before he [*Mayor Walker*] left for Florida stop Judge [*Charles W. Appleton*] reported favorable progress and expected see his boss [*Owen D. Young*] today and advise me Monday stop His boss [*Owen D. Young*] poor health ordered away for months but if he [*Owen D. Young*] says yes we can get extension will keep you advised."

N.B. The italicized matter in brackets is not part of the text but sets forth the explanation, given in the testimony of the cryptic designations employed.

After the General Electric refused to have anything to do with financing the Equitable, it appears that efforts to obtain financing were made in Philadelphia but were suspended before realization in accordance with the suggestion contained in the following telegram from Smith to Fageol.

"John [*Hastings*] made mistake as his boy friend [*Mayor Walker*] did not want further negotiations with Philadelphia banker [*Albert M. Greenfield*] but says go ahead with Brooklyn party [*Brooklyn Manhattan Transit Corporation*] Chairman Board [*Gerhard M. Dahl*] agreeable and like [s] you things look bright."

N.B. The italicized matter in brackets is not part of the text but sets forth the explanation, given in the testimony of the cryptic designations employed.

Up to this time the Brooklyn Manhattan Transit Corporation was not in the good graces of the City Administration because of its opposition to the application of the Equitable Coach Company for a Certificate of Convenience and Necessity. Mr. Leroy T. Harkness, a former member of the State Transit Commission, suggested to Mr. Gerhard M. Dahl, Chairman of the Board of the Broklyn Manhattan Transit, that it would be to the best interest of the Brooklyn Manhattan Transit if this opposition ceased. Mr. Dahl acquiesced; so Mr. Harkness then got into touch with Senator Herrick, whom he knew to be an intimate friend of the Mayor and also friendly with the Equitable group, in an effort to determine the attitude of the Administration toward unified surface transportation in Brooklyn, under the leadership of the Brooklyn Manhattan Transit. Senator Herrick was receptive to the idea and also indicated that he thought both the Equitable group and the City Administration would look upon it with favor.

Subsequently, Herrick, Harkness and Dahl met at luncheon

and discussed the general situation, including a change in the
Equitable franchise whereby the Brooklyn Manhattan Transit
would acquire the right to operate buses in Brooklyn.

Once again Senator Hastings was brought into the picture
and once more he took an active part in those negotiations.
During one of those conferences, Fageol is alleged to have
shown Mr. Harkness the outline of the plan finally to unify
all the traction interests in the Equitable Coach Company.
These conferences began in the spring of 1928 and finally
culminated in December of that year in the so-called "readjustment agreement." This agreement obligated the Brooklyn
Manhattan Transit to assume liabilities in the sum of
$686,000, as outlined in a schedule annexed thereto.

This agreement came before the Board of Estimate and
Apportionment in an application for leave to carry out its
terms. Objection was made on the ground that it embodied
a financial statement by the terms of which a slush fund was
made possible. Senator Hastings had been paid many thousands of dollars by the Equitable group, yet his name, nowhere, appeared in its schedule of moneys expended.

Both Mr. Dahl and Mr. Harkness testified that after this
readjustment agreement was signed the attitude of the Administration toward the Brooklyn Manhattan Transit changed.

As a result of these "slush fund" charges and the many
demands for ascertainment of the true facts, the Mayor
authorized the Finance Department to make an investigation
into all of the affairs of the Equitable. In a few preliminary
hearings in that investigation, Fageol and the others testified,
but neither they nor the Mayor nor Delaney volunteered
the information that Senator Hastings was an active pro-
moter of the Equitable franchise, in that he was the recipient
of many thousands of dollars from the Equitable group, or
that he was to have a stock interest in the corporation, when,
as and if issued. And yet the Mayor testified "it was sent to
the man [meaning Comptroller Berry] who was against it,
and the only man who did not vote for it, on the theory that
from him the strictest and most severe kind of an examination

and investigation could be had.... It wasn't necessary for me to suggest witnesses nor to send witnesses." When Comptroller Berry was on the stand, he testified:

"Q. Now when this Equitable group realized that they were confronted with a real investigation, what did they do?

"A. They complained that they were being asked unfair questions, and that their books were being subpœnaed, and things of that kind, and there was a complaint made to me. So at the next hearing I went up there and sat with Mr. Prial and I ruled all the questions he asked were perfectly fair and that they ought to come out and then they removed from the investigation. In other words, they withdrew from it.

"Q. And while you had the power, as I understand it, to administer an oath to witnesses, you were without power to subpœna them, is that right?

"A. In that particular case I was.

"Q. So that when they withdrew, there was no way that you could go ahead with the investigation?

"A. No."

Comptroller Berry further testified that he did not, at that time, nor even at the time he was on the stand in this Investigation, know that Hastings was active in the Equitable. He further testified that the Equitable group did not produce their books or vouchers or anything else to show for what purposes they had spent this $686,000. And he testified further to the fact that after this abortive inquiry, Mayor Walker did nothing to promote any more thorough investigation.

When its franchise was granted the Equitable was ordered to begin operations within ninety days. Because of its inability to satisfy the Transit Commission of its financial responsibility it applied to the Board of Estimate for extensions of time. All of these extensions, save one, were moved before the Board of Estimate by the Mayor. Finally, on April 3, 1929, the Transit Commission handed down its opinion denying the application of the Equitable for a Certificate of Convenience and Necessity. That was the end of the Equitable.

It appeared that on August 8, 1927, two days before the

franchise contract was signed, J. Allan Smith, the Trustee of the Equitable group fund to secure bus franchises, arranged with the Equitable Trust Company to purchase a $10,000 letter of credit for Mayor Walker. The next day Mr. Hoffman, the bank's representative, called at the office leased jointly by Smith and Senator Hastings, and there received from Smith $10,000 in cash, giving Smith his receipt therefor. On the following day, Hoffman returned to this office, where he met Hastings, who then took him to City Hall. Hoffman there delivered to the Mayor the letter of credit.

The next day the Mayor left for Europe in company with Mrs. Walker, Senator Herrick, Senator Downing, Hector Fuller and Commissioner McCormack at the instance and at the expense of Rodman Wanamaker "to obtain information regarding housing, park systems and other municipal activities."

Although the letter of credit was exhausted on September 20 by a withdrawal of $3,150, and although he had no account with the Equitable Trust Company in Paris or New York, the Mayor, on the next day, drew a draft on himself in the sum of $3,000 payable in New York.

This draft arrived in New York before the party returned. Mr. Loasby of the Equitable Trust Company called on Smith, who had arranged the original credit, to pay it, which he finally did out of his own pocket in January, 1928.

When the Mayor was asked to explain the overdraft, he testified that he drew it on the Equitable Trust Company because Senator Downing asked him to do so, and that he drew it not for his own use, but for the use of others in the party. Although he drew this draft on a bank where he had no account, he himself took no steps upon his return to determine whether or not it had been paid. He claimed that he did not know that it had been paid by Smith.

Mr. Smith explained that he received the $10,000 in cash from Hastings, and that he asked to be permitted to buy this letter of credit from the Equitable Trust Company so he could throw some business to his friend Mr. Loasby, President of that Trust Company, and thus do him a favor. He also testified that he did not know where Hastings got the original $10,000, but as to the overdraft he thought that Hastings had told him that he got the money from Sentor Downing; further, that he did not want to pay the overdraft but finally did and from time to time thereafter he had been repaid by Hastings in cash, in various amounts.

It was Mayor Walker's claim that he and other members of the party for whose benefit the letter of credit existed, had made cash contributions to the late Senator Downing for this purpose. The Mayor said that his contribution was $3,000 and that he never benefited beyond this amount.

CHAPTER XXVII

THE SISTO, BLOCK AND SHERWOOD STORIES

ENTRY into the taxi business in New York City is no longer free and open. Since January, 1932, the Board of Taxicab Control has been in existence and no taxi can operate on the city streets unless its owner first secures from this Board a Certificate of Convenience and Necessity and also a license. The Mayor alone has the power of appointment and removal of the five members of this Board. Preliminary to its establishment and in April, 1930, the Mayor, in vetoing a bill for increased taxi fare, appointed a Taxicab Investigating Commission. In the following September, this Commission reported to the Mayor in favor of "taxicab service under a single franchised corporation." This, according to Colonel George W. Mixter, a member of this Commission and later a member of the Board, was a "little philosophizing" rather than a "practical thing." Although no "single franchised corporation" was set up, substantially the same result, *i.e.*, a monopoly, was made possible through the creation of this Board. The Mayor sponsored the Municipal law which created this Commission.

There were two large operating companies which were vitally interested in the passage of a law regulating competition in the taxicab business. The Checker Cab Manufacturing Company, a Parmelee Subsidiary, was one and the Terminal Cab Company, a General Motors Subsidiary, was the other.

J. A. Sisto and Company and Samuel Ungerleider and Company, investment bankers, were for a time jointly interested in the flotation of the Parmelee Company securities.

J. A. Sisto happened to be in Atlantic City in the summer of 1929, and there he met and talked with the Mayor. Sisto was at that time interested in stock of the Cosden Oil Company. There was some discussion among the group there

264

assembled as to the Mayor's participation in this "pool." John J. McKeon testified that the Mayor said he couldn't buy any "if it was five cents a share." Sisto had a similar recollection of the conversation. The Mayor, however, says that he accepted an invitation to participate and that although he put up no money and signed no commitment he would have paid his share of the loss had there been any. Following this conversation, Sisto purchased 1,000 shares of this stock at a cost of $45,000. About five months later he sold it at a profit of $87,960. Sisto testified that although he did not feel obligated to give any part of this to the Mayor, he did so out of admiration for him. Accordingly he sent to the Mayor through McKeon $26,000 worth of bonds. Corroborative of Sisto's testimony that no part of these profits belonged to the Mayor is the fact that he, Sisto, in his tax return for 1929, listed these 1,000 shares as his and charged himself with the entire profit.

Ten of these bonds of the par value of $10,000 were debenture bonds of the Reliance Bronze and Steel Corporation, convertible into stock at the option of the holder. The Mayor testified that when he received them in December, 1929, he put them in his "safe," and a day or two later, while talking with Mrs. Walker over the telephone, he told her that he "had put some bonds in the safe for her," and that she still had them. Nevertheless, the interest coupons for the year 1930 were deposited in an account in his name in the Federation Bank and Trust Company. The Mayor sought to avoid the effect of this by testifying that this account was really Mrs. Walker's, and that these coupons were deposited "probably by Mr. Sherwood because he transacted any little business she had and took care of her accounts—audited them, and paid bills for her and did other services for her." This deposit was made on December 29, 1930.

On or about February 3, 1931, the City of New York awarded a $43,000 contract to the Reliance Bronze and Steel Corporation. Section 1533 of the City Charter provides in part, as follows:

"No . . . other officer of the Corporation, shall be or become interested, directly or indirectly, as . . . stockholder or otherwise, in or in the performance of any contract . . . , the expense, price or consideration of which is payable from the City Treasury, . . ."

The section goes on to say that if such officer shall "knowingly acquire an interest as above described in any contract . . . unless the same shall be devolved upon him by law," he shall "on conviction thereof, forfeit his office, and be punished for a misdemeanor. . . ."

The burden of the Mayor's explanation is that this $26,000 in bonds represented "profits of an ordinary, lawful business transaction"; that he didn't know of this contract and that he gave the bonds to Mrs. Walker.

It also appeared that during the time Samuel Ungerleider and Company was interested in the sale of Parmelee securities it purchased from Russell T. Sherwood a block of 1,000 shares of Ungerleider Financial stock for $51,960. This was some $22,000 in excess of the market price. This, Mr. Ungerleider swore, was pursuant to a repurchase agreement made the year before when Sherwood purchased this stock. While insisting that such a transaction was not unusual, he admitted that it was only made where there was a special reason and that such agreements were usually in writing. He testified that the special reason in this case was a request therefor by McKeon, but McKeon denied making any such request. No written agreement with Sherwood as to this was ever produced.

This money was deposited in one of the Sherwood accounts from which withdrawals were made for the benefit of the Mayor.

The Terminal Cab Company took an indirect route to further its interests. It employed the ubiquitous Senator Hastings, paying him over a period of time $26,000. Mr. Seymour, its General Manager, testified:

"A. Yes. I was quite certain that he could be of assistance. I knew Senator Hastings was a politician. It was obvious by the office which he holds, and that was not an inconsequential consideration, because we knew that our competitor . . . at least we had reason to believe . . . was well entrenched politically. They had been in business here for a great many years, and it was a factor that we could not be unmindful of."

Mr. Seymour did not agree with Colonel Mixter's assertion that he did not consider Hastings an expert authority on taxicabs. Colonel Mixter testified that "so far as Hastings appeared at all, he appeared in our minds as the messenger from the Mayor." Hastings never informed the Colonel that he was the paid employee of the Terminal Cab Company that was actively seeking this regulatory law.

The Mayor swore in three members of this Commission, including Colonel Mixter, in his apartment in the Mayfair. Hastings was in the Mayor's apartment at that time.

On another occasion Seymour visited Hastings, and on this occasion he found present, Frank P. Walsh, Chairman of the Taxicab Investigation Commission. Mr. Walsh will also be remembered in connection with his trip to California with the Mayor and Hastings when the Mayor was to plead for the release of Mooney. Hastings made the arrangements and the party traveled de luxe in a private car. Up to the date of Hastings' testimony, although it had been billed to him in the sum of $2,000, Hastings had not paid the Pullman Company. But he testified ". . . it will be paid, like every other debt of mine will be paid." Locally Mr. Walsh will be remembered as Counsel to Hastings in the lawsuits brought to compel him to testify. By means of these lawsuits Hastings delayed Counsel in the completion of his case for over two months. The disclosures in regard to Senator Hastings furnish some indication for his statements about Judge Seabury, and also may give some basis for his hesitancy in submitting to examination.

The Senator made a motion to vacate a subpœna of the Committee which was served on him on January 4, 1932. This was denied. Still he refused to appear and, consequently, was cited for and held in contempt and sentenced to imprisonment for thirty days, and the Sheriff of any county was directed "to apprehend him and bring him before the Committee or a duly constituted sub-committee in response to the subpœna."

Finally, on March 3, 1932, the Court of Appeals handed down an opinion written by Chief Judge Cardozo, affirming the denial of Hastings' motion to vacate the subpœna and modifying the order adjudging him in contempt.

Chief Judge Cardozo said in part:

> "He may be prosecuted for a misdemeanor (penal law Sec. 1329). . . . He may be punished as for a contempt by the Legislature itself (Legislative law Sec. 4). There is no statute, however, whereby the failure to obey a subpœna issued by the Legislature may be punished by the judiciary as constituting a contempt of court. . . ."

District Attorney Crain, however, did not prosecute him for a misdemeanor. The Legislature, then in session, did not punish him for contempt, nor did it pass a statute empowering the courts to punish future offenders. It was not until after all this that Hastings appeared and testified.

One Sunday afternoon the Mayor telephoned Mr. Paul Block and asked him to go for an automobile ride, and since he was there, to bring his ten-year-old son Billy. While Mr. Block and Billy were waiting for the Mayor, the following colloquy, as testified to by Mr. Block, took place:

> ". . . and the youngster said 'How much salary does the Mayor get' and I told him $25,000, [laughter; gavel] which was his salary at that time.
>
> " 'Does the City give him a home?,' And I said, 'No, they don't.' I recall he said, 'Does it give him an automobile?' And I said 'Yes, but not to Mrs. Walker.'
>
> " 'Well,' this youngster said, 'can he live on what he gets?' [Laughter] And I said, 'Well, I suppose he can, but it probably is a difficult problem.'
>
> "And, Judge, I want you to believe me that it entered my mind then that I was going to try to make a little money for him. [Laughter; gavel.]"

Some time after this Mr. Block, according to his recollection, had the following conversation with the Mayor:

"A. I recall I said to the Mayor, 'Jimmie, I am going to try and make a little money for you. I am going to open a joint account for us and see if I can make a little money for you. . . .'

"Q. Now, what did the Mayor say to you?

"A. As I recall it, he said 'Oh, you oughn't to do that, Paul,' and I said, 'Yes, I am going to do it.' Something like that was said between us."

In answer to the charges then pending before the Governor the Mayor said:

"The transaction with Mr. Paul Block involved a joint brokerage account. The profits derived from the operation of that account were not 'gratuities.' The legal and moral liability of each party to the account was equal and definite, well fixed and established. If there had been a loss, my obligation to the brokers would be as great as that of Mr. Block and could not be disputed."

While on the stand Mr. Block was asked the following questions and in response gave the following answers:

"Q. Well now, in your conversation with the Mayor as to the circumstances under which the account was to be opened, there was never any agreement, was there, that if that account should result in a loss, Mayor Walker would pay a proportion of that loss?

"A. There was never a discussion of that, but may I say as I said to you once before?

"Q. Yes.

"A. If there had been a loss in that account I would not have allowed him to stand it."

Mr. Block said he would characterize this transaction as "profits" rather than a "gift" or "donation" but finally he testified:

"Q. At any rate, Mr. Block, it was, as far as the Mayor was concerned, something for nothing?

"A. Yes, certainly. [Laughter; gavel.]"

While the Mayor was on the stand he characterized this transaction as a "beneficence," and in regard to his liability for any loss said:

"Q. Did you agree to stand any of the loss that might arise in the course of trading in that account?
"A. I was ready to.
"Q. Did you ever have any agreement to that effect?
"A. Mr. Block made no agreement about the matter.
"Q. Don't you know that it was the understanding that you should not so contribute?
"A. There was no understanding that I should not. The subject was never discussed."

Mr. Block stressed the point that "this of course I figured was for my friend Jimmie Walker, rather than for the Mayor of New York—but he hapened to be the Mayor." Nevertheless, although he had known James J. Walker "for years before he was the Mayor," Counsel asked him the following question and he gave the following answer:

"Q. Hadn't he been given any money by you before he became Mayor? . . .
"A. Never. The first account was in February, 1927, and he was Mayor then, wasn't he?"

The fact remains that this account was opened in February, 1927, upon the credit of Mr. Block without any contribution by the Mayor, and without any written agreement by him to share any loss that might ensue. It was originally opened under the designation of "P.B. & J.J.W." This was later changed to "P.B. & M.B." According to a letter to Paul Block from his brother Max, this was done at the suggestion of an Internal Revenue Agent, "because, while he could see that there was nothing discreditable about such transactions, some people might suspect ulterior motives, and he would advise that instead of having the Mayor appear as one of the two parties of this joint account, it would be better to substitute another name."

From the time the account was opened until it was closed

on August 6, 1929, the Mayor and Paul Block each withdrew some $246,000 after deducting taxes of approximately
$70,000 on the share of each.

The Mayor testified, "Mr. Block always gave me the money
from time to time." It is undisputed that save for one instance
the Mayor received his share in checks which he cashed. The
only item paid out by check was to an unnamed person. Mr.
Block testified that he delivered this $7,500 check to the
Mayor. The latter admits that it was drawn on his authoriza-
tion but testified that he never got the check; that it was
delivered to the unnamed person by the broker.

The examination continued:

"Q. Now, what did you do with the cash, Mr. Mayor?

"A. Took it home and put it in a safe. Not a vault, not a tin
box,—a safe in my house. [Laughter; gavel.] I mean, to distin-
guish that, seriously."

The Mayor ascribed two reasons for this; first, so that it
would be available for Mrs. Walker and himself and, secondly, "That these moneys were all tax paid, and I never
deposited them in a bank where they might be confused with
or associated with moneys that were not tax paid." The fact
remains, however, that between March 9, and June 15, 1927,
he received $102,000. No tax was due, and none was paid on
this until 1928. Further, the mere mingling of tax paid moneys
with other moneys would not make the former taxable over
again.

Senator Hastings was one of the organizers of the Robert
Beyer Corporation. He induced Mr. Block to invest in this
Corporation and introduced Dr. Beyer to the Mayor. In the
spring of 1927, Hastings, Paul Block and his son Billy, the
Mayor, Delaney, the Chairman of the Board of Transportation, and "a lot of distinguished people" went to Dr. Beyer's
laboratory. The Senator testified that they all went there
to witness the manufacture of gold. But he also testified:

". . . He claimed he could manufacture a new synthetic tile; he
claimed he could make tile with a coal process, and at considerably

reduced cost, and would be able to underbid any competitor for any particular job, whether it be a subway or whether it be a private building."

The Senator said that he "very probably" tried to have it approved "for use in subways" as well as for other uses. Indeed, he, in company with Dr. Beyer, subsequently called at Chairman Delaney's office for the purpose of securing the approval of the engineers of the Board of Transportation, on Dr. Beyer's representation that a considerable saving would be effected. Subsequently, Mr. Lucas, Division Engineer of the Board of Transportation, submitted a report of tests made on samples of this tile in which he stated that the tile appeared "to be almost identical in quality and kind with our standard station finish tile." As a matter of fact no tile was sold to the city. The Senator, in March, 1929, sold out his interest for $50,000 in cash. No wonder he believed that Dr. Beyer could make gold.

Doctor William H. Walker is a brother of the Mayor. He is medical examiner to the Department of Education at a yearly salary of $6,500. He is also medical examiner to the City Pension Retirement Board for which he receives $25 for each of the eighteen or twenty sessions which are held by the Board in the course of a year.

Although Doctor Walker has never been officially designated by the Corporation Counsel to act for the city in its workmen's compensation cases, he has been actively associated with four of the doctors so designated, who enjoy a practical monopoly of this practice. These four doctors are Thomas J. O'Mara, Harris Feinberg, Alfred B. Cassasa, and Edward L. Brennan. Doctor Walker shared offices wtih Doctors Feinberg, Cassasa and Brennan. In addition, he had a joint bank account with Doctor Feinberg and a joint bank account and safe deposit box with Doctor Brennan.

To these four associates of Doctor Walker are sent the cases of almost every city employee who has sustained injuries in the course of duty. The cases in Manhattan and

Queens go to Doctors Cassasa and O'Mara, those in Brooklyn to Doctor Brennan and those in the Bronx to Doctor Feinberg.

Since, in general, the cases received by these doctors involve injuries of a less serious nature, the major part of their treatment consists of massage and baking treatments, for which they are paid by the city at the rate of $2 a visit. In addition X-rays are taken by these doctors in many of these cases at increased cost to the city.

The doctors' bills are in the first instance submitted to the office of the Corporation Counsel. The only check made as to the accuracy of these bills was to multiply the number of visits shown in the bill by the uniform fee of two dollars. No effort was made to determine whether the visits were made, or whether the treatments were actually given. No check was made as to whether or not the treatment was for a condition resulting from the accident, or whether the number of treatments given was necessary.

Illustrative of one of the cases put in evidence was the following colloquy between Counsel and witness:

"Q. That is, Edward Baren had injured his left thumb while in the pursuit of his duty for the city?

"A. Apparently, it looks like left; they put two asterisks, or something else. It is left. I assume it—

"Q. All right we will accept it as left thumb. Now, this bill that Doctor Cassasa presents (is for) a home visit and then it covers an item for strapping of the foot, does it not? [Laughter; gavel.]

"A. Yes, sir."

Then there was the instance where an employee's injury was designated as an injury to the right toe, and Doctor Feinberg rendered a bill for four X-rays of the hand. In another, the injury was described as a "bruised third finger, right hand," for which Doctor Cassasa presented a bill for twelve visits. Among other instances of like character was a "laceration of the right second finger" for which a bill was rendered for fifteen visits and a sacroiliac support.

During the period from January 1, 1929, to January 31, 1932, these four doctors were paid by the city fees aggregating $216,001.55. The office of the Corporation Counsel approved these payments, and warrants for that amount were countersigned by the Mayor's Chief Clerk.

Doctor Walker denied splitting with these doctors the fees which were paid by the city, but was forced to admit that he split some city fees with Doctor Feinberg. He also admitted endorsing some city checks which Doctor Feinberg received and depositing them in their joint account. He also admitted endorsing and depositing, in this Walker-Feinberg account, some city checks received by Doctor Cassasa. Many instances were shown where one of these four doctors received a city check for his services, and at or about that same time the doctor drew his check payable to Doctor Walker for exactly half of the amount so received. It was the Doctor's contention that these checks were in payment for services he performed for this doctor in other than city compensation cases. Doctor Walker testified that for the usual services he rendered to these doctors his charges would vary, dependent on the circumstances.

> "Q. That being the case, doesn't it seem strange to you that in these particular city compensation cases you received exactly one-half, even to the odd number of dollars and the odd number of cents,—doesn't that seem very strange?
>
> "A. I didn't even know it was so until now.
>
> "Q. Now that you do know it is so, doesn't it seem very strange to you?
>
> "A. It is evidently a coincidence. . . .
>
> "Q. Hasn't it happened so often that it is rather suggestive of the fact that it was not the result of mere coincidence but was the result of plan or design?
>
> "A. No."

Regarding his brother's testimony, the Mayor said:

"Any one who knows him knows that he is an earnest, plugging type who is lost in a situation like this. If any one had been there to advise him he would have made a far different showing."

Russell T. Sherwood was for some years sort of a "book-keeper" in the law office of Warren and McIntyre with which James J. Walker was associated before he became Mayor. There came a time when Sherwood applied to the Bank of Manhattan Trust Company for a position in their New Business Department. One Michael F. Dee, a lawyer in New York, wrote a letter of recommendation in which he said in part:

"Mr. Sherwood, with his country-bred attitude of being chiefly a listener, soon became the clearing house of the interests of all connected with the organization [Blauvelt & Warren, later Warren & McIntyre] and was implicitly trusted by everybody, and it was recognized that the confidence reposed in him by any one of the interests were entirely safe in his keeping. . . ."

When Sherwood applied for this job he stated that his former salary was $3,000 per annum and extras. This new job with the bank was at a salary of $10,000 per year. Mr. Rowley, President of the Manhattan Company, readily admitted that Sherwood's acquaintance with the Mayor and other department heads was "in his favor."

Sherwood started working at the Bank in January, 1930. While there he became very friendly with Frederick C. Harris, Secretary of the Manhattan Company.

On August 11, 1931, the Committee issued a subpœna requiring his attendance, but Sherwood evaded service. He went first to Atlantic City. When he was discovered there, another effort was made to serve him. Again he disappeared and went to Chicago. From there he went to Mexico City where he was married. While he was honeymooning in Mexico City he was served, pursuant to statute, with an order of the Supreme Court of the State of New York, requiring his attendance as a witness in New York City before the Committee. This order he disobeyed and once more disappeared. For the violation of this order he was adjudged in contempt by the Supreme Court and fined $50,000. Furthermore, he lost his $10,000 a year job with the bank.

Sherwood was wanted as a witness only in connection with the Committee's examination into the affairs of Mayor Walker. Sherwood was not a city official. Why then should he have disappeared—given up a $10,000 a year job and suffered a $50,000 fine? On August 13, 1932, Sherwood had kept himself beyond the reach of the Committee's subpœna for over a year.

Sherwood and the Mayor had many financial dealings together. It was Sherwood that handled some payments to the "unnamed person." It was Sherwood with whom the Mayor had a joint safe-deposit box in 1924. This was changed to a larger one in 1930 still in the joint names of the Mayor and Sherwood.

Mr. Harris testified that two days after the subpœna for Sherwood had been issued, Sherwood came to the bank and took out of safe-keeping two packages "contents unknown" that "were bound together with a strap." Sherwood visited Harris in Asbury Park toward the end of August, but Harris did not inform the Committee as to Sherwood's whereabouts. After leaving Asbury Park, Sherwood went to Chicago, which Harris knew but did not inform the Committee. Harris spoke with Sherwood over the long distance telephone while the latter was in Mexico City. Again Harris failed to inform the Committee of this fact.

Harris testified that he received a letter dated October 1, 1931, from Sherwood, who was then in Chicago. In this letter he asked Harris to go to his safe-deposit box (as a matter of fact it was the same box held jointly by Sherwood and the Mayor) and get his will. The word "will" was underlined. Harris said he had no idea why Sherwood underlined this word, for when he opened the box there was nothing else there but "paper clips and rubber bands." Between the time he saw Sherwood in Asbury Park and the receipt of this letter Harris called upon the Mayor. He called because he thought that it would help him to "cultivate the acquaintance of the Mayor of the City of New York," whom he had already met on several previous occasions.

Under date of October 6, 1931, Sherwood, then in Mexico City, wrote Harris a short note advising him where he could be reached. He said nothing about receiving his will. After the receipt of this letter and after he had been to the safe deposit box, Harris called Sherwood on the telephone "to congratulate him on being married." After this telephone call Harris again talked with the Mayor at City Hall. He said that he hadn't meant to call on the Mayor, but as he was passing City Hall he saw a crowd in the plaza and so he dropped in to ask the Mayor what the crowd was. Some time later Harris again saw the Mayor at the latter's apartment. This visit was occasioned by Harris' reading in the paper that the Mayor was sick. At the time of these conversations the Mayor and Harris both knew that Sherwood was a fugitive from the process of the Committee. Even though they both were Sherwood's friends, they say that they did not mention Sherwood's name.

The Mayor admits that Sherwood took care of some of Mrs. Walker's business affairs; that he and Sherwood opened a joint safe-deposit box in 1924; that Sherwood came to City Hall, where he got the Mayor's salary checks which he later deposited and that he also made other deposits for the Mayor. The Mayor testified: "I haven't seen a checkbook of my own or a stub or canceled voucher in six years." These, he testified, were at the office of Warren and McIntyre and that Sherwood made out "most of the checks," and brought them to the Mayor for his signature. The Mayor admitted that Sherwood made payments to the captain of the "steam launch" or "yacht" which Mrs. Walker sometimes used; and that he made payments on behalf of the Mayor to both Mrs. Walker and to his (the Mayor's) sister; that it was Sherwood who delivered $31,200 in cash and took delivery of stock which the Mayor had purchased in that amount; that it was Sherwood in whose name the Mayor directed stock to be issued by the Century Circuit Company in payment to James J. Walker and his associates for alleged legal services; and that it was Sherwood who deposited a check in his account given in payment of legal services rendered by James J. Walker and his associates.

From January 1, 1926, down to the time that Sherwood fled the jurisdiction, there passed through his bank and brokerage accounts, exclusive of transfers, almost a million dollars, of which over seven hundred and twenty thousand dollars was in cash.

One of these Sherwood accounts was with the Central Hanover Bank and Trust Company. This account was marked "Special."

One William J. Scanlan had at one time or another represented to various people that he could be reached by telephone at Cortland 7-1000. This was in fact a telephone in City Hall. Scanlan was a salesman for the Butler Manufacturing Company. On October 29, 1927, Scanlan received a commission of $10,000, for the sale to the city of ten street sweepers, which he had "boosted" to the Mayor, and thereafter a $6,000 check from Scanlan to Sherwood was deposited in the Sherwood special account. Sherwood also deposited in this "Special" account a check for $51,960, which he received from Samuel Ungerleider and Company for stock then selling on the Exchange for about $30,000. There were also deposited in this account dividends on the above described Century Circuit stock and coupons from five Consolidated Gas Company bonds owned by Mrs. Walker.

Photostatic copies of the checks drawn on this account by Sherwood, between August 27, 1929, and November 5, 1931, show payments to and on behalf of members of the Mayor's family in the sum of $22,000. One item was in payment of the annual rent for the safe deposit box in the joint names of Sherwood and the Mayor.

To this situation the Mayor answered that he gave cash

to Sherwood for the payments to the Mayor's wife and sister, and that Sherwood must have kept the cash and issued checks.

There were purchased from the Sherwood accounts for the unnamed person, securities costing approximately $58,000. In addition it was Sherwood who purchased, for $10,000 in cash, a letter of credit to this same unnamed person, and then later, cash sums increasing this letter of credit by $6,500 were supplied by Sherwood.

Also, Sherwood, on March 25, 1927, opened an account with the brokerage house of Hornblower and Weeks, with a deposit of $100,000 in cash which he then stated was not his money. This account was designated "Investment Trustee Account." Between that date and August 9, 1927, when this account was closed, not a single share of stock was traded in—the account being used solely as a reservoir for the accumulation of cash to the extent of $261,000. In this account on June 17, 1927, two items of $25,000 each in cash were deposited. Two checks, each for $25,000, were drawn on the Block account, on June 9 and June 16, 1927, respectively. Both checks were drawn by Baruch and Company and reduced to cash. The checks themselves were redeposited by Baruch and Company. The first check was redeposited in the account of Baruch and Company on June 16, and the second on June 22, 1927. The Mayor and Paul Block both testified that payments to the Mayor for this account were made in cash. The Mayor further testified in regard to these two checks, as follows:

"... The cash was given to me, whether before the check was cashed or afterwards, and then the check went back into the account of the broker who gave me the cash."

Therefore, under the method of dealing in this account the Mayor might have had $50,000 in cash on June 16, 1927.

On August 9, 1927, Sherwood drew out, in cash, the entire amount of this account—some $261,000. This closed the account.

Nowhere in any of the Sherwood accounts is there any record of any deposit or other disposition of this money.

There is no need to describe the turbulent and stormy sessions of the Committee while Mayor Walker was on the witness stand. The courtroom was packed by Tammany adherents, while those who had official passes were kept waiting in the courthouse rotunda and never did get in because the room was already filled.

The first day's examination concerned the Equitable Bus Company and its franchise. Although the Mayor's memory failed him in regard to specific matters of inquiry, he took the opportunity to make speeches about the traction interests. He made futile attempts to "wisecrack" away logical inferences from admitted facts. Only when the interruptions of the Tammany Minority became so violent as to prevent any progress at all, did he assist in quieting them. Grandiloquently he referred to the Constitutional provisions under which he claimed he might refuse to testify, and then with magnificent gesture waived their benefit. That was the first day.

His examinaion on the second day came down to more specific questions—his "beneficences,"—the Sisto matter and Russell T. Sherwood. He no longer made speeches as he had the day before. He interjected the word "persecution." He became exceedingly careful in his answers and took a less self-assured attitude. He left the stand the loser in what the public press characterized as a "duel" between himself and Counsel, as an analysis of his testimony shows. It was the triumph of cold facts over mere denials, evasions and speeches to a friendly, partisan audience.

Within two days after the hearings closed Governor Roosevelt gave out a newspaper interview stating in effect that if there was any evidence against any public official it was the duty of the Committee and Counsel to submit it to him and that he would act promptly and decisively.

Judge Seabury, construing this newspaper statement as a

challenge, immediately accepted it and issued a statement
assuring the Governor that in a day or two he would submit
the evidence and an analysis of it to him. This promise he
carried out within five days, accompanying the papers referred to, containing specifications of conclusions that arose
from the proven facts, with an analysis of the evidence. Mr.
William Jay Schiefflin embodied these conclusions or specifications in formal charges which he filed with the Governor. The
Governor, after stating that he regarded the specifications
contained in Judge Seabury's letter as charges, sent them together with Mr. Schiefflin's formal charges to Mayor Walker,
notifying him to make answer to them. Before the Governor
sent these specifications and charges to the Mayor he submitted them to Messrs. Mack and Conboy for their consideration.

After the lapse of thirty-five days the Mayor filed his
answer. In it he denied the conclusions which Judge Seabury
had claimed arose naturally and reasonably from the evidence;
he also asserted that some of the matters referred to in the
charges and specifications had arisen during his first term as
Mayor and that the Governor was without jurisdiction to
consider them. The Mayor's answer was also replete with
personal abuse of Judge Seabury and animadversions upon
the motives of the Committee.

Within a few days after the Mayor filed his answer Judge
Seabury replied in detail to the Mayor's answer ignoring,
however, all personal attacks either directed against himself
or the Committee. Such was the status of the removal proceedings against Mayor Walker at the time this book went
to press. The City of New York and the Country await the
action of Governor Roosevelt.

CHAPTER XXVIII

THE COMMITTEE

AFTER the Resolution to investigate the government of New York City had been passed by both Houses of the Legislature and the appropriation had been assured, speculation was aroused as to what would be the makeup of the Committee, particularly the Democratic or Minority side. Later, after deliberation by the Legislative leaders, it was determined and announced that the Honorable Samuel H. Hofstadter, the only Republican Senator from New York City, was to be the Chairman.

The other Republican members of the Committee were chosen from various parts of the State. All the Democratic or Minority members chosen, were from New York City. The Republicans, generally speaking, were in favor of a complete and thoroughgoing investigation. The Democrats, on the other hand, were opposed to any investigation which might reveal facts reflecting on the Organization or any of its members.

After Senator Hofstadter had been appointed Chairman, he wrote to Judge Samuel Seabury, of New York City, requesting him to act as Chief Counsel to the Committee. This invitation Judge Seabury accepted on certain conditions which he laid down in his letter of April 8, 1931, to Senator Hofstadter. The letter reads:

"April 8, 1931.

"Hon. Samuel H. Hofstadter
   Chairman of the Joint Legislative Committee appointed to Investigate the City of New York.
   Senate Chamber,
   Albany, New York.
"My dear Senator Hofstadter:
   "I accept the designation as counsel of the Joint Legislative

282

Committee appointed under and pursuant to the concurrent resolution of the Senate and Assembly of the State of New York for a city-wide investigation of the government of New York City and the county governments within its geographical areas.

"This acceptance is based on the assurances which I have received and which I have no doubt express the wishes of every member of that Committee, that, in the discharge of my duties as counsel, I shall have an absolutely free hand. This freedom of action is to leave me entirely unembarrassed in the presentation to the Committee of such evidence as I deem to be pertinent, and in the selection of my staff, including the reporters who are to take the testimony at the private hearings.

"The task involved in acting as the Committee's counsel, as I visualize it, is to present for the consideration of the Committee the true facts as they exist in the complicated structure known as the Government of the City of New York and the local instrumentalities of government operating within the limits of that City, and to present evidence as to such constructive proposals as shall make possible beneficial changes in the Charter of the City.

"It is now over a generation since the Charter of the City has been revised. Since that time the complexities of City life have been greatly increased and changes are necessary to eliminate waste and corruption, and to increase the ability of the City to minister more adequately to the governmental needs of its people. Constructive proposals are of paramount importance, but they must spring from the practical needs of the people living within the City. A discussion of them would be premature until the facts inherent in the actual situation have been fully disclosed.

"If the investigation which the Legislature has directed is to be of value, it must be thorough and comprehensive. If it is to be of this character a large number of well-equipped lawyers, investigators, accountants, stenographers and clerks will be necessary. The task of investigating the government of the City of New York and the county governments within its territory is a gigantic one. The work can be brought within the realm of possibility only by effective organization and a competent staff of assistants.

"The expenses of such an investigation will obviously exceed the sum of $250,000 already appropriated. I am informed that this amount was expended in the recent Connolly investigation. In view of my knowledge of what will be required, I take the responsibility of earnestly urging that the amount of the appropriation be increased at this time by $250,000.

"In addition to the staff of lawyers, investigators, accountants and clerks which will be necessary, there will also be expenses incurred in furnishing, with proper equipment, the offices which are to be selected. The work of reporting the minutes at the public and private hearings will, of itself, be an item which will be necessarily large. It seems to me that it is the part of wisdom to recognize this situation at the outset, so that the Legislature may, before adjournment, if it seems fit, make provision for carrying out, in an effective way, the investigation which it has ordered.

"The task which I assume in response to your invitation is a legal one and I shall discharge it in the manner in which a lawyer acting as counsel for a private client should discharge his duty. I shall discharge it to the best of my ability and without regard to any political consideration or influence whatsoever. In endeavoring to disclose the situation as it is, the spirit which shall guide me in the discharge of my duties as counsel to the Committee is well expressed in the fine old oath which grand jurors were required to take, *viz.*:

" 'You will diligently inquire and true presentment make. . . . You shall present no one for envy, hatred or malice; neither shall you leave any one unpresented for fear, favor, affection, hope of reward or gain, but shall present all things truly as they come to your knowledge, according to the best of your judgment.'

"To the letter and spirit of this oath I pledge myself faithfully to adhere in the discharge of my duty as counsel.

"I remain, Sir, with great respect,
                              "Very truly yours,
                                   (sgd) "Samuel Seabury."

This letter in its terms was accepted by the Chairman, who then issued a call for the first meeting of the Committee at the Bar Association in New York City on April 20, 1931. The meeting was held. Everything passed off very smoothly. The Democrats joined in and seconded the motions made, and gave to all the appearance of coöperation and helpfulness. How false this impression turned out to be is now a matter of public record. The opposition began to gather at the next

session held on May 14, 1931, and, ever since, has been grow-
ing more determined and frantic as the evidence has been
adduced.

At the first meeting Assemblyman Moffat, one of the majority members of the Committee, introduced a resolution
authorizing the Committee as a whole to appoint sub-
committees of one to hear examinations in private. This motion was seconded by Assemblyman Louis Cuvillier, one of
the Democratic Minority. It was put to a vote and unanimously passed.

At the second session, Assemblyman Cuvillier introduced
a resolution declaring that all hearings should be held in
public, because neither in its preamble nor in the Resolution
proper was there any provision that private hearings might be
held before a sub-committee. As a matter of fact the Resolution, in so many words, provided for the creation of sub-
committees.

At the first meeting Mr. Cuvillier had said: "The way I
look upon the Committee, it is to do this work, and we will
proceed to do it in a dignified, orderly way. We do not want
to lower it like a meeting of schoolboys, but to proceed in
a dignified way. . . ." At the close of the same session, he had
this to say of Counsel: "I think we could not have selected
better Counsel than Judge Seabury to carry on the work, being
a native of New York State and a former Judge of the Bench
of New York City, and having the interest at heart of the
City, we feel that we are safe in his hands." Could the reader
look through the minutes of all the sessions of the Committee,
he would at once see how Mr. Cuvillier subsequently demonstrated the sincerity of these remarks. A few examples taken
from his endless speeches, interruptions and motions may not
be amiss to illustrate his recorded attitude.

At the opening of the second meeting, Mr. Cuvillier moved
that Counsel be excluded from the room. What point there
was in this except to insult Counsel was never discovered. He
next moved that the Committee refuse to grant immunity to any
witness. If this action had been taken it would have prevented

much of the evidence coming out due to the witnesses' fear
of prosecution. Not satisfied with this, he next moved that
the Committee then adjourn (May 14, 1931) and "refuse to
proceed any further with its deliberations, on the grounds
stated, and so report to the Legislature to be convened the
first Wednesday in January, 1932." The grounds he had stated
were that the whole Resolution was unconstitutional. Thus
it was at the second session that the only motions he made
were to hamper and hamstring the work which he had said he
so much wanted to carry out in an orderly way.

The third Committee meeting opened with Mr. Cuvillier
going into a long disquisition attempting to show that the
two appropriations for the Committee's work were unconstitutional. This view he endeavored to jam through in spite
of his reasons, and have the Committee declare its own appropriation invalid. Needless to say, the Committee refused
to go on record as approving any such suggestion. Later, at
the same meeting, he moved that the Committee adopt a resolution declaring that the Committee was without power to investigate the Courts in the City. This power was so plainly
stated in the Joint Resolution that for this motion, he could
not get even a Democratic second.

Another attempt to obstruct the work of the Committee
came at a later meeting after the Doyle case had been decided by the Court of Appeals and the question of the "immunity laws" was to be presented to a Special Session of the
Legislature for action. On this occasion, Mr. Cuvillier voted
against the Committee's resolution to petition the Governor
to call this special session to pass on these laws giving the
Committee power to grant immunity to witnesses, without
which it was impossible to make them testify. In assigning
his "reasons," he talked for three full pages of stenographic
minutes.

He made countless other motions, among which was one
to investigate the affairs of the assistants on the legal staff up
to the time of their employment by the Committee. This idea

apparently was prompted by an article in a newspaper. This motion died of its own ineptitude.

These dilatory and destructive motions and obstructions were comparatively few when compared with his constant mumbling interruptions at the public hearings. It is impossible, without printing a supplement to this book, to record them all. One or two types of interruptions will suffice.

Early in the investigation Mr. Cuvillier in some way learned of a case decided some time ago in the Court of Appeals, commonly known as the Barnes case. That case, in brief, decided that Barnes, the leader of Albany County, need not divulge the price at which, nor the manner by which he acquired certain stock in the J. B. Lyons Printing Company. That decision had no application to this Investigation. One salient distinguishing fact is that Barnes was not a public officer holding a position of public trust and, therefore, owing no duty of that nature to the public.

However that may be, the case has been referred to, read and re-read so many times that even the most casual spectator became sick of it. To have stopped the reading of it would have deprived the Minority of one method of obstruction, so no matter what the occasion was, nor who the witness was, all of a sudden the proceedings would stop, a sort of droning would begin on the Bench, the audience would sink back to get comfortable, the Chairman and other Committeemen would look around with a knowing smile, the stenographer would jump up and put his note book on the Bench right under the droning sound, on and on it would go until finally Assemblyman Cuvillier, who had been reading, would become tired and then, lifting his head, he would announce, in his only audible words, that he objected to the question on the grounds set forth in the "Barnes Case." The Chairman would overrule the objection in a little set speech and the proceedings would again resume. Without the semblance of exaggeration this procedure happened at least one hundred and fifty times. It delayed and obstructed the work of the Committee for days. Every subject, no matter how remote, was so reduced and distorted that it was brought within the decision of the Barnes case. If the objection had been taken seriously by any one, the whole Investigation would have been stopped long ago.

Assemblyman Cuvillier had another stock objection which he would use when the Barnes case failed to delay the proceedings long enough, and that is a quotation from the State Constitution to the effect that "The doors of each house shall be kept open except when the public welfare shall require secrecy." It is useless to catalogue the occasions on which this objection was urged because, to a person not having seen the Democratic Minority in action, any illustration that might be given would seem to be almost impossible. Suffice it to say this stock objection ran the Barnes case a close second in delaying the proceedings.

There was another type of interruption used. It might be called the legally meaningless type. This type of interruption was used to impress some one with a show of legalistic phraseology. For instance, and only one illustration is given, though there are countless others, in the examination of one of the Sherwood sisters, Counsel asked the witness whether or not she had recently received a letter from Russell, her fugitive brother. Before the woman could answer, up spoke Mr. Cuvillier and objected on the ground that the question called for a conclusion. That such could be the case seems incredible, but to make it even sillier, when the Chairman overruled his objection, the Assemblyman took an "exception" which, of course, means nothing at all save where an appeal from the ruling lies. The examples given are, as said above, but types, their number is impossible to determine. When the substance of the objections is analyzed, it is plain to see that the only purpose was to delay and befog the issue. There could be no other purpose to such a continuous mumble of sputtering objections for a period of fourteen months, except to hinder and obstruct. It must be said, however, that the only purpose accomplished was one of delay because Counsel refused to let the real issue be confounded and confused.

Another member of the Minority whose interruptions form a considerable part of the record was Senator John J. McNaboe. It is fortunate that his remarks are matters of public record so that future generations may peruse and learn from the mouths of the men themselves, what type of person was once elected to represent them.

On one occasion it so happened that a police officer was testifying as to conditions in Bronx County coming under his observation. Counsel had finished questioning. Mr. McNaboe then took up his examination. This, as all other examinations by the Minority, was designed to destroy the effect of testimony given and to confuse the whole situation. This particular witness refused to be misled by Senator McNaboe's questions. This so exasperated Mr. McNaboe that finally he screamed, ". . . and I think this man is a skunk."

Again after Doctor Doyle had been adjudged in contempt of the Committee and the Court of Appeals had held that he must answer the question as to whether or not he had ever bribed a public official and after Doctor Doyle had answered "no," the Committee then took a vote to determine whether or not the witness Doyle had purged himself of his contempt. Before voting on that proposition, Mr. McNaboe made a speech in support of his position that Doyle had purged himself, saying in part:

". . . There is innuendo, presumption and suspicion. There is a forceful attempt to keep a sick man in jail until he does talk. If that is the spirit of these United States, if that is the spirit of this State, if that is the spirit of the Legislative Committee, I say it is high time for somebody to rise up in great protest and stop placing feeble persons in jail because they don't give you the answer that you expect to get. I say, Dr. Doyle, if I were in your place, I would remain in jail until hell freezed over. . . . I vote to purge the witness."

Space permits of only one or two other types of remarks made by Senator McNaboe; one type took the form of irrelevant and ill-tempered outbursts, as the following quotations show:

> "You cannot shut me up. I am as much a Senator as you are. I am not out of order. . . .
> "That is it, slam down the Democrats, every chance you get. Twist the stories in headlines and slam it down all you want. . . .
> "I will protest with the loudest voice that I can summon to my command at the insinuations, innuendoes. . . . (gavel)
> "The insinuations that are being cast about here are un-American and unfair. . . . (Laughter—gavel)
> "I am not going to be shouted down by you every time I ask a question. . . .
> ". . . I would suggest, Mr. Chairman, that you get a piledriver. . . .
> "I have more rights than you have."

The other type of remark was a continuous stream of insults to Counsel. Such remarks as these were made:

> "I ask Counsel to stop talking when I am speaking to the Chairman. . . .
> "Counsel has no standing here when I am talking to the Chairman. . . .
> "I will not be shouted down by an employee of this Committee. . . .
> "Counsel is trying to entrap the witness. . . .
> "Look at the minutes . . . if you wish to see clearly the frameup which our Counsel and his hitherto silent satellite have attempted on a member of this Committee. . . ."

It is not necessary to complete the list. The examples given are few in comparison with the total number made. These few, it seems, bespeak the man who made them and need, therefore, no other comment. As to the remaining two Democrats of the Minority it is sufficient to mention their names. They are John J. Dunnigan, a Senator from the Bronx, and an Assemblyman from Brooklyn named Irwin Steingut.

The Republican or Majority side of the Committee, conducted themselves in a commendable manner. They behaved like gentlemen and refrained, from start to finish, from hindering or delaying the progress of the Investigation. The Chairman, Samuel H. Hofstadter, handled his office, and it was a very difficult one, in a skillful manner. He presided over all the public hearings of the Committee in a dignified and judicial manner.

Too much cannot be said by way of commendation of the fine spirit shown by Senator Wheatley and Assemblymen Potter and Lamont. These gentlemen dealt with the subjects in hand in a large and generous way. The other Republican, Assemblyman Moffat, was diligent in his attendance at the public hearings, and manifested great interest in the work of the Committee.

CHAPTER XXIX

CONCLUSION

THUS, the tale is told. It is necessarily but a sketch of the true situation existing in New York City. The Investigation was limited in its money, in its duration and in human endurance. Could it have gone on indefinitely, a greater and more panoramic picture would have been painted. Some day that may be done. If so, the actual condition of the City will be revealed. The whole story then can and will be told.

What then is this insolence of office? It is not a new thing. It has been an ever-present parasite on government since the beginning. It was the same in the days of the Greek City States; it was the same in Rome. It was this that led Cicero to ask Cataline, who, after his treachery had become known, had the effrontery to take his place in the Roman Senate, "how long will you abuse our patience?"; it was the same in England in the days of the feudal lords and the absolute monarchs before Magna Charta and the rise of the Commons; it was the same in the days of the Louis in France and was one of the causes of that Revolution; it was the same in the days of the Kaisers in Germany and was instrumental in hastening the outbreak of the World War; it was the same under the Romanoffs in Russia and contributed to their overthrow; and it is the same now in our own Federal, State and Municipal governments where, as in the earlier days, a powerful and relentless political machine has all the agencies of government in its grip. The thing itself may be defined as the attitude which those in power, who feel they cannot be touched, have towards a helpless and machine-controlled public. It is the attitude which causes them to say, despite the evidence produced, well—what are you going to do about it? Has that attitude been proved in the testimony adduced before the Committee and demonstrated in the pages of this book? The facts themselves, in a brief résumé, must answer.

First—The Magistrates' Courts Investigation. Witness after witness shaded and qualified his testimony by cutting fine corners and raising false distinctions in his answers; witness after witness, members of the Tammany organization, was conclusively demonstrated to have been unfit for the position which he held,—was shown to have been utterly devoid of any sense of civic decency and to have regarded his job, which was a public trust, merely as a grab bag and a step to a more lucrative place in the City Government. Witness after witness insulted the intelligence of the whole city by the ridiculously childlike and impossible stories which they told in explanation of their fortunes. Were any of these people afraid of any prosecution whatsoever resulting from their testimony? The answer is—No. The reason is that the Tammany organization protects, to the very limit, even its most insignificant officeholder. In return, it expects, and it receives, when it is on trial, a conspiracy of silence, together with a complete collapse of the memories of those of its members who testify.

The administration itself endeavored to belittle and becloud the disclosures made, tried to laugh the Investigation off, saying, in effect, that the City should pay no attention to it as soon all would blow over and be forgotten. This was their attitude up to the time the disclosures were brought home to them. After that time their attitude and method of attack changed from laughter to abuse of Counsel.

Second—The Investigation into the District Attorney's Office: The same tactics were in a general way pursued by the District Attorney, his witnesses and his Counsel. The same historical attitude of the officeholder—well, I'm here, what are you going to do about it?—was taken by the District Attorney himself.

Third—The City-wide Investigation: Again, the same attitude of insolence was found while the City-wide Inquiry was under way. As damning fact was piled on damning fact, the one and only chorus which arose again and again from the Minority was—wait until election, then you will see! Not once did it occur to them that perhaps the electorate was sick and disgusted with the Tammany Hall crowd and was determined to turn them out. Once again the same incredible stories were told as to fabulous fortunes. The same cries of political ambition and desire to wreck the whole Democratic party in New York City. The same freedom from fear of prosecution was exhibited by many witnesses; the same cries of destruction of the City Government and its financial credit. The same cheap endeavors to becloud and belittle the whole Investigation.

There were one or two acts which, more than any words could tell, bespoke the attitude of insolence which characterized the whole City Administration. One was the action taken by the Mayor in regard to Dr. Schroeder, of the Department of Sanitation.

Dr. Schroeder was a close personal friend of the Mayor's. He was his personal physician as well as head of the Department of Sanitation. This Department had at the time of the Investigation a budget appropriation of approximately thirty-two million dollars. From this amount the only apparent benefit that the taxpayers received was a brightly dressed band, some gayly painted garbage trucks and some rubbish cans gaudily painted in variegated hues. One of the Department's Commissioners had resigned because he refused to tolerate longer the "illegal" actions of Dr. Schroeder. The Mayor himself was at the time under charges of a serious nature, raising the question of his own fitness to hold his office. Nevertheless, to insure the continuance of his personal friend and physician in office until 1938 at a salary of $22,500 a year, the Mayor secretly accepted Dr. Schroeder's resignation as Commissioner of the Department for the balance of his then term, which was to have expired in 1935, and immediately reappointed him as Commissioner for a term which extended his tenure of office three years, that is, until 1938—thus sad-

dling on the already overburdened taxpayers the further sum
of $67,500, as salary for Dr. Schroeder.

Another example typical of this attitude of insolence
towards the taxpayers, was the speech which the Mayor made
suggesting and recommending that each of the 147,000 city
employees waive his rights to receive one month's pay out
of his total salary for the year. This he offered as a cure for
the swollen budget of the City. Nowhere did he recommend
that the unnecessary and wasteful offices of the City Government be discontinued. Nowhere did he recommend that the
Commissioners and others give up their City-owned automobiles with the private chauffeurs. Nowhere did he suggest
that the already inflated salaries of high City officials be
deflated. Nowhere did he recommend that a single one of the
147,000 City officeholders be discontinued. That he couldn't
do, for that is how Tammany makes and holds votes. To
sum it up, nowhere in that speech was there any suggestion
of a careful and scientific budgetary retrenchment and reduc-
tion. It was a brazen attempt to curry the good will of the
voters and to have it appear that, by this temporary and
superficial method, the budget, and, therefore, the taxes,
would be reduced. There are countless other examples but
space forbids their telling.

There is the story and there is their answer,—a challenge
to civic honesty—What are you going to do about it?

ACKNOWLEDGMENT

THIS picture would not be truly painted were the important part played by the newspapers omitted. To the Press of the city much credit is due for their unbiased and complete reports of each day's proceedings. Much of the success of the Investigation is itself due to this. The newspapers themselves were fortunate in having the services of the men and women who attended on all three investigations, because through their actions they gained the confidence of Judge Seabury in all the capacities in which he served. He, too, gained and held their confidence throughout the long assignment. That in itself, they said, was a very unusual thing in the experience of newspaper men. Theirs was a mutual trust. Because of this, these men and women were enabled to gain a deeper insight into the spirit behind the three investigations. Because of this deeper insight, the Public itself received a truer and fuller picture than they otherwise could have had.

The world moves on and events that are past fade from the memory and become forgotten. For this reason, and because they and the Investigations should be remembered together, we wish to include and list the names of the Counsel who assisted Judge Seabury in these Investigations. These gentlemen came together unknown to one another. Soon they became welded in a unit of service. By his actions they soon learned to know that their leader was one whose only interest was to better a revolting and unfortunate situation in the City of New York, and because of this, to them a spirit of high endeavor was born. Their services throughout the two years were of the highest order. They gave unreservedly of their time and services to a public cause. Their reward lay chiefly in the knowledge gained that their labors were well done and were not in vain. As time passes they will have no regrets for having given of themselves. In fact, as soon as the real worth of these investigations is realized their endeavors will be looked upon somewhat with a spirit of envy by those who were not a part of their labors and their struggles.

Those who served in the Magistrates' Courts Investigation in addition to Mr. Isidor J. Kresel, who acted as Chief Counsel, were:

> Henry J. A. Collins
> Irving Ben Cooper
> Robert M. Davidson
> James H. Goodier
> Philip W. Haberman, Jr.
> Sydney Handler
> Harold Melniker
> William B. Northrop
> Jacob Gould Schurman, Jr.
> Harland B. Tibbetts

In the Investigation of the District Attorney's Office:

> John Kirkland Clark
> Henry J. A. Collins
> Philip W. Lowry
> Robert Morris
> William B. Northrop
> Jacob Gould Schurman, Jr.
> Robert K. Simonds

In the City-wide Investigation:

Henry J. A. Collins	Carroll Hayes
W. Randall Compton	Oren C. Herwitz
Irving Ben Cooper	Henry T. Hunt
John R. Davies	Herbert Levien
Robert M. Davidson	George B. Levy
James H. Goodier	Philip W. Lowry
Harry D. Guthrie, Jr.	Harold Melniker
Philip W. Haberman, Jr.	Joseph G. Miller
Sydney Handler	J. G. Louis Molloy

William B. Moore
Robert Morris
William G. Mulligan, Jr.
William B. Northrop
William B. Parsons

Jacob Gould Schurman, Jr.
Harland B. Tibbetts
George Trosk
Walter B. Walker
John C. Walsh

INDEX